Evolutionary and Neurocognitive Approaches to Aesthetics, Creativity, and the Arts

Edited by

Colin Martindale
University of Maine

Paul Locher
Montclair State University

Vladimir M. Petrov
State Institute for Art Studies (Moscow)

Foundations and Frontiers in Aesthetics
Series Editors: Colin Martindale and Arnold Berleant

LONDON AND NEW YORK

First published 2007 by Baywood Publishing Company, Inc.

Published 2018 by Routledge
2 Park Square, Milton Park, Abingdon, Oxon OX14 4RN
52 Vanderbilt Avenue, New York, NY 10017

First issued in paperback 2018

Routledge is an imprint of the Taylor & Francis Group, an informa business

Copyright © 2007 Taylor & Francis

All rights reserved. No part of this book may be reprinted or reproduced or utilised in any form or by any electronic, mechanical, or other means, now known or hereafter invented, including photocopying and recording, or in any information storage or retrieval system, without permission in writing from the publishers.

Notice:
Product or corporate names may be trademarks or registered trademarks, and are used only for identification and explanation without intent to infringe.

Library of Congress Catalog Number: 2006043022

Library of Congress Cataloging-in-Publication Data

Evolutionary and neurocognitive approaches to aesthetics, creativity, and the arts / edited by Colin Matindale, Paul Locher, Vladimir M. Petrov.
    p. cm. -- (Foundations and frontiers in aesthetics)
  Includes bibliographical references and index.
  ISBN 0-89503-306-2 (cloth)
   1. Aesthetics--Philosophy. 2. Art--Philosophy. 3. Creative ability. 4. Evolutionary psychology. I. Martindale, Colin. II. Locher, Paul, 1941- III. Petrov, V. M.

BH39.E95 2006
153.3'5--dc22

2006043022

ISBN 13: 978-0-415-78369-9 (pbk)
ISBN 13: 978-0-89503-306-2 (hbk)

 Printed in the United Kingdom by Henry Ling Limited

Table of Contents

Preface.. v

CHAPTER 1
What Art Is and What Art Does: An Overview of Contemporary Evolutionary Hypotheses
   Ellen Dissanayake...................................... 1

CHAPTER 2
An Evolutionary Model of Artistic and Musical Creativity
   Gregory J. Feist....................................... 15

CHAPTER 3
The Adaptive Function of Literature
   Joseph Carroll.. 31

CHAPTER 4
Does Reading Literature Make People Happy?
   Willie van Peer, Alexandra Mentjes, and Jan Auracher..... 47

CHAPTER 5
Cognitive Poetics and Poetry Recital
   Reuven Tsur.. 65

CHAPTER 6
The Alphabet and Creativity: Implications for East Asia
   Wm. C. Hannas.. 89

CHAPTER 7
Creativity, Gender, History, and the Authors of Fantasy for Children
   Ravenna Helson....................................... 101

CHAPTER 8
Trends in the Creative Content of Scientific Journals:
Good, But Not as Good!
Robert Hogenraad 117

CHAPTER 9
The Information Approach to Human Sciences, Especially Aesthetics
Vladimir M. Petrov 129

CHAPTER 10
Art and Cognition: Cognitive Processes in Art Appreciation
Helmut Leder and Benno Belke 149

CHAPTER 11
Literary Creativity: A Neuropsychoanalytic View
Norman N. Holland 165

CHAPTER 12
A Neural-Network Theory of Beauty
Colin Martindale 181

CHAPTER 13
Neural Correlates of Creative Cognition
Oshin Vartanian and Vinod Goel 195

CHAPTER 14
Creativity, DNA, and Cerebral Blood Flow
Rosa Aurora Chávez-Eakle 209

CHAPTER 15
Artistic Creativity and Affective Disorders: Are They Connected?
Dennis K. Kinney and Ruth L. Richards 225

Index 239

Preface

In this book, we bring together chapters describing exciting new advances in the study of aesthetics, art, and creativity. The chapters focus either directly or indirectly upon evolutionary and biological approaches to these topics. All known societies produce art, literature, and music. This universality suggests that they must serve functions that are quite fundamental. Dissanayake gives an overview of 10 evolutionary explanations of the importance of the arts. Her own theory, and other similar theories, are that the arts serve an adaptive function that is essential to the survival of a society. As well as adaptive fitness, Darwin saw sexual selection as an evolutionary force. Some current evolutionary theories of art hold that it exists because of sexual selection. That is, artists produce art in order to maximize their chances of mating with a desirable member of the opposite sex. This might be the case with some popular singers, but Dissanayake argues that it is implausible that sexual selection could be the main reason for the existence of art. With this, I certainly agree. A third type of evolutionary explanation of the arts is that they exist as a secondary result of the existence of something else that is adaptive. For example, poetry could not exist without language. This is certainly true, but cannot explain why poetry is universal to all societies rather than occurring only in some societies. In his chapter, Feist works out explanations of art and music based upon both adaptation and sexual selection. In contrast, Carroll presents a purely adaptationist explanation of the function of literature. In their chapter, van Peer, Mentjes, and Auracher offer an essentially evolutionary explanation of why people enjoy reading literature.

Language is of course the stuff of literature. Tsur investigates an interesting problem in poetic meter. Much English poetry is supposedly in iambic pentameter; however, unless one misaccents syllables, hardly any of it really is. As he points out, in the first 160 lines of *Paradise Lost*, only two exactly follow the pattern of strong and weak accents called for by iambic pentameter. In reading poetry, one is supposed to place accents where they belong rather than accenting syllables so that they are forced to be iambic pentameter. Read correctly, poetry in iambic pentameter sounds "right" even though the accents do not follow the rules for this meter. By examining sound spectrographs, Tsur offers an explanation for this. There is more to syllables than whether they are accented or not. Chinese and Japanese officials freely admit that they have what they call a "creativity problem." Chinese and Japanese tend to be able to improve upon Western innovations, but tend not to innovate themselves. The problem is that if innovation decreases in the West, this will have profoundly bad economic and other problems for the East. Hannas argues that this problem arises from the nature of the writing systems that they use. Their ideograms stand for syllables rather than phonemes. He argues that this leads them not to analyze words or, by extension, ideas into their component parts. Putting old ideas together in new ways is the essence of creativity. If one does not analyze an idea into its component elements, he or she will be unable to put these elements together in new ways. Hence, the person will not be creative.

A number of theorists have argued that evolution is not confined to biology but may be found on the sociocultural level as well. In her chapter, Helson describes how the personality of the author is related to the type of fantasy stories that he or she writes. She also describes very clear and marked historical trends in the traits of the main characters of such works. Hogenraad approaches scientific writing from the point of view of sociocultural evolution and also describes very clear historical trends in the content of such writing. Petrov presents a theory of evolution based upon modern information theory. Though the theory is very general, he focuses upon aesthetic evolution.

Leder and Belke offer a general neurocognitive framework for the investigation of the appreciation of art. Holland gives us a similar framework that can be used for the explanation of literary creativity. In my chapter, I move to a more concrete level and offer a neural-network explanation of the perception of beauty. Space prevented me from explaining in any detail how an almost identical theory for the explanation of creativity could be formulated. I could only remark that perception of beauty of the "perception" of a creative idea are isomorphic. In their chapters, Vartanian and Goel as well as Chávez-Eakle describe fascinating new research using brain-imaging techniques while people are engaged in creative thought. Both find that the frontal lobes and the right hemisphere are crucial in such thought. A good deal of research suggests that creativity is related to affective disorders. In their chapter, Kinney and Richards deal with exactly how they are related. Affective disorders are in large part genetic, as is creativity. If there is an evolutionary selection pressure for creativity, it could act as an indirect selection pressure for affective disorders. The research of Kinney and Richards suggests that creativity is not associated with extreme affective disorder but with milder forms that would not usually be diagnosed as mental disorders. Enthusiasm is necessary for creativity, but extreme mania or depression are detrimental to it.

Colin Martindale

CHAPTER 1

What Art Is and What Art Does: An Overview of Contemporary Evolutionary Hypotheses

Ellen Dissanayake

Although art theorists today have enlarged their purview of what should be included in a concept of art, contemporary psychologists of art frequently base their studies on outdated ideas and assumptions arising from the fine-art tradition of Western Europe (and possibly some "high" cultures of Asia). It is ironic that psychologists, as scientists, seek universal general explanatory principles and yet rely on a restricted sample of objects, whereas academic art theorists (at least today) accept as art a broad variety of manifestations in modern Western and non-Western societies, yet deny that there are any general principles underlying their psychological nature or function.

Both contemporary art theory and, to a large extent, traditional psychology of art have ignored evolutionary psychology based on the writings of Charles Darwin (1871). Yet at least five observations suggest that the arts have been adaptive during human evolution and are an inherent part of human nature. That is to say (a) the arts are present in every culture that is or has been known; (b) in most traditional societies, individuals and groups devote an excessive amount of time, energy, and material resources to the arts, far more than would be expected for a superfluous activity; (c) the arts attract attention and invite participation and indeed provide enjoyment and pleasure; (d) very young children are predisposed to make and enjoy the arts; and (e) the arts are usually concerned with biologically important subject matter.

Although the arts are products of cultures and vary from place to place, we now know that from birth and during their early years, humans are biologically predisposed to be cultural beings, evident both in innate abilities (to interact with others, imitate, play, and speak) and emotional needs (for attachment to familiars, mutual interaction, and positive regard by their associates). Similarly, capacities to engage in the arts are biologically predisposed, and I suggest that a "behavior of art" can be considered a biological adaptation.

In the past decade or so, evolutionary psychologists have proposed hypotheses about the nature and adaptive function of art. In Part A of this chapter, I shall summarize nine of these, and in Part B, describe my own hypothesis and how it fits into the general adaptationist discourse about what art is and what it does. Space unfortunately does not permit examination of subtle aspects of the nine other views (or indeed my own), and their proponents may feel themselves unfairly, because too summarily, presented. My intention in Part A is to provide a general overview, with references that can lead interested readers to the works mentioned.

It should be pointed out that virtually all evolutionary psychologists agree that the ultimate function of any adaptive behavior is to positively affect inclusive fitness; that is, the individual's survival and reproductive success. Contributions to fitness may not be obvious, and most individuals rarely, if ever, consciously reflect on the ultimate motivation behind their "proximate" actions and responses or the reasons they give for behaving and responding as they do.

Despite this shared axiom, controversies among evolutionary psychologists are lively, and the relatively new field of evolutionary approaches to the arts awaits a unifying set of principles about its subject. The disparate approaches and theories in part reflect the complexity and confusion of notions about human "art," which is not even a word or concept in the majority of human societies. The subject of art, both within and outside of evolutionary psychology, is reminiscent of the famous elephant described by several blind men. What one concludes about the trunk may not pertain to what another has to say about the tail, ear, or foot. Any one view is not obviously relevant to any other, which makes discussion difficult and even unprofitable; and some hypotheses are based at least in part on unexamined presuppositions about art that may or may not be shared by other investigators. Some have to do with art as an artifact (a work, an object); a quality or feature (such as beauty); a cue to something else (such as creativity or skill); or as an activity or behavior. Some studies presuppose more than one meaning, inadvertently sliding from one aspect of art to another. The variety of suggestions about art's adaptive function then arise from (a) differences in what the writer takes to be "art" or (b) different ideas about the ways in which fitness is positively affected; that is, its proximate manifestations. In the nine hypotheses described in the next section, what art is or what art does will in some cases seem partial, tangled, or obscure, and often difficult to compare with another hypothesis.

A. NINE HYPOTHESES ABOUT WHAT ART DOES

Any suggestion of the function (the adaptive consequences) of art—what art does—presumes a notion of what art is. Many hypotheses about art's function simply presuppose that art is one thing, thereby excluding other things. For example, "art" typically refers to paintings, sculptures, and other visual art, thereby disregarding not only music and literature but dance and performance (which are perceived visually). Those who treat art as adaptive may also specifically equate it with *beauty,* or *creativity and imagination.* Yet there are beautiful things (sunsets, flowers) that are not art, and creativity or imagination may be expressed in such nonart activities as teaching or problem solving (to call such activities "art" because they make use of creative thought is only synecdoche). *Skill* seems to be inherent in art (as its etymology attests, where "art" means correct understanding of technical principles, such as the art of fly-fishing or of surgery). Yet I claim that art need not be skillful. A hypothesis about the adaptive value of "beauty" or "creativity" or "skill," I argue (see Part B), is not the same as a comprehensive hypothesis about the adaptive value of the larger category, "art," or even of an individual art.

(1) Typical of what might be called a neurocognitive approach to function are fascinating and erudite books by Solso (1994) and Zeki (1999), whose titles or jacket copy explicitly refer to visual art and the brain. These studies do not take an overt adaptationist perspective but suggest that "by knowing more about the workings of the brain in general and of the visual brain in particular, one might be able to develop the outlines of a theory of aesthetics that is biologically based" (Zeki, 1999, p. 1); or "Art is part of us and we are part of art. Mind and art are one" (Solso, 1994, p. xv). For Zeki, the function of art is to search for the constant, lasting, essential, or enduring features of objects, surfaces, faces, or situations and thus **to acquire a deeper knowledge of them**. Ramachandran and Hirstein (1999), in a similar vein, consider art's purpose to be to enhance, transcend, or even distort or caricature reality and thereby help a viewer to **solve perceptual or cognitive problems**. The examples on which these studies are based are preponderantly masterpieces of Western fine art.

(2) Among a plethora of functions proposed by evolutionary psychologists is that offered by practitioners of *soi-disant* "evolutionary

aesthetics" (formerly "Darwinian aesthetics"), which considers art as an adaptive behavior that **promotes selective attention and positive emotional responses to components of the environment that lead to "good" (adaptive) decisions and problem solving** (Orians, 2001), and are thus considered "beautiful." The earliest studies were of evolved preferences that direct choices of desirable—safe, productive—landscapes (see review in Ruso, Renninger, & Atzwanger, 2003), but subsequent studies have included preferences for sexually relevant features such as waist-hip ratio (of females), body odor (of men), or symmetrical facial features (in both sexes), all of which signal health, fertility, and good mating opportunity (see, e.g., Voland & Grammar, 2003). Just as neuro- and cognitive scientists assume that their work on perceptual preferences is relevant to understanding art, so do writers on evolutionary aesthetics; for example, "Darwinian aesthetics is the method to determine the cues in great art that make it great (i.e., determine the actual information that human aesthetic mechanisms process during aesthetic valuation of art)" (Thornhill, 1998, p. 568). Whereas neurocognitive approaches tend to be restricted to Western visual masterworks, evolutionary aesthetics errs in the other direction, using the terms art, aesthetic value, and beauty quite broadly, including almost any feature that is preferred and therefore promotes a "high likelihood of survival and reproductive success" (Thornhill, 1998, p. 544). Both views are similar in assigning a problem-solving function to the arts, whether through perceptual mechanisms or adaptive cognitive modules in the brain.

(3) Geoffrey Miller (2000, 2001) is the best known of several scholars who are concerned with **art as creativity and/or virtuosity that contributes to mating opportunity**. "Human art capacities evolved in the same way [as aesthetic ornamentation in other species], with aesthetic judgment evolving in the service of mate choice" (Miller, 2001, p. 20). The peacock's long, glossy, beautifully marked tail feathers are literally "a drag" that "tie him down" and make him vulnerable to predators. Like human art, the peacock's fabulous tail would seem to be useless and even detrimental, since valuable energy is required to maintain such an appendage as well as to erect and suitably quiver it. Yet admiring peahens choose to mate with individuals who present them with the most magnificent, symmetrical display. In a similar manner, human body ornamentation, literary language, song, dance, and other artful performance are proposed to have evolved over generations through sexual selection by females. Like the peacock's tail, the arts are advertisements of fitness, "honest, costly signals," because the strength, vigor, intelligence, skill, and creativity required for their display cannot be "faked" by less well-endowed males. Miller's

hypothesis (see also Feist, 2001; Voland, 2003) fits well with evolutionary aesthetics, as described above, since it is concerned with preferences for signals (the arts) of adaptive benefits (here are good genes).

(4) A similar reliance on costly signaling theory to propose a function for the arts is not stated but implied in a hypothesis that considers the extremes of religious behavior to have evolved as **honest signals of commitment** (Irons, 2001). Although religion seems to facilitate intragroup cooperation, there are potential difficulties with assessing a member's trustworthiness and commitment (the "free rider" problem), which are solved by requiring behaviors that are "hard to fake." Although Irons and other scholars who address religious behaviors (e.g., Sosis, 2003) describe such difficult, costly practices as penitence, sacrifice, or self-mutilation and do not mention the arts, art-filled ceremonial behavior is also costly and is intrinsic to most if not all religions and fits into this category (see Part B).

(5) A function for art that has been attributed for more than a century to play and make-believe in both animals and children (e.g., Groos, 1898, 1901) has been given new life within evolutionary psychology. John Tooby and Leda Cosmides (2001) claim that the capacity to engage in fictional, imagined worlds **provides risk-free practice for later life when similar circumstances might arise**. Like advocates of evolutionary aesthetics (see above), they use the words "aesthetic" and "beauty" to refer to advantageous features or activities that humans evolved to pay attention to or choose. And just as neurocognitivists specifically address visual art (see above), Tooby and Cosmides are concerned here with fictional narrative and propose a similar adaptive function: "[the bundled representations in narratives] have a powerfully [sic] organizing effect on our neurocognitive adaptations, even though the representations are not literally true" (Tooby & Cosmides, 2001, p. 21). Fictions make adaptive information available to cognitive systems that are involved with foresight, planning, and empathy.

Because by far the most work using evolutionary approaches to the arts is on literature (see Carroll, 2004 and this volume), I shall not discuss other hypotheses about literary art specifically here. I will say, however, that like the neurocognitivists (see above), most adaptationist studies of literature deal with modern Western (written) examples (for notable exceptions, see Easterlin [2002], Gottschall [2003], Scalise Sugiyama [2001]), although there are notable differences between oral and written communication. Darwinian literary studies have tended to be concerned with subject matter more than, or even to the exclusion of, form, tone, and other artful devices that are important components of oratory or recitation, surely the earliest forms of literary language.

(6) Several evolutionary theorists have proposed variants of the idea that the arts function to **manipulate and control other people**. For example, Aiken (1998a, 1998b) focuses on the capacity of art to evoke emotion, and thereby to affect and even coerce the thought and behavior of other individuals. Although she admits that "art has, in fact, many purposes" (Aiken 1998b, p. 227), it is clear that insofar as it directs attention to messages, it can be used for propaganda to the benefit of the art maker (or *patron* of the art maker; that is, the person who invests in the production of beauty [Voland, 2003, p. 257]). Power (1999) offers a version of art as manipulation and deception, proposing that visual art originated when ancestral females (participating as a group) painted their bodies with red ochre in order to attract males (who assumed they were menstruating and hence fertile and receptive to courtship and eventual insemination), thereby gaining gifts of meat, a valuable resource.

(7) In contradistinction to the preceding views, which are all accounts of how the arts have evolved as the result of competition (for resources necessary for survival, for prestige, for mates) or in order to manipulate and deceive others, several writers have emphasized that the arts additionally **enhance cooperation and social cohesion and continuity**—by augmenting the impact of ritual, thereby reinforcing religion's power to cement group cohesion (Boyd, 2005); by indicating group membership with dress or badges (Aiken, 1998a); by means of behavioral coordination and neural entrainment through rhythmic movement and ritualized participation in temporally organized performances (Dissanayake, 2000); and by inculcating "descent amity" (Coe, 2003). Based on extensive fieldwork in Spain, Colombia, Ecuador, and the southwestern United States, Coe's "ancestress hypothesis" describes how traditions are transmitted within kin groups, especially by mothers to children, by means of visual art (although performances of all kinds would also be relevant), encouraging cooperation among those identified as co-descendants of a common ancestor.

(8) Archaeologists, in particular, note that at some point in the past, humans developed the ability to create and use symbols, which conferred obvious fitness benefits. "Art" is frequently included by prehistorians in a list of other symbolic behaviors developed by early humans, along with language, notation and other information storage systems, and burial of the dead with grave goods, all of which reflect and **contribute to higher thought and intelligence**, thereby implying plausible adaptive value.

(9) Finally, an influential hypothesis of *nonfunction* for the arts should also be mentioned—the argument that art has no adaptive value

in itself but is **merely a byproduct of other adaptations**. The canonical example of this view is the analogy with strawberry cheesecake, which humans have evolved to like because during the Pleistocene, when sugar and fat were scarce, it was advantageous to consume high calories when they became available, rather than to continue ingesting tubers or leaves (Pinker, 1997, pp. 524-525). Like sugar, fat, alcohol, recreational drugs, masturbation, and pornography, the arts exploit cravings that in other contexts are or were adaptive. They allow us "[to press] our pleasure buttons" (Pinker, 1997, p. 525). In a subsequent book, Pinker (2002, pp. 404-406) proposes other sources for art as by-product: the hunger for status, the aesthetic pleasure of experiencing adaptive objects and environments, and the ability to design artifacts to achieve desired ends. These are motivations that direct choices, like those proposed by adherents of the assumptions of evolutionary aesthetics (as above).

My own hypothesis of art's function can be added to the nine general positions just described. Before presenting it, it is necessary to discuss in more detail what the term art refers to.

B. WHAT IS ART?

If one considers small-scale "traditional" or "subsistence" societies—groups of foragers that are more like ancestral societies than recent, specialized, technologically complex societies with developed agriculture and writing—we see that the primary context for the arts of music, dance, dramatic performance, poetic language, and visual display is various kinds of ritual ceremony. Indeed, it can be said that ceremonies (if not "ritual," a larger category and different concept) are constituted of arts and would not exist without them. In ceremonies, the arts attract attention, sustain interest, coordinate group effort, and provide emotional excitement and satisfaction. One could postulate then that the arts arose in human evolution as adjuncts to ceremonial behavior rather than as independently evolved activities.

What is more, in ceremonies, the arts are typically performed simultaneously, a feature that is not evident in modern societies' arts, which are usually manifested and conceptualized as separate entities (i.e., visual art, instrumental and vocal music, dance, poetry, literature, drama) and subentities or genres.

Additionally, as several arts may occur at once, an entire group may make the art or participate in its performance. The Trobriand *masawa*, or ceremonial seagoing canoe, is constructed by a group—owned, used, and enjoyed communally (Malinowski, 1922). According to Chernoff

(1979, p. 23), "[t]he most fundamental aesthetic in Africa [is that] without participation, there is no meaning."

Such rethinking of how the arts may have been originally manifested suggests that adaptive hypotheses about art based on only one art, only one artist (as fitness-maximizer at the expense of others), or only one function require modification. Perhaps "art" is better conceptualized as a superordinate or prototypical behavioral category, with individual arts being types, with sometimes different functions. Like attachment behavior, composed of individual behaviors of crying, clinging, looking at, moving toward, and so on, art behavior or "artification" (see below) is the overarching motivational system or adaptation, composed of dancing, singing, decorating, carving—the various arts. Note that the individual manifestations of both attachment and of artification may vary and may occur within other contexts. If named individually without reference to their adaptive overarching psychobiological motivation system, they could seem a chimera-like cobbling together of already existing behaviors (Dissanayake, 1995).

Another principle of evolutionary psychology may also require rethinking—the fixation on individual competition, thereby ignoring or repudiating the obvious fact that individuals require group life and that adaptations for social and emotional coordination have been equally important, themselves contributing to the ultimate ends of survival and reproduction. Judging from innumerable examples of actual practices of the arts in subsistence societies, they overwhelmingly tend to bring individuals together and create social accord and cooperation (as suggested in #7, Part A).

A common assumption in many of the nine hypotheses is that the defining feature of art inheres in other characteristics, such as symbol use, beauty, play, skill, narrative, costly signals, or creativity and imagination. Yet these are not in themselves art, but broader entities that some but not all instances of art may have or use. It remains for their proponents to say specifically what makes artful instances of these characteristics or techniques different from nonartful examples: a carelessly scrawled map for getting from here to there, for example, or an infant's flawless complexion, an idle doodle, winning an auto race, a joke or lie, a convoy of heavily armed soldiers, or the novel idea of manufacturing a warmable toilet seat. In other words, when proposing an adaptive or functional value for "art," one still must distinguish what makes specifically artistic symbols, beauty, play, skill, narrative, costliness, or imagination different from other instances of these features; that is, one must still specify what *additional* capacity selection could have acted upon. Some of these characteristics are associated with art in the modern Western high-art tradition, but do not obtain universally.

An emphasis on masterworks is restrictive, even though "artifiers" in all societies often intend to do their best and "get it right" and also generally equate "the good" and "the beautiful" (see below). An emphasis on things like lakes and body odor casts the net too wide. Simply liking them does not tell us anything about art.

My own view differs from others not only in suggesting that the arts originated and developed in association with "religion"—specifically its behavioral manifestation, ritual ceremony—but in viewing art itself as being not an entity or a quality but *a way of doing or treating something*; that is, a behavior of art, or "artification." When "artifying," I suggest, *one intentionally makes ordinary reality extra-ordinary through certain operations: formalization, elaboration, repetition, exaggeration, and (sometimes) manipulation of expectation, or surprise.* The first four of these operations are also characteristic of what has been called "ritualization" of communicative displays in other animals, thereby making them more conspicuous or distinctive. Importantly, human mothers and other caretakers spontaneously (unintentionally) perform such operations on their vocalizations, facial expressions, and gestures when interacting face-to-face with small infants who respond to (and *elicit* and *prefer*) such behavior in vocal, visual, and kinesic communications from their elders, suggesting an evolutionary source for a capacity to make and respond to the behavioral components (i.e., formalization and so forth) of artmaking (Dissanayake, 2000).

In dance, ordinary bodily movements or gestures, "artified" by means of the operations just named, become extraordinary. Similarly, the words of ordinary speech become poetry and the paralinguistic or expressive features of the voice become song. Ordinary materials (clay, wood, stone, fiber, cave walls), objects (bodies, hair, utensils), surroundings, themes, or ideas become extraordinary when formalized and elaborated (often, but not always, using the adaptive or "beautiful" shapes, colors, and motifs that neurocognitivists and investigators of evolutionary aesthetics reveal). People do not simply *prefer* salubrious landscape features. Some—artists—*draw additional attention* to them through formalization and elaboration, and it is this "moreness" or *extra*ordinariness that characterizes art. Often a cognitive or sensory preference will be *obscured* by artification (archaic words, magical syllables), rendering useless its contribution to how we behave in similar circumstances in the future.

Artification may look like creativity, but familiarity with traditional societies makes clear that "creativity" and individual showing off are typically, if not always, discouraged. Certainly cultural behavior changes over time. But as Coe (2003, p. 47) points out, "when art history is viewed across the ages, what is obvious is continuity and resistance to change." Once again, a modern Western view of art prejudices thinking about ancestral arts.

Skill, too, varies when many individuals participate and when participation is valued as much as or more than virtuosity. Much traditional art is performative, even ephemeral, not permanent and contemplative as in the Western "high art" tradition. For example, the Yolngu of Australia may cover and destroy paintings within minutes of completion (Morphy, 1992).

Evolutionary explanation is needed not only for why artists often use creativity, beauty, and skill, or why we admire these attributes. The more fundamental question is why humans have an irrepressible penchant for making some things special, weird, strange, unusual, sometimes ugly—extraordinary—as in ceremonies, and elsewhere.

WHY DO (DID) PEOPLE EVER BEGIN TO DO IT—TO ARTIFY?

One plausible motivation for artification, only implicitly addressed by investigators of religious behavior (see #7, Part A), has to do with the wish to influence outcomes of uncertain but vital (biologically important) circumstances, such as subsistence, being safe, prosperous, and healthy, or traversing important life stages from birth to death—the subjects of "religious" art-filled ceremonies in every society that has been known. Humans, who can remember the past and imagine recurrences of desired or feared happenings in the future, feel the need to *do something* about uncertainty.

I suggest that ancestral artifications (formalizing and elaborating voice and movement, responsiveness to which is part of human nature from infancy) with other people provided, through rhythmic and behavioral temporal coordination, a tenth plausible function for art: that of **relieving tension and anxiety and instilling a sense of coping with uncertainty** by making individuals feel part of a group and even connected to a higher power. Hormones released during prolonged stress are debilitating to a wide range of somatic functions, including immune system activity, mental performance, growth and tissue repair, and reproductive physiology and behavior (Sapolsky, 1992). Individuals who engaged in anxiety-reducing group ceremonies would likely have been more fit than those who went their own isolate, anxious ways.

How might an artified response to stress have first occurred? Malinowski (1922) and Mead (1976/1930) each describe a group of individuals in New Guinea (Trobriand Islands, Manus) who, during a terrifying storm, chanted charms together in a singsong voice.

Repetitive, self-soothing kinesic and vocal behaviors occur in everyone, first appearing in infancy. "Doing something" such as moving and vocalizing rhythmically with others or another is even more soothing. It is not hard to imagine that if the storm subsided peaceably, movements and utterances might become more formalized and elaborated and gradually become a "storm (or danger) prevention ceremony," performed as a safeguard even without an immediate cause.

The widespread practice of lamenting the loss by death or separation from a loved one seems to me another plausible model for an origin of early human art, where a natural behavior like weeping and moaning in grief became formalized and elaborated in song/poetry and shared with others to relieve feelings of helplessness, despair, and the anxiety attendant on the interruption death brings to the life of an individual or group.

The reactions of people in the United States after the September 2001 attacks illustrate the therapeutic nature of artification and participation in art-filled ceremony. Individuals spontaneously gathered in parks, churches, and other special places to listen to song, liturgy, and poetry; walked solemnly holding candles and flags; wrote poems to be placed in public places—none of these ordinary behaviors—and found solace in doing these things with others.

The Art and Anxiety hypothesis challenges the Art as By-product claim. There are numerous instances of art behavior that counter the suggestion that people are merely pressing pleasure buttons. Laments, funerary arts, crawling through a kilometer of narrow, wet tunnels to paint (or view) bison on cave walls are not done for entertainment and fun.

Sugiyama and Scalise Sugiyama (2003, p. 182) suggest that costly signals may operate "on several frequencies, capable of sending a variety of messages." Thus, ceremonial extravagances like time-consuming preparations of ritual spaces or paraphernalia (e.g., masks, costumes, musical instruments, arduous performances, and elaborate patterned scarifications at initiation) need not be interpreted only as costly signals for attracting mates or only as unfakable proof of commitment, but also as "indexical" of or correlative to the importance to individuals and groups of their beliefs and practices (Tambiah, 1979). It seems plausible that having a sense of meaningfulness and competence is cognitively and emotionally adaptive to human individuals and groups, especially when compared to its opposite—lack of meaning and not knowing how to cope.

If the behavioral category of art may have a variety of functions, the nine hypotheses described in Part A are not *wrong*, but partial. My hypothesis of ceremonial artifications that promoted group coordination and reduction of individual stress seems to me to fit the facts of what is known about the arts in small-scale societies more comprehensively than others. Additionally, it provides a plausible origin for a general behavior/motivation (to artify) from which individual arts could emerge and eventually assume other functions and characteristics. My hypothesis emphasizes movement, rhythm, repetition, formalization, and the psychological effects of temporal organization as primary, suggesting that visual arts (e.g., ornamenting bodies, artifacts, and surroundings) may have evolved separately and were added to temporally constructed artifications in order to provide additional emphasis.

REFERENCES

Aiken, N. E. (1998a). *The biological origins of art.* Westport CT: Praeger.
Aiken, N. E. (1998b). Power through art. *Research in Biopolitics, 6,* 215-228.
Boyd, B. (2005). Evolutionary theories of art. In J. Gottschall & D. S. Wilson (Eds.), *Literature and the human animal* (pp. 147-176). Evanston, IL: Northwestern University Press.
Carroll, J. (2004). *Literary Darwinism: Literature and the human animal.* New York and London: Routledge.
Chernoff, J. M. (1979). *African rhythm and African sensibility.* Chicago: University of Chicago Press.
Coe, K. (2003). *The ancestress hypothesis: Visual art as adaptation.* New Brunswick NJ: Rutgers University Press.
Darwin, C. (1871). *The descent of man and selection in relation to sex.* London: Murray.
Dissanayake, E. (1995). Chimera, spandrel, or adaptation: Conceptualizing art in human evolution. *Human Nature, 6*(2), 99-117.
Dissanayake, E. (2000). *Art and intimacy: How the arts began.* Seattle WA: University of Washington Press.
Easterlin, N. (2002). Hans Christian Andersen's fish out of water. *Philosophy and Literature, 24*(2), 443-454.
Feist, G. J. (2001). Natural and sexual selection in the evolution of creativity. *Bulletin of Psychology and the Arts, 2*(1), 11-16.
Gottschall, J. (2003). Patterns of characterization in folk tales across geographic regions and levels of cultural complexity: Literature as a neglected source of quantitative data. *Human Nature, 14*(4), 365-382.
Groos, K. (1898). *The play of animals.* New York: D. Appleton & Co.
Groos, K. (1901). *The play of man.* New York: Appleton.
Irons, W. (2001). Religion as a hard-to-fake sign of commitment, In R. Nesse (Ed.), *Evolution and the capacity for commitment* (pp. 292-309). New York: Russell Sage.
Malinowski, B. (1922). *Argonauts of the Western Pacific.* London: Routledge & Kegan Paul.
Mead, M. (1976/1930). *Growing up in New Guinea.* New York: Morrow.

Miller, G. (2000). *The mating mind: How sexual choice shaped the evolution of human nature*. New York: Doubleday.
Miller, G. (2001). Aesthetic fitness: How sexual selection shaped artistic virtuosity as a fitness indicator and aesthetic preferences as mate choice criteria. *Bulletin of Psychology and the Arts, 2*(1), 20-25.
Morphy, H. (1992). From dull to brilliant: The aesthetics of spiritual power among the Yolngu. In J. Coote & A. Shelton (Eds.), *Anthropology, art, and aesthetics* (pp. 181-208). Oxford: Clarendon.
Orians, G. H. (2001). An evolutionary perspective on aesthetics. *Bulletin of Psychology and the Arts, 2*(1), 25-29.
Pinker, S. (1997). *How the mind works*. New York: Norton.
Pinker, S. (2002). *The blank slate: The modern denial of human nature*. New York: Viking Penguin.
Power, C. (1999). "Beauty" magic: The origins of art. In R. Dunbar, C. Knight, & C. Power (Eds.), *The evolution of culture: An interdisciplinary view* (pp. 92-112). Edinburgh: Edinburgh University Press.
Ramachandran, V. S., & Hirstein, W. (1999). The science of art: A neurological theory of aesthetic experience. *Journal of Consciousness Studies, 6*, 15-51.
Ruso, B., Renninger, L., & Atzwanger, K. (2003). Human habitat preferences: A generative territory for evolutionary aesthetics research. In E. Voland & K. Grammar (Eds.), *Evolutionary aesthetics* (pp. 279-294). Berlin: Springer Verlag.
Sapolsky, R. M. (1992). Neuroendocrinology of the stress response. In J. R. Becker, S. M. Breedlove, & D. Crews (Eds.), *Behavioral endocrinology* (pp. 287-324). Cambridge MA: MIT Press.
Scalise Sugiyama, M. (2001). Food, foragers, and folklore: The role of narrative in human subsistence. *Evolution and Human Behavior, 22*, 221-240.
Solso, R. L. (1994). *Cognition and the visual arts*. Cambridge MA: MIT Press.
Sosis, R. (2003). Why aren't we all Hutterites?: Costly signaling theory and religious behavior. *Human Nature, 14*(2), 91-127.
Sugiyama, L. S., & Scalise Sugiyama, M. (2003). Social roles, prestige, and health risk: Social niche specialization as a risk-buffering strategy. *Human Nature, 14*(2), 165-190.
Tambiah, S. J. (1979). A performative approach to ritual. *Proceedings of the British Academy, London LXV* (pp. 113-169). Oxford: Oxford University Press.
Thornhill, R. (1998). Darwinian aesthetics. In C. Crawford & D. L. Krebs (Eds.), *Handbook of evolutionary psychology: Ideas, issues, applications* (pp. 543-572). Mahwah, NJ: Erlbaum.
Tooby, J., & Cosmides, L. (2001). Does beauty build adapted minds? Toward an evolutionary theory of aesthetics, fiction and the arts. In H. P. Abbott (Ed.), *On the origin of fictions: Interdisciplinary perspectives* (pp. 6-27). Madison WI: University of Wisconsin Press and *Substance, 30*(1&2).
Voland, E. (2003). Aesthetic preferences in the world of artifacts—Adaptations for the evaluation of 'honest signals'? In E. Voland & K. Grammar (Eds.), *Evolutionary aesthetics* (pp. 239-260). Berlin: Springer Verlag.

Voland, E., & Grammar, K. (Eds.). (2003). *Evolutionary aesthetics*. Berlin: Springer Verlag.
Zeki, S. (1999). *Inner vision: An exploration of art and the brain.* Oxford: Oxford University Press.

CHAPTER 2

An Evolutionary Model of Artistic and Musical Creativity

Gregory J. Feist

The human brain is truly a marvelous and awe-inspiring thing. It has between 50 and 100 billion nerve cells, each of which has between 2,000 and 5,000 neural connections that are approximately a hundred trillion synaptic connections! (Gerasimov, 1998; Passer & Smith, 2001). But we mustn't forget: it is a brain like all other brains. Its function is to organize and interpret information from the five basic sensory modalities. All brains of all living creatures possessing brains do the same thing. It is just that the modern human brain carries out these functions more complexly, abstractly, and symbolically than any other animal the world has ever seen (not to get too grandiose with our own abilities!).

One of the wonders of the human brain is that it is capable of both appreciating and creating sensory experiences that inspire a sense of wonder, beauty, and awe; that is, create and appreciate art. That particular patterns of sound, markings, light waves, gustatory and tactile sensations, and verbal and linguistic forms are preferred and appreciated over other patterns and forms of the same is intriguing and ultimately what this chapter in specific and this book in general are concerned with. The question that begs to be addressed, to paraphrase the rock group "The Talking Heads," is "How did we get here?" From a long-term perspective, there is one glaring answer: evolution.

SELECTION THEORIES OF CREATIVITY AND AESTHETICS

What people find "beautiful" is not arbitrary, but rather has evolved over eons of hominid sensory, perceptual, and cognitive evolution

(Aiken, 1998; Barrow, 1995; Berlyne, 1971; Coss, 1968; Dissanayake, 1988, 1992; Feist, 2001; Miller, 2000a, 2000b; Orians & Heerwagen, 1992; Tooby & Cosmides, 2001). Two broad categories of evolutionary theory can be distinguished in aesthetics: natural selection and sexual selection theories, with the former focusing on solutions that solve survival problems and the latter on solutions that solve social and reproductive problems.

The natural selection theories subsume explanations that focus on arousal and habituation as well as those that focus on the needs for safety, survival, and order (Barrow, 1995; Berlyne, 1971; Coss, 1968; Darwin 1871; Orians, 2001; Orians & Heerwagen, 1992). The fundamental argument is that people prefer sensations and perceptions that feel safe and orderly, ultimately ones that have survival value. Art and aesthetic preferences are no exception. For example, Orians and Heerwagen (1992) conducted a study of landscape features and found that participants prefer the safe and protected savannas—forested and mountainous—over the more vulnerable tundra and desert settings. Moreover, Orians (2001) has argued that we have evolved preferences for certain kinds of ancestral environments. Evolved preferences revolve around the basic problems of survival: safety, food acquisition, shelter, and choosing associates for reproduction, foraging, protection, and gaining status. Our preference for the beautiful developed out of our adaptive responses to these basic problems of survival.

Sexual selection theories, on the other hand, emphasize fitness and mate value (Dissanayake, 1988, 1992; Miller, 2000a, 2000b; Power, 1999). That is, producing works of art signals one's fitness (intelligence, creativity) to potential mates. Only people who can "afford it" (i.e., are fit and talented enough) can spend their time doing art. Perhaps the most cogent argument for the power of sexual selection pressures in art and aesthetics comes from Geoffrey Miller (2000a, 2000b). He contends that human creative and aesthetic abilities have evolved through sexual selection pressures and mate choice because they are reliable signals of fitness (e.g., good health and superior intellectual capacity). Miller contends that one form of sexual selection through which aesthetic preferences have evolved in humans is called "the handicap principle" (Zahavi & Zahavi, 1997). In brief, the basic idea of the handicap principle states that "ornamental" and "wasteful" signals (often in males) evolve because they provide an indication of superior fitness. These traits must come with a cost or a handicap if they are to accurately signal fitness; that is, they must have high costs in order to be reliable. By having a cost, they cannot be easily faked, and only the most fit individuals can afford them. Mate choice operates to maximize fitness of offspring by developing a preference for such "extravagant displays." The heavy and bright plumage of the peacock is the prototypical case for such handicapping. Art and music may be such "handicaps" for humans.

A few theorists have attempted to bridge the natural and sexual selection perspectives (Feist, 2001; Thornhill, 1998). For example, Feist (2001) argues that both natural and sexual selection pressures have shaped the human capacity to be creative, but different forms of selection have shaped different forms of creativity. From an evolutionary perspective, it is important to distinguish two forms of creativity; namely, whether the behaviors have direct survival value (i.e., as seen in technical or applied creative behavior) or whether they don't (i.e., as seen in aesthetic, ornamental or artistic behavior). The more applied forms of creativity—technology, engineering, and tool making—are probably more under natural selection pressures in that they have direct implications for surviving to reproductive age. On the other hand, the more ornate and aesthetic forms of creativity— music, dance, wit, and art—are probably more under sexual selection pressures, in so far that they implicitly (unconsciously) signal an individual's genetic, physical, and mental fitness, and are deemed attractive by members of the opposite sex. They, in fact, would be the kinds of traits we would want our offspring to possess. Wit, intelligence, creativity, and charm would make some individuals more attractive to members of the opposite sex than others, and over eons of human evolution, sexual selection pressures would result in a wide range of individual differences in these traits (in contrast to natural selection pressures, which tend to attenuate individual differences over time). In short, I argue that both forms of selection have been important in shaping human creative potential and behavior over the millennia, but that each form of selection has shaped a distinct form of human creativity.

INTELLIGENCE, CREATIVITY AND AESTHETICS AS CO-OPTED ADAPTATIONS

Related to the question of selection is the question of whether these traits are adaptations or co-opted by-products of adaptations (Buss, Haselton, Shackelford, Bleske, & Wakefield, 1998; Gould, 1991; Thornhill, 1997; Williams, 1966). As Darwin first recognized, mental structures and their corresponding processes (intelligence, creativity, symbolic and abstract thinking) are most certainly part of the evolutionary process. "A great stride in the development of the intellect will have followed, as soon as the half-art and half-instinct of language came into use.... The higher intellectual powers of man, such as those of ratiocination, abstraction, self-consciousness, etc., probably follow from the continued improvement and exercise of the other mental faculties" (Darwin, 1871, p. 633).

As implied here by Darwin, explicit, rational theories are not evolved "adaptations," but their implicit foundations may be. A few scholars, to be sure, have recently argued that human intellect, creativity, and wit are biological adaptations that have been shaped not by survival and natural selection pressures, but rather by courtship and sexual selection pressures (e.g., Miller, 2000a, 2000b). But most modern scholars on evolution of mind see art, music, consciousness, rationality, and science more as co-opted by-products of adaptations rather than adaptations directly (Buller & Hardcastle, 2000; Buss et al., 1998; Feist, 2001, in press; Gould, 1991; Pinker, 1997; Thornhill, 1997; Tooby & Cosmides, 1992; Williams, 1966). That is, basic cognitive processes of perception, concept formation, and domain specific intelligences might be adaptations; but specific creative outcomes, as Darwin suggested, of these processes are probably by-products and not under direct selection pressure. Art, science, mathematics, and philosophy were not what our brains evolved to do, but once they developed the cortical power for abstract, symbolic, and metacognitive thought, these specific creative activities simply required the right cultural and historical ingredients to become manifest.

For example, John D. Barrow (1995, 1998) makes an interesting and intriguing proposal that human aesthetic sensitivities evolved as by-products from the basic perceptual discrimination of symmetrical and nonsymmetrical forms. Living things possess greater symmetry than nonliving things, and one's ability to distinguish living from nonliving obviously has fundamental ramifications for survival as well as reproduction. Knowing what can be eaten and what can't is basic to survival, but in addition, symmetrical forms, especially in facial features, are intuitively and automatically deemed more attractive than less symmetrical forms; and even four-month-old human infants have this preference for symmetrical faces. In this sense, aesthetic preferences are related in humans and nonhumans to reproductive outcomes. We are attracted to symmetrical forms in bodies, as current evolutionary theorists suggest, due to their advertising greater genetic fitness.

EVOLVED DOMAINS OF MIND

Natural and sexual selection pressures have predisposed and constrained the human mind toward certain kinds of sensations and functions. These functions are specific mechanisms and cognitive domains that solve specific problems. Domains of mind have some degree of physical/neuroanatomical status (i.e., localized to particular brain regions), but they are also conceptual and heuristic entities. As defined by Rochel Gelman and Kimberly Brenneman, a domain is a "given set of principles, the rules of their application, and the entities to which they apply . . ." (Gelman & Brenneman, 1994, p. 371). That is, domain specific principles are interrelated and operate within a specific class of problems that have been crucial for survival and reproductive success. Domains are similar to but not synonymous with modules, for the latter are encapsulated information units that process inputs (perceptions) (cf. Fodor, 1983). Domains are universal and part of human nature, and they concern knowledge of the social (people), animate (animals), and inanimate (physical objects) worlds; being able to count, quantify (number), and communicate (language) our ideas about these worlds; appreciating and creating aesthetically pleasing arrangements of visual images (aesthetics); and being sensitive to and appreciative of rhythm, pitch, timing in sounds (music) (Aiken 1998; Dissanayake, 1992; Feist, 2001; Gardner, 1983; Pinker, 1997; Wallin, Merker, & Brown 2000). Because this chapter is concerned with art, I focus my attention on the two specific domains that underlie art; namely, folk art and music. In other places, I have discussed in more detail the domains of mind involved in the psychology of scientific thinking (Feist, in press).

Domains of Mind as Domains of Art

Art (aesthetics) is the sensitivity to, production of, and appreciation and preference for particular visual forms, figures, and color combinations over others. Defined this way, I equate "art" in this narrower sense with "visual art" (painting and drawing). Aesthetics in general, and visual art in particular, inherently involve emotional responses of like/dislike, which provide signals for our well-being. Indeed, a sense of aesthetics is an inevitable outcome of our sense of safety, order, and well-being, as well as other principles of perception (Aiken, 1998; Barrow, 1995; Dissanayake, 1992; Feist, 2001; Feist & Brady, 2004; Gardner, 1983; Miller et al., 2000; Orians, 2001; Orians & Heerwagan, 1992; Ramachandran & Hirstein, 1999; Zeki, 1999).

Music is the capacity to produce, perceive, and appreciate rhythmic, melodic sounds that evoke an emotional response in oneself and others. It can also be defined as the ability to perceive changes in pitch to be harmonically or rhythmically related. As one ethnomusicologist wrote recently: "All of us are born with the capacity to apprehend emotion and meaning in music, regardless of whether we understand music theory or read musical notation" (Tramo, 2001, p. 54).

Evidence for Domains

To call something a domain requires specific criteria, otherwise it risks being an arbitrary enterprise. I argue there are seven criteria, the majority of which must be met if a capacity is to count as a domain of mind: archeological, comparative, developmental, universal, precocious talent and giftedness, neuroscientific, and genetic (cf. Feist, in press; Gardner, 1983). In short, nothing less than the combined interdisciplinary evidence from archeology, primatology, developmental psychology, anthropology, giftedness/education, neuroscience, and genetics is required before something can be classified as a domain. Now is neither the time nor place to present a systematic review of all the evidence for each domain. Instead, I will briefly review the two main domains relevant to art and aesthetics; namely, visual art and music, and three out of the seven criteria (fossil, neuroscientific, and developmental).

Fossil Evidence

Fossil evidence for the artistic/aesthetics domain is somewhat older than for music. The oldest findings for art implements and objects (beads, ochre) possibly reach back 75 to 350 thousand years (Barham, 1998; Fullagar, Prince, & Head, 1996; Henshilwood, d'Errico, Vanhaeren, van Niekerk, & Jacobs, 2004). These findings, however, are somewhat controversial and disputed as to their symbolism, intentionality and purpose. By approximately 40 kyr there is undisputed evidence for symbolic art objects found in Europe and Australia—for instance, the Hohlenstein-Stadel statuette and the Chauvet, Cussac, and Lascaux cave paintings (cf. Mithen, 1996; White, 1992).

Music also has ancient origins that are not always identifiable in the archeological record. Like number, archeological evidence for ancient music-making is almost nonexistent in species other than *H. sapiens*, because the earliest forms of musical expression, such as song, dance, and wood instrumentation, do not fossilize. Like many of these domains of mind, the fossil record concerning music must no doubt inherently underrepresent what our ancestors did and were capable of. Dean Falk (2000) speculates, for instance, that music, like language, *began* evolving about 2 million years ago in humans, but did not reach mature development until perhaps only a couple hundred thousand years ago. Wooden instruments and drums might have been the first material form of music, but the first archeological evidence of musical instrumentation is that of a bone "flute" from only about 45 kyr and has been attributed to Neanderthal (Kunej & Turk, 2000). Another bone flute has been dated to 36 kyr (Hahn & Münzel, 1995). So, there is quite a gap between the probable origins of music and the archeological record.

Neuroscience Evidence

If something is to be a domain, it will most likely have specific and relatively dedicated neural networks most involved in processing that particular kind of information. Although it is clear there is no "art" or "music" center in the brain, and that many structures are integrated in artistic and musical experience, recent neuroscientific evidence has begun to uncover the neurological architecture behind artistic and musical behavior.

Bruce Miller and colleagues, for instance, have reported a very intriguing finding concerning the preservation or enhancement of visual or musical creativity and degeneration of linguistic and social skills with the onset of frontotemporal dementia (FTD) in the left hemisphere (Miller et al., 2000). More specifically, patients who manifested creative ability were more likely to have dementia in the anterior region of the left temporal lobe and yet have a relatively intact frontal lobe. There were exceptions, with some also having frontal damage, and these patients tended to show visual rather than musical skills. To be sure, creative abilities are not the norm with FTD patients, and therefore these patients must have some specific subset of the dementia. Miller and others refer to this phenomenon as "paradoxical functional facilitation" and believe that in intact individuals, these regions can inhibit certain artistic skills, and when these brain regions degenerate, the skills paradoxically become manifest.

Ramachandran and Hirstein (1999) have published a neurological theory of aesthetic experience in which they propose eight neurological principles of aesthetic production and response—"a set of heuristics that artists either consciously or unconsciously deploy to optimally titillate the visual areas of the brain" (Ramachandran & Hirstein, 1999, p. 15). A number of these principles are relatively well-known from Gestalt psychology and traditional theory of aesthetics (e.g., grouping, isolation, and contrast), but the one they spend the most time on is somewhat novel; namely, the "peak shift effect." Once a behavior is reinforced for responding to a particular stimulus, the behavior is even more exaggerated when the animal is presented with a more extreme version of the stimulus. For instance, if a rat is taught to discriminate a square from a rectangle that has a 3:2 aspect ratio, it will respond even more frequently to a rectangle with a 4:1 aspect ratio. Ramachandran and Hirstein (1999) argue that this exaggerated effect plays a fundamental role in aesthetic production and response. Artists exaggerate certain qualities of an image (form, shape, color, movement) because they are consciously or more often unconsciously amplifying traits or differences that provoke an aesthetic response in the brains of others. Exaggerating sexual qualities in particular has been a common technique throughout the history of world art. Ramachandran and Hirstein also tie their argument into runaway sexual selection theory (i.e., female choice results in exaggerated male ornamental signals of fitness, such as bright plumage or coloring).

As neuroscientists, Ramachandran and Hirstein (1999) also integrate these findings into what is known about brain function. For instance, they argue that much of the visual or auditory processing in art can actually occur after emotional processing of the limbic system has occurred. They propose a "progressive bootstrapping" model in which limbic and cortical regions process incoming information progressively in stages, whereby "partial 'solutions' or conjectures to perceptual problems are fed back from every level in the hierarchy to every earlier module to impose a small bias in processing" (Ramachandran & Hirstein, 1999, p. 23). In this sense, they are in fact arguing for a close interplay between the "hot" affective response system and the "cold" cortical response—or in more common terms, cognition and emotion.

Another neuroscientist has coined the phrase "neuroaesthetics" in an attempt to crystallize the research and theory on the biological underpinnings of art and aesthetics (Zeki, 1999). In fact, Zeki (1999) argues that brain function and art are both attempting the same basic functions; namely, to depict objects as they are and to form concepts. Art, moreover, is the process of distilling only the essential and permanent characteristics of objects or experiences and expressing and representing them in an external and communicable medium.

Regarding neuroscientific evidence for music, brain structures and brain development appear to be both influences of and influenced by musical interest and training. There are many complications in the neuroscience of music; for example, whether people are musicians or not; whether they are listening, playing, or reading music; and whether they are male and female, to name but three of the more noteworthy qualifications. Nevertheless, certain principles have emerged from the literature, of which I will but highlight some of the key findings.

One general finding is that brain structures are somewhat different in musicians compared to nonmusicians. For instance, the motor cortex, cerebellum (Hutchinson, Lee, Gaab, & Schlaug, 2003; Sergent, Zuch, Terriah, & MacDonald, 1992), planum temporale (PT) of the temporal lobes (Ohnishi et al., 2001), and the corpus callosum (Schlaug, Jäncke, Huang, Staiger, & Steinmetz, 1995) are larger in musicians than nonmusicians. The larger PT of musicians interestingly is limited to musicians with perfect pitch. Granted, these findings are more correlational than causal, but they do suggest the brain can be shaped by musical training as it is from other forms of environmental stimulation (e.g., Rosenzweig, Krech, Bennett, & Diamond, 1962). Lending support to this argument is the fact that there is a direct and proportional correlation between the degree of activation of the left auditory cortex most associated with music (planum temporale) and the age at which music training was begun (i.e., the earlier, the larger the area of activation; Ohnishi et al., 2001).

It is not terribly surprising to learn that neuroscientists have confirmed the importance of the auditory cortex (temporal lobe) in musical experience (e.g., pitch and melody). What is a little more surprising is the relative asymmetry of this effect, with the right auditory cortex (the planum temporale) being more activated than the left while listening to music; at least this is the case for nonmusicians (Schlaug et al., 1995). Another general finding of the neuroscience of music is that melody, pitch, and harmony call more on the right hemisphere activity than on left, especially the right prefrontal cortex and right paralimbic regions (Blood, Zatorre, Bermudez, & Evans, 1999; Falk, 2000; Tramo, 2001; Zatorre, Evans, & Meyer, 1994). These findings are consistent with evidence concerning the right hemisphere's role in emotional processes. Moreover, timing, sequencing, and rhythm—important elements of music—are complex abilities, but seem to mostly activate the cerebellum, the supplementary motor cortex, the premotor cortex, the basal ganglia, and parietal cortex (Janata & Grafton, 2003; Tramo, 2001). Finally, when musicians read music, only the visual-spatial region of their parietal lobe becomes active, suggesting that musicians read notes in space, hence the connection between music and spatial ability (see Falk, 2000; Hassler, Birbaumer, & Feil, 1985; Sergent et al., 1992).

Developmental Evidence

Children, especially young children, offer a glimpse into human nature insofar as traits and abilities that develop in children the world over and prior to major cultural influences, suggest a central nervous system that has been built to do certain activities and solve particular problems. Traits that are manifested automatically, spontaneously, and show a regular developmental sequence suggest an evolved domain of mind. Art and music meet this criterion.

Developmental evidence for art makes it clear that drawing is a completely normal, ubiquitous, and automatic activity of childhood. Most every child goes through a period of drawing, even if ability levels vary greatly. As a visually based and nonverbal medium, it may even be more basic, intuitive, and common than writing.

Although no research has been conducted on general art/aesthetic preferences in newborns, research on attractiveness in the human face with newborns has shown convincingly (similar to infant preference for consonantal music) an aesthetic preference for attractive over less attractive faces by infants as young as four months of age (Langlois, Ritter, Roggman, & Vaughn 1991; Rubenstein, Kalakanis, & Langlois 1999). Infants are obviously not being told to or reading in a magazine that they should look longer at the attractive face and yet this is what they do quite consistently.

The development of art comes in different forms: the development in understanding and appreciation of other people's art and the development in producing art. Regarding the former, Howard Gardner and Ellen Winner conducted some of the first studies of the development of understanding of art (Gardner, 1982). Gardner and Winner report three stages of the child's understanding of art: young childhood (ages 4 to 7), middle childhood (age 10), and adolescence (ages 14 to 16). Young childhood is marked by a "mechanistic view" in which art is thought to be produced more by machines (factories) than humans. Middle childhood is the age of "realism" where how realistic the image is the main criterion of its quality. If it is a good reproduction of reality, it is good. If not, it is not good. By adolescence, a "relative" phase develops, in which individual taste becomes the main criterion by which the quality of art is evaluated.

Regarding the development of producing art, Gardner (1982) also reports that in early childhood (up to about age 8 or 9), children are prone to much spontaneous, impressionistic, and fanciful drawing; around age 8 to 10 their interest in drawing wanes and takes a more literal and realistic turn. Many older children reject and are even become hostile toward unrealistic depictions that "just can't happen." Then by adolescence, children often return to a more impressionistic, abstract, and fantasy-laden artistic phase. This has been dubbed by Gardner a "u-shaped model" of artistic development (with peaks being in early childhood and late adolescence). Adult artists are those who are able to return to the preliteral age of childhood and express impressionistic, unconscious thoughts and feelings.

Similarly, Golomb (1987, 2002) reviewed evidence for how artistic skills develop normally from early to late childhood. In one study, Golomb (1987) gave the same four drawing tasks to 411 children 3 to 14.

She found that as children got older, they were more likely to use principles of grouping and similarity, with early undifferentiated alignments becoming more ordered with age. Moreover, compositional ability developed up through age 9 and then leveled off, with no differentiation between 9 and 14 year olds. The leveling off in general artistic development after age 10 is somewhat perplexing given the significant linguistic and mathematical development that occurs after this age. Golomb (2002) also reviewed evidence from the Goodenough Draw-a-Person test that shows progression up until approximately age 10 and then a leveling off. Older compared to younger children do include more elements in their drawings, are less linear, maintain their attention longer toward completing a drawing, and exhibit other technical accomplishments. Finally, Golomb argues that these developments do not occur in stage-like Piagetian fashion and are not correlated with intelligence and only loosely with intellectual/cognitive development.

Regarding developmental evidence for music, Sandra Trehub is the leading expert in the field of the development of music perception and appreciation in infants. The main conclusions from her research, and others like it, is that infants as young as 6 months are incredibly sensitive to lapses or anomalies in tone, pitch, or scale. Infants will orient toward an anomalous note whether the sequence is culturally familiar or unfamiliar, and they can hear differences between two adjacent notes, changes in rhythm, and perceive and remember melodic contour (Trehub, 2000; Trehub, Bull, & Thorpe, 1984; Trehub & Thorpe, 1989). Moreover, Zentner and Kagan (1998) demonstrated that 4- to 7-month-old infants prefer (i.e., looked longer and were less active during) consonant musical intervals compared to dissonant intervals (cf. Gardner, 1982). Winner (1996) reports that all children begin to produce their own spontaneous music around age 18 months, but by age 5 their spontaneous singing declines (unless they are gifted).

Gelman and Brenneman (1994) argue that inherent first principles guide attentional and cognitive processing of numeric and musical stimuli, and therefore development in these domains is guided by first principles. The musical brain is not blank, but rather disposed toward certain structural preferences in tone, rhythm, contour, and pitch. Rhythm and beat are easy and automatic partly because they involve auditory pattern recognition, but music theory is not. Much like formal math, music theory is not part of normal auditory development and therefore is more difficult and requires training. First principles can both facilitate and hinder learning (Gelman & Brenneman, 1994).

CONCLUSIONS

Aesthetic and creative experience is part of being human; it is part of our nature. Indeed, one could argue that creativity and aesthetics are *the* distinguishing and signature characteristics of modern humans. Other species of hominid did not have the creative and aesthetic abilities of *H. sapiens sapiens*. They no doubt had some capacities for these experiences, but their form and structure must have been quantitatively if not qualitatively distinct from our own.

In our own attempt to understand these unusual and unique experiences and capacities of modern humans, humans have developed a number of theories. I have focused on evolutionary-based theory in both its natural and sexual selection form. Survival and reproduction are no doubt the major ancestral problems we and all species have confronted, and anything that confers advantages in these domains is generally selected for. Although not obvious on the surface, artistic and musical ability and sensitivity do in fact bestow survival and reproductive benefits. They signal fitness (only the most clever and creative individuals produce works that no one else is capable of) and help distinguish animate from inanimate (symmetrical)—hence what might be predator or prey. They also suggest to us what kind of environment might be most sustainable for human survival.

Not that art and music are evolved biological adaptations. Most theorists, myself among them, argue instead for their status as co-opted by-products of other adaptations. I do argue, however, that they are evolved and specific domains of mind and present fossil, neuroscientific, and developmental evidence for why I believe this to be so. As long as we have complex brains, we will continue to prefer certain combinations of sounds, sights, tastes, and linguistic patterns over others. In other words, we will continue to be "*Homo aestheticus*" (Dissanayake, 1992).

REFERENCES

Aiken, N. E. (1998). *The biological origins of art*. Westport, CN: Praeger.
Barham, L. (1998). Possible early pigment use in south-central Africa. *Current Anthropology, 39,* 703-710.
Barrow, J. D. (1995). *The artful universe*. Boston: Little-Brown.
Barrow, J. D. (1998). *Impossibility: The limits of science and the science of limits*. Oxford, UK: Oxford University Press.
Berlyne, D. E. (1971). *Aesthetics and psychobiology*. New York: Appleton-Century-Crofts.
Blood, A. J., Zatorre, R. J., Bermudez, P., & Evans, A. C. (1999). Emotional responses to pleasant and unpleasant music correlate with activity in paralimbic brain regions. *Nature Neuroscience, 2,* 382-387.

Buller, D. J., & Hardcastle, V. G. (2000). Evolutionary psychology, meet developmental neurobiology: Against promiscuous modularity. *Brain and Mind, 1,* 307-325.

Buss, D. M., Haselton, M. G., Shackelford, T. K., Bleske, A. L., & Wakefield, J. C. (1998). Adaptations, expatiations, and spandrels. *American Psychologist, 53,* 533-548.

Coss, R. G. (1968). The ethological command in art. *Leonardo, 1,* 273-287.

Darwin, C. (1871). *The descent of man.* London: Murray (reprinted in 1998 by Prometheus Books).

Dissanayake, E. (1988). *What is art for?* Seattle, WA: Washington University Press.

Dissanayake, E. (1992). *Homo aestheticus: Where art comes from and why.* New York: The Free Press.

Falk, D. (2000). Hominid brain evolution and the origins of music. In N. L. Wallin, B. Merker, & S. Brown (Eds.), *The origins of music* (pp. 197-216). Cambridge, MA: MIT Press.

Feist, G. J. (2001). Natural and sexual selection in the evolution of creativity. *Bulletin of Psychology and the Arts, 2,* 11-16.

Feist, G. J. (in press). *The scientific mind: Foundations for the psychology of science.* New Haven, CT: Yale University Press.

Feist, G. J., & Brady, T. R. (2004). Openness to experience, non-conformity and the preference for abstract art. *Empirical Studies of the Arts. 22,* 77-89.

Fodor, J. A. (1983). *The modularity of mind: An essay on faculty psychology.* Cambridge: MIT Press.

Fullagar, R. L. K., Prince, D. M., & Head, L. M. (1996). Early human occupation of northern Australia: Archeology and thermoluminescence dating of Jinmium Rock-Shelter, Northern Territory. *Antiquity 70,* 751-773.

Gardner, H. (1982). *Art, mind, & brain: A cognitive approach to creativity.* New York: Basic Books.

Gardner, H. (1983). *Frames of mind: The theory of multiple intelligences.* New York: Basic Books.

Gelman, R., & Brenneman, L. (1994). First principles can support both universal and culture-specific learning about number and music. In L. A. Hirschfeld & S. A. Gelman (Eds.), *Mapping the mind: Domain specificity in cognition and culture* (pp. 369-390). New York: Cambridge University Press.

Gerasimov, V. (1998). Information processing in the human body. Website: http://vadim.www.media.mit.edu/MAS862/Project.html (accessed August 22, 2004).

Golomb, C. (1987). The development of compositional strategies in children's drawings. *Visual Arts Research, 13,* 42-52.

Golomb, C. (2002). *Child art in context: A cultural and comparative perspective.* Washington, DC: American Psychological Association.

Gould, S. J. (1991). Exaptation: A crucial tool for evolutionary psychology. *Journal of Social Issues, 47,* 43-65.

Hahn, J., & Münzel, S. (1995). Knochenflöten aus dem Aurignacien des Geissenklösterle bei Blaubeuren, Alb-Donau-Kreis. *Fundberichte aus Baden-Württemberg, 20,* 1-12.

Hassler, M., Birbaumer, N., & Feil, A. (1985). Musical talent and visual-spatial abilities: A longitudinal study. *Psychology of Music, 13,* 99-113.

Henshilwood, C., d'Errico, F. Vanhaeren, M., van Niekerk, K., & Jacobs, Z. (2004). Middle stone age shell beads South Africa. *Science 304,* 404.

Hutchinson, S., Lee, L. H., Gaab, N. & Schlaug, G. (2003). Cerebellar volume and musicians. *Cerebral Cortex, 13,* 943-949.

Janata, P., & Grafton, S. T. (2003). Swinging in the brain: Shared neural substrates for behaviors related sequencing and music. *Nature Neuroscience, 6,* 682-687.

Kunej, D., & Turk, I. (2000). New perspectives on the beginnings of music: Archeological and musicological analysis of a middle Paleolithic bone "flute." In N. L. Wallin, B. Merker, & S. Brown (Eds.), *The origins of music* (pp. 235-268). Cambridge, MA: MIT Press.

Langlois, J. H., Ritter, J. M., Roggman, L. A., & Vaughn, L. S. (1991). Facial diversity and infant preferences for attractive faces. *Developmental Psychology, 27,* 79-84.

Miller, B. L., Boone, K., Cummings, J. L., Read, S. L., & Mishkin, F. (2000). Functional correlates of musical and visual ability in frontotemporal dementia. *British Journal of Psychiatry, 176,* 458-463.

Miller, G. (2000a). Evolution of human music through sexual selection. In N. L. Wallin, B. Merker, & S. Brown (Eds.), *The origins of music* (pp. 329-360). Cambridge, MA: MIT Press.

Miller, G. F. (2000b). *The mating mind: How sexual choice shaped the evolution of human nature.* New York: Doubleday.

Mithen, S. (1996). *The prehistory of the mind: The cognitive origins of art and science.* London: Thames and Hudson.

Ohnishi, T., Matsuda, H., Asada, T., Aruga, M., Hirakata, M., Nishikawa, M., Katoh, A., & Imabayashi, E. (2001). Functional anatomy of musical perception in musicians. *Cerebral Cortex, 11,* 754-760.

Orians, G. H. (2001). An evolutionary perspective on aesthetics. *Bulletin of Psychology and the Arts, 2,* 25-29.

Orians, G. H., & Heerwagen, J. H. (1992). Evolved responses to landscapes. In J. H. Barkow & L. Cosmides (Eds.), *The adapted mind: Evolutionary psychology and the generation of culture* (pp. 555-579). New York: Oxford University Press.

Passer, M. W., & Smith, R. E. (2001). *Psychology: Frontiers and applications.* New York: McGraw Hill.

Pinker, S. (1997). *How the mind works.* New York: Norton Books.

Power, C. (1999). 'Beauty magic': The origins of art. In R. Dunbar, C. Knight, & C. Power (Eds.), *The evolution of culture* (pp. 92-112). New Brunswick, NJ: Rutgers University Press.

Ramachandran, V. S., & Hirstein, W. (1999). The science of art: A neurological theory of aesthetic experience. *Journal of Consciousness Studies, 6,* 15-51.

Rosenzweig, M. R., Krech, D., Bennett, E. L., & Diamond, M. C. (1962). Effects of environmental complexity and training on brain chemistry and anatomy:

A replication and extension. *Journal of Comparative and Physiological Psychology, 55,* 429-437.

Rubenstein, A. J., Kalakanis, L., & Langlois, J. H. (1999). Infant preference for attractive faces: A cognitive explanation. *Developmental Psychology, 35,* 848-855.

Schlaug, G., Jäncke, L., Huang, Y., Staiger, J. F., & Steinmetz, H. (1995). Increased corpus callosum in musicians. *Neuropsychologia, 33,* 107-1055.

Sergent, J., Zuch, E., Terriah, S., & MacDonald, B. (1992). Distributed neural network underlying musical sight-reading and keyboard performance. *Science, 257,* 106-109.

Thornhill, R. (1997). The concept of evolved adaptation. In G. R. Bock & G. Cardew (Eds.), *Characterizing human psychological adaptations* (pp. 4-22). New York: Wiley.

Thornhill, R. (1998). Darwinian aesthetics. In C. B. Crawford & D. L. Krebs (Eds.), *Handbook of evolutionary psychology: Ideas, issues, and applications* (pp. 543-572). Mahwah, NJ: Erlbaum.

Tooby, J., & Cosmides, L. (1992). The psychological foundations of culture. In J. Barkow, L. Cosmides, & J. Tooby (Eds.), T*he adapted mind: Evolutionary psychology and the generation of culture* (pp. 19-136). Oxford, England: Oxford University Press.

Tooby, J., & Cosmides, L. (2001). Does beauty build adapted minds? Toward an evolutionary theory of aesthetics, fiction, and the arts. *SubStance, 30,* 6-27.

Tramo, M. J. (2001). Music of the hemispheres. *Science, 291,* 54-56.

Trehub, S. (2000). Human processing predispositions and musical universals. In N. L. Wallin, B. Merker, & S. Brown (Eds.), *The origins of music* (pp. 427-448). Cambridge, MA: MIT Press.

Trehub, S. E., & Thorpe, L. A. (1989). Infants' perception of rhythm: Categorization of auditory sequences by temporal structure. *Canadian Journal of Psychology, 43,* 217-229.

Trehub, S. E., Bull, D., & Thorpe, L. A. (1984). Infants' perception of melodies: The role of melodic contour. *Child Development, 55,* 821-830.

Wallin, N. L., Merker, B., & Brown, S. (2000). *The origins of music.* Cambridge, MA: MIT Press.

White, R. (1992). Beyond art: Toward an understanding of origins of material representation in Europe. *Annual Review of Anthropology, 21,* 537-564.

Williams, G. C. (1966). *Adaptation and natural selection: A critique of some current evolutionary thought.* Princeton, NJ: Princeton University Press.

Winner, E. (1996). *Gifted children: Myths and realities.* New York: Basic Books.

Zahavi, A., & Zahavi, A. (1997). *The handicap principle: A missing piece of Darwin's puzzle.* New York: Oxford University Press.

Zatorre, R. J., Evans, A. C., & Meyer, E. (1994). Neural mechanisms underlying melodic perception and memory for pitch. *Journal of Neuroscience, 14,* 1908-1919.

Zeki, S. (1999). *Inner vision: An exploration of art and brain.* Oxford: Oxford University Press.
Zenter, M., & Kagan, J. (1998). Infants' perception of consonance and dissonance in music. *Infant Behavior & Development, 21,* 483-492.

CHAPTER 3

The Adaptive Function of Literature

Joseph Carroll

> What those vast cerebral expansions that emerged during the Pleistocene probably provided was a vast symbolic capacity that enabled foresight, hindsight, and the brain-power to peer into other minds and to entertain alternate courses of action, thereby allowing humans to create the cultures that dominate our modern world....
> What makes humans unique, perhaps more than anything else, is that we are a linguistically adept story-telling species. That is why so many different forms of mythology have captivated our cultural imaginations since the dawn of recorded history (Panksepp & Panksepp, 2000, pp. 126-127).

Literature is only a special case of artistic activity, but its artistic medium is language, and that makes it a case of exceptional interest. Darwin himself boldly conjectured that the development of language was the single most important factor in the evolution of the modern human mind, and similar conjectures have been formulated within the context of the most recent knowledge about human evolution (see Bickerton, 2002; Bradshaw, 2002; Darwin, 1981; Dunbar, 1993; Mellars, 1996; Mithen, 1998; Stringer & Gamble, 1993.) Language is a medium both of knowledge and of social interaction. Through language we come to understand the world in forms abstracted from the sensory present, extending over time, and organized into conceptual classes and relationships. And through language, more than through any other device available to us, we negotiate our social relations with one another—share our thoughts and feelings, bond, dominate, submit, order, inquire, and otherwise manipulate each other. Literature assimilates all these language functions and turns them to the general purposes of art. (The arts of language are oral in their inception but have been extended into "literature" by the prosthetic device of writing. In what follows, I shall speak only of "literature," but shall ask you always to understand that word as shorthand for the concept "literature and its oral antecedents.") The most general purpose that literature fulfills is that of creating emotionally charged images of our experience in the world. By means of such images, we orient ourselves to the world, organize our own sense of values and motives, and thus regulate our behavior. Our linguistic communities form spheres of action. Through the medium of verbal imagination, literature makes vividly present to us both the nature of those communities and our own place within them.

In previous publications (Carroll, 1995, 2004), I have identified literature as a form of "cognitive mapping," meaning that literature is a special case of the general function of intelligence—that of orienting the individual organism to the environment. The kinds of verbal representations we call literature differ from science and other forms of cognitive mapping that are purely factual in orientation. Unlike science and practical records, plans, and directives, literature is not impersonal. It incorporates the subjective, emotional, or qualitative aspect of human experience in two specific ways. First, whatever the subject of a literary representation might be, that subject is seen from a perspective that is imbued with passion and value. It is made meaningful to human needs, to desires, fears, and the sense of wonder. Second, very often human beings are the subjects of the representation. Even when the subjects are mythical creatures or animals, they are almost always anthropomorphized in such a way that they are only slightly displaced versions of human creatures—creatures acting with recognizable human passions and perceiving the world with sense organs, affective responses, and conceptual categories much like our own.

The views I am propounding about the adaptive function of literature presuppose that both the mind in general and literature in particular actually have an adaptive function. That assumption distinguishes these views from the two other chief hypotheses that have been put forward to account for the evolutionary origin of art: Geoffrey Miller's theory (2000) that the human brain and its artistic manifestations are both products of "sexual selection," and Steven Pinker's theory (1997) that art is a parasitic by-product of other cognitive functions that are themselves adaptive. Before explaining more fully the implications of my own adaptationist hypothesis, I shall examine these two competing ideas.

Miller has argued that the hypertrophic human mind did not evolve to serve the general purposes of survival. It evolved instead, he suggests, as an equivalent to the peacock's tail—as a showy but adaptively useless ornament designed only to attract members of the opposite sex. The peacock's tail is a handicap for the peacock—it has a certain metabolic cost and renders the peacock more visible and vulnerable to predators—but it is not a functionally complex organ, and it is evidently not very useful for any purpose other than of attracting peahens. The human brain is more metabolically expensive than the peacock's tail; and it is anatomically expensive also, making for a difficult and dangerous birth followed by a life easily susceptible to mortal injury. Most importantly, it is astonishingly, functionally, complex, and it is patently useful for all the general purposes of life—for finding food and shelter, warding off danger, using tools, and negotiating with conspecifics for the purposes of concerted collective action. The supposition that an organ of this character could have arisen purely as a form of sexual display is, on its face, so implausible as to barely warrant serious consideration.

If we move on from the brain in general to the question of art in particular, the supposition of sexual display is less immediately and grossly implausible, but is still weak and shaky on its own terms and has little positive explanatory power (see Dissanayake, this volume). It falsely implies that art is mainly an activity produced by young males as part of their mating repertory, and though it says nothing in particular about what art actually contains or does—about its subjects, its techniques, or its effects—it implies, wrongly, that the chief function of art would be the display of individual brilliancy and that this brilliancy would be of a sort most likely to stimulate the sexual response systems of nubile females. These implications bear little correspondence to the facts. Most art in its origins is probably closely bound up with religious ceremonies and rituals; it is collective, public, and communal. The subjects of art prominently include sex and mating, since they involve all matters of intense emotional concern among humans; but they also involve parenting, friendship, the forces of nature, war, spiritual awe, death, and any number of other possible human concerns not notably identified with sexual excitation. The audience for art is the human race—males and females, children, adolescents, young adults, the middle-aged, and the elderly.

Pinker has a dual thesis about the evolutionary origins of art. Unlike Miller, he presupposes that the brain and mind evolved to solve adaptively important problems. In keeping with the cognitive science bent of orthodox evolutionary psychology, he treats the brain as an information processing device, and he tends to regard this device in a mechanistic and utilitarian light. The brain is there, like a computer, to generate information in the most efficient and accessible way. The information it generates concerns food, danger, sex, and social exchange. The brain needs to get a certain amount of work done, and the most efficient way to accomplish any given task is to automate it: to render it the reliable outcome of predictable stimuli triggering "proximal" mechanisms—neurological, hormonal, physiological—that produce appropriate adaptive behaviors. The presence of hunger triggers foraging or hunting behavior; the sight of nubile females triggers mating behavior. The presence of conspecifics triggers social exchange mechanisms and so on. Once such proximate mechanisms are in place, they can be triggered by stimuli introduced artificially and produce results that have no direct adaptive advantage. For instance, pornographic images can stimulate sexual response mechanisms. Sexual excitation not directed toward effective reproductive activity would be a parasitic by-product of a proximal mechanism originally "designed" for adaptive purposes.

Pinker's theory of art locates it within both the areas of brain activity he identifies: utilitarian information processing and parasitic by-products. In his view, as a source of utilitarian information, the arts, and especially literature, can be adaptively functional. Literary scenarios can present simulacra of adaptively important information—practical information about the environment, the location of resources or danger, and the behavior of conspecifics (also see Sugiyama, 2001). Pinker himself does not go into detail about the functions of narrative form, but one could easily enough fill out this part of the argument with suppositions—like those of Jerome Bruner (1990) or Mark Turner (1996)—that the mind most easily and normally processes information in narrative form. In addition to this utilitarian function, in its guise as a parasitic by-product, art would activate cognitive responses—sensory and conceptual—that had evolved for more functional purposes. Music would parasitize hearing, for example, and the aesthetic aspects of literature would parasitize the faculties of language.

The two functions Pinker assigns to art are in fact part of what art can do. Literary art can and does provide practical information. After finishing *Madame Bovary*, I earnestly vowed that if I ever chose to commit suicide, I would find some method less gruesome than that of swallowing arsenic. Art can also provide pornographic stimulation or the equivalent of that in various kinds of wish-fulfillment fantasies. (Like Freud, Pinker thinks of verbal narratives primarily as forms of wish fulfillment.) In "The Kugelmass Episode," Woody Allen has a character enabled, by magical means, to enter into the world of *Madame Bovary* in order to have intimate sexual relations with the title character. Pinker is not wrong in identifying these functions of literature—that of conveying practical information and that of serving to stimulate pleasurable fantasies as a form of hedonistic self-exploitation—but as an account of the evolutionary origins and the psychological functions of art, this account is drastically incomplete. It fails to get to the heart of the matter.

Much of the information conveyed in literature is of no direct practical utility, and if practical information were the only point at issue, much of that information could be conveyed more effectively by other means. (I did not need to read a long novel to learn that there are ways to kill one's self less horrible than that of taking arsenic.) Pleasurable fantasy is a relatively minor form of artistic activity, and it can hardly account for tragedy or for any painful realist representation. The death of Hercules in the fiery shirt of Nessus can satisfy the pornographic lusts of very few people, and almost no one closes Madame Bovary with the satisfied sense of having lived a vicarious life more thrilling and charming than his or her own. (The liaison in "The Kugelmass Episode," predictably enough, did not work out very well.) No reader or theatergoer has much to be pleasurably gratified about at the end of *Electra*, *King Lear*, or *L'Assomoir*, except in the cessation of torment, anguish, and grief.

Though Pinker himself tends to regard literature as primarily a form of wish fulfillment, his theory does not absolutely require that literature consist solely of pleasurable fantasy. It requires only that literature hijack cognitive processes that might have evolved to fulfill adaptive functions to which literature does not directly contribute. Likely candidates for these supposedly more primary processes would include language, mechanisms for sequencing events, and mechanisms of social exchange. The success of the hijacking would depend on activating the sources of pleasure with which those adaptive functions are associated—for instance, the pleasures of speech, the linking of ideas into sequences, and social grooming. The hijacking hypothesis offers a causal, evolutionary explanation different from the idea that art has an intrinsic adaptive function, but the hijacking hypothesis does not contain any arguments that preclude or undermine the idea of an intrinsic adaptive function. The two hypotheses, the idea of art as hijacking and the idea of an intrinsic adaptive function to art, are simply alternative, competing evolutionary hypotheses about the origin and nature of art. If we can identify good reasons for believing that art has intrinsic adaptive functions, those reasons would take precedence over arguments that fail to identify such functions but that also fail to stipulate reasons such functions could not exist.

In order to gain an adequate understanding about the adaptive function of literature and to assimilate whatever is worth keeping in the ideas of practical information and pleasurable cognitive stimulation, we must invoke a fundamental principle of adaptive design—the principle of costs and trade-offs. Every adaptation has its costs—metabolic costs, opportunity costs, dangers, and limitations. Any adaptation that is maintained in relative stability does so not because it is a perfect design, but because it constitutes a stable tension between costs and benefits within a relatively stable ecology. The human brain is the most metabolically expensive organ in the human body, and our best understanding of the benefits this organ provides, sufficient to counterbalance its costs, is that it enables humans to respond flexibly and intelligently to the challenges of a variable environment. That general hypothesis has a certain prima facie plausibility, and over the past several years evolutionary anthropology and cognitive archaeology have been giving support, in depth and detail, to that commonsense understanding of the matter (see Foley, 1996; Irons, 1998; MacDonald & Hershberger, 2004; Potts, 1998). Animals vary in the degree to which they are ecologically specialized. Koalas, at one end of the scale, can live only on eucalyptus leaves. Humans, at the other end, have become so flexibly capable of adapting to almost any environment that they can reasonably be said to have specialized, as a species, in adaptive flexibility. Their upright posture and opposable thumbs have contributed to that specialization, but overwhelmingly the most important component of it is the large human brain, with its capacity for abstracting from local detail, identifying complex and hierarchically organized goals at many removes from any immediately perceived object, and adapting means to ends through logically organized sequences.

Such advantages do not come cheaply. In addition to the metabolic expense, the increased danger of childbirth, and the labor and risk attendant on extended childhood dependency, the human mind presents one disadvantage that is intrinsic to its very character as an organ of mental flexibility: the disadvantage attendant to confusion. The key aptitude in cognitive flexibility is the capacity to detach observation and reflection from programmed sequences of stimulus and response. To the modern human mind, alone among all minds in the animal kingdom, the world does not present itself as a series of rigidly defined stimuli releasing a narrow repertory of stereotyped behaviors. It presents itself as a vast and perplexing array of percepts and contingent possibilities. The human mind is free to organize the elements of its perception in an infinitely diverse array of combinatorial possibilities. And most of those potential forms of organization, like most major mutations, would be fatal. Freedom is the key to human success, and it is also an invitation to disaster. This is the insight that governs E. O. Wilson's penetrating explanation for the adaptive function of the arts. "There was not enough time for human heredity to cope with the vastness of new contingent possibilities revealed by high intelligence. . . . The arts filled the gap" (Wilson, 1998, p. 225).

If instincts are defined as stereotyped programs of behavior released automatically by environmental stimuli, then we can say that in humans, art takes the place of instinct. That does not mean what the cultural constructionists would have it mean—that culture is autonomous and infinitely various, and that it generates all motive and content in human experience. Humans have flexible response systems, but those systems are still constrained and guided by what Wilson (1998) calls "epigenetic rules" and what Kevin MacDonald (1995) calls "evolved motive dispositions." Cultures vary widely in the way they prepare food, but no culture varies in the need to prepare food, and beneath superficial differences in food sources and styles of preparation, the variation in food all over the world is strictly constrained by the universal properties of the human gustatory and digestive systems. In no culture do humans consume wood, as termites do.

The function of literature and the other arts is to fashion an imaginative universe in which the forces at work both in the environment and inside human beings are brought into subjectively meaningful relations to one another. That is not the same thing as providing practically useful information or providing an objectively accurate map of the external environment. A subjectively meaningful cognitive map can directly influence motives and values, but more broadly it provides points of reference within which humans can adjust their sense of the relative value and significance of all the emotionally and motivationally significant aspects of their experience. Literature and the other arts are devices of orientation, like compasses, sextants, and sonar, and they are vital to personal development, to the integration of individual identities within a cultural order, and to the imaginative adjustment of the individual to the whole larger world in which he or she lives.

Because they have vital adaptive functions, literature and the other arts are themselves motivated as emotionally driven needs. The need to produce and consume imaginative artifacts is as real and distinct a need as hunger, sex, or social interaction. Like all such needs, it bears within itself, as its motivating mechanism, the impetus of desire and the pleasure and satisfaction that attend upon the fulfilling of desire. That kind of fulfillment is not a parasitic by-product of some other form of pleasure, nor merely a means toward the end of fulfilling some other kind of need—sexual, social, or practical. Like all forms of human fulfillment, the need for art can be integrated with other needs in any number of ways. It can be used for sexual display or the gratifications of sexual hunger or social vanity, and it can be used as a medium for social bonding, but it is nonetheless, in itself, a primary and irreducible human need.

Literature represents and articulates human experience. In order to understand how literature works, we have to understand human nature. Human nature is the source of literature, and also its central subject matter. So, what is human nature? For the nearly three millennia of our preserved literary history, information on that subject has been given to us by poets, dramatists, storytellers, philosophers, and sages of all sorts. The majority of all literary writers and literary theorists have at some point invoked "human nature" as their central point of reference, the authority for their utterance, and the norm through which they justify one depiction for its truth, and condemn another for its falsity. What is it to which these authors and theorists are appealing? When authors or ordinary people say, "Oh, that's just human nature," what do they have in mind? They almost always have in mind the basic set of motivational dispositions that regulate human life history—the basic animal and social motives: self-preservation, sexual desire, jealousy, maternal love, the favoring of kin, the need to belong to social groups, and the desire for social status. Usually, certain universal characteristics of social morality are also meant: the resentment of wrongs, the gratitude for kindness, the intuitive sense of the integrity of contractual relations, the disgust at cheating, the naturalness of revenge, and the appropriateness of reciprocal generosity. And finally, all of these substantive motives are complicated and elaborated by the ideas that enter into the folk understanding of ego psychology: the primacy of self-interest and the prevalence of self-serving delusion, manipulative deceit, vanity, and hypocrisy (for adaptationist perspectives on this aspect of human nature, see Buss, 2001; Hogan, 1983).

As this third set of aspects suggests, the casual conversational phrase, "Oh, that's just human nature" has very often something of a cynical ring to it, but the weight of evaluation can also be placed on the positive side of the scale. Viewing an act of selfish deceit, one would not be surprised to hear the comment, "Well, that's just human nature," but neither would it be surprising to hear that phrase used to account for filial love, tender gratitude, admiration for honest dealing, and indignation at injustice (on the moral content of human nature, see Arnhart, 1998; Frank, 1988; J. Q. Wilson, 1993). Literature can emphasize either tonality, satiric contempt, or affirmative warmth, and in literature, as in life, one often hears both tonalities intermingled, as it is in the work of most canonical English novelists, where bitter depictions of cruelty and duplicity alternate with strong portraits affirming generosity, affection, and decency.

The literary and philosophical traditions articulate a folk knowledge of human nature. Until very recently, that folk knowledge was a source of psychological information superior to anything available within the established academic disciplines of the social sciences. In *Descent of Man, and Selection in Relation to Sex* (1981), Darwin offered a pioneering effort to analyze human motives and human social psychology within the context of evolutionary anthropology. The result was a work of genius and a classic of moral psychology, a work that still richly repays careful study. But the actual knowledge available to Darwin about the details of human evolution were scanty, and psychology, as an empirical discipline, did not yet exist. For a period of about 40 years, from the time of *Descent of Man* up to the second decade of the twentieth century, some anthropologists, psychologists, and literary authors explored the evolutionary and naturalistic dimensions of human nature; but that sort of psychology was still largely speculative and "humanistic" in character. Beginning in about the second decade of the twentieth century, an anti-evolutionary revolution took place in the social sciences, and for all the middle decades of the century, up until the 1970s, the bulk of all work done in cultural anthropology and psychology, to say nothing of sociology and political science, was oriented not to an evolutionary understanding of human nature but rather to the false idea of cultural autonomy—the idea that human culture had decisively severed all connections between biological constraint and human motives and cognitions (see Degler, 1991). The chief alternatives to mainstream cultural constructivism in humanist psychology were the speculative and often deeply erroneous conceptions of Freud and the equally speculative, highly suggestive, but more diffuse and mystical speculations of Jung. The sociobiological revolution that began in the 1970s has now made it possible, for the first time in our history, to begin to construct an objective, empirically derived framework of knowledge about human nature. For the first time, as a result, it is now possible to create a framework for literary criticism that is independent of the folk traditions of human nature that are embedded in literature and philosophy.

The new Darwinian framework is independent of the folk tradition, but it is also integral and continuous with that tradition. The literary folk traditions are constituted by the intuitions of the best minds in our cultural history. Those intuitions, in their collective mass, are not simply wrong. As a general guide to human nature, they are certainly more reliable and adequate than any of the theoretically misguided or idiosyncratic and highly charged psychological systems that emerged in the behaviorist and psychoanalytic traditions. Nonetheless, in the works of all individual authors, the manifestations of folk intuitions are likely to be limited and biased, constrained and partially distorted, both by the specific cultural ecologies in which they are produced and also by the peculiarities of the authors' individual temperaments. No single literary text can bear within itself a comprehensive and fully adequate framework of knowledge within which to assess itself. A critic who wishes to give an independent analysis of a literary text—something more than a summary and paraphrase—has no choice but to create some kind of framework that is not simply identical with the structure of meanings within that text.

Until the present time, in the absence of a scientifically grounded knowledge of human nature, all interpretive literary study had only one of two alternatives: (a) either to operate impressionistically within the general lexicon of folk literary knowledge, assessing each individual work in relation to that general pool; or (b) to adopt some speculative, theoretical system as a framework, and to use it either in a purely discursive, intuitive way or to follow some pseudosystematic elaboration of technical terms. The former alternative is that of old-fashioned, humanistic, belle-lettristic criticism. With heavy admixtures of mystical, romantic philosophy, and with some attention to commonsense methods in the formal analysis of images, tone, theme, and linguistic structures, that alternative formed the basis for what was known as the "New Criticism," the school of interpretive literary criticism that dominated academic literary study from the 1940s through the 1970s (see Abrams, 1997). Alongside the New Criticism, the second alternative, that of speculative theory, functioned as a loyal opposition or robust minority, under the aegis of various theoretical systems, but most prominently and persistently under those of Freud, Marx, and Jung. (For instance, Lionel Trilling, one of the chief belle-lettristic literary essayists of the midcentury period, was a devoted Freudian; the magisterial and massively influential scholar Edmund Wilson was closely affiliated with Marxism; and the chief literary taxonomist of the twentieth century, Northrop Frye, was heavily dependent on the archetypal psychology of Jung.)

In the past 25 years or so, old-fashioned belle-lettristic impressionism has been relegated to the casual reviewing of books and movies. In academic criticism, Jung has now all but disappeared, but Freud and Marx flourish more strongly than ever. They would not themselves, presumably, be very happy with the uses to which their concepts have been put. They were both scientific materialists and determinists, and in current literary study, their ideas about psychological and social organization have been assimilated into the radically irrationalist and antirealist doctrines of poststructuralism—doctrines derived from French theorists such as Jacques Derrida, Michel Foucault, and Jacques Lacan. Poststructuralist notions have now, for at least two decades, dominated academic literary study, and those notions have actively and aggressively suppressed the idea of an underlying biologically constrained human nature. The two key tenets of poststructuralism are the idea that language or "discourse" creates reality and the idea that all meaning is "indeterminate" or infinitely ambiguous. Within this scheme of things, all of science is itself nothing more than a cultural discourse designed to support oppressive and arbitrary structures of political power.

Any literary theorist who advocates a Darwinian or adaptationist theory of literary study necessarily steps outside the range of poststructuralist doctrine that currently dominates literary study and steps instead into the range of "consilience": the idea of the unity of all knowledge within the framework of modern science. For the purposes of literary study, what a Darwinian understanding of human nature can provide is a framework of analysis that is concordant with the phenomenal or phenotypic surface of representations in literary texts but that is more adequate, as causal explanation, than any single depiction of human nature in any literary work, or any single conception of human nature in the mind of any individual author. The Darwinian understanding of human nature is more adequate, as causal explanation, than the explanations within literary works because it is more general, more complete, more analytical, more ideologically neutral, more empirically grounded, and more adequately integrated with the total body of scientific knowledge.

Literary authors before 1859 could themselves hardly have been evolutionary adaptationists, and even now many authors have still not concerned themselves seriously with the anthropological and biological underpinnings of the behavior they intuitively depict and the motives and feelings they intuitively express. But human nature is the common medium, the *lingua franca*. It is the currency in which authors must trade if they are to make connections with the intuitive understanding of their audience. Individual authors can and do deviate in all sorts of ways from populational averages, just as individual people do. There is nonetheless a recognized common ground—common motives, common forms of emotional response, and common forms of perception, observation, and reflection. All differences of temperament or sensibility register themselves and have meaning for us by reference to that common ground. Our individual identities, with their peculiarities of culture and temperament, are like cottages scattered around the edge of a village common. Each cottage has its differences of shape or furnishing, but each shares the common features that are derived from commonality of materials, of historical origins, and of function. In all the cottages, design subserves the basic needs of shelter and domestic organization, and the life that is carried on in each is linked, by shared interests and occupations, to the communal life of the village.

Literature is in one crucial respect unlike many subjects of scientific study. Rocks, chemicals, electromagnetic waves—all of those are insentient phenomena. Literary texts are intentional structures of meaning. In this respect, literary study closely parallels the modern personality theory that is based on "lexical analysis"—the statistical analysis of words from the dictionary that define features of personality (see John & Srivastava, 1999; Saucier & Goldberg, 1996). Authors speak their minds and know what they are saying. In interpreting literary utterances, as in interpreting the utterances of people with whom we converse, we might well posit motives or implications of which the author is not conscious. And in interpreting the utterances of authors, as in interpreting the utterances of other people, we are free to explain or judge the utterances in whatever way seems best to us. We seldom simply concur, in neutral and passive accord, with what anyone says, in books or in life.

An author has a meaning, and a reader assesses that meaning. Where then does meaning reside? In the author's intentional structure of meaning? In the reader's encompassing meditation on that meaning? In both. The author's intentional structure of meaning is like an object studied by science, a rock or chemical. As scholars, we have a primary obligation to give as exact and faithful an account of that meaning as possible. We should never say an author "meant to say" something other than what that author meant to say—so far as we can judge of that—but having given a faithful account of what the author meant to say, we are free to encompass that intentional utterance within the larger, more comprehensive framework of our own analytic and interpretive structures, including our attributions of motives that might have animated the author and our assessment of implications the author might himself or herself indignantly repudiate. People do not always wish to acknowledge the scope or drift of what they say, or take responsibility for it; and authors, whatever else might be said about them, are people.

Admission into the canon is like admission into an athletic hall of fame; it is a virtual guarantee of certain kinds of excellence. Canonical literary authors are demonstrably figures of genius. They have wide observation, penetrating insight, towering imaginative power, and preternatural faculties of articulate utterance. Few individual literary critics are ever in a position to claim that their individual perspectives are more comprehensive, more encompassing, than those of individual authors. Literary criticism will always require talent and insight, but science is a collective enterprise, and in using the consilient framework of adaptationist knowledge about human nature, individual literary critics have recourse to a collective understanding that is greater than the understanding of any single individual, no matter how great a mind that individual might have. That collective understanding is the synthetic product of the combined efforts of whole communities of research extending over generations. By participating in that collective understanding—including its ethos of empirical constraint and its chastity of factual affirmation—individual literary critics and scholars can rightly claim to encompass the works of genius and to submit those works to scientific observation and analysis.

In literary texts, "point of view" has a special status as the central locus of meaning. In the most narrowly restricted, technical sense, "point of view" means only the formal method an author adopts for the purposes of narrating a story. In that sense, a story can be told "in the first person," from an "omniscient third-person perspective," or from various modifications of third-person or participant perspectives (see Booth, 1996). In a broader sense, "point of view" signifies the total set of meanings and observations that characterize an individual mind—the characteristic values and styles, the forms of perception, the emotional tone, the conceptual repertory. In that sense, the meaning of intentional structures in a literary text is the articulation of a specific point of view: that of the author.

In most literary texts, other points of view are also represented. Indeed, they are the chief subjects of representation. Characters act or behave, but they also think and feel, and their thoughts and feelings are ultimately of more account, in the construction of meaning, than their acts. In most literary works, there are multiple points of view. The various characters interact, as people do in life. They intuit each others' feelings and motives, or try to; they try to persuade or otherwise manipulate each other; and they judge each other. The author himself or herself has a point of view, and that point of view has ultimate authority within the text. Within the author's own intentional structure of meaning, the point of view of each character derives its significance from its relation to the author's point of view. It is the author who gets to impose the ultimate, encompassing interpretation of the represented events. It is the author who decides what things mean.

Whatever their other motives might be, characters, authors, and readers share one fundamental motive: the need to affirm a certain understanding of the world. All human beings have that need, and satisfying that need is the central, irreducible motive in all literary art. In the absence of instinctive, stereotyped response, humans are compelled to locate their action within some imaginative context, and literature is one of the chief forms through which such contexts are created. All individual literary representations instantiate an emotionally charged understanding of the world. Articulating that understanding satisfies the mind of the artist, and the primary motive readers have for reading is to participate in that understanding and to share in that satisfaction. As common readers, Darwinian literary critics enjoy and appreciate literature in this primary way. As scholars, they also seek to encompass literary works within the explanatory context derived from an adaptationist understanding of human nature.

REFERENCES

Abrams, M. H. (1997). The transformation of English studies: 1930-1995. *Daedalus, 126,* 105-132.
Allen, W. (1980). The Kugelmass episode. In *Side effects* (pp. 59-78). New York: Random House.
Arnhart, L. (1998). *Darwinian natural right: The biological ethics of human nature.* Albany: State University of New York Press.
Bickerton, D. (2002). From protolanguage to language. In T. J. Crow (Ed.), *The speciation of modern homo sapiens* (pp. 103-120). Oxford: Oxford University Press.
Booth, W. (1996). Distance and point of view: An essay in classification. In M. J. Hoffman & P. D. Murphy (Eds.), *Essentials of the theory of fiction* (pp. 116-133). Durham, NC: Duke University Press.
Bradshaw, J. L. (2002). The evolution of intellect: Cognitive, neurological, and primatological aspects and hominid culture. In R. J. Sternberg & J. C. Kaufman (Eds.), *The evolution of intelligence* (pp. 55-78). Mahwah, NJ: Lawrence Erlbaum Associates.
Bruner, J. (1990). *Acts of meaning.* Cambridge, MA: Harvard University Press.
Buss, A. (2001). *Psychological dimensions of the self.* Thousand Oaks, CA: Sage.
Carroll, J. (1995). *Evolution and literary theory.* Columbia: University of Missouri Press.
Carroll, J. (2004). *Literary Darwinism: Evolution, human nature, and literature.* New York: Routledge.
Darwin, C. (1981). *The descent of man, and selection in relation to sex* (2 vols. in 1), J. T. Bonner & R. M. May (Eds.). Princeton: Princeton University Press. (Original work published 1871.)
Degler, C. (1991). *In search of human nature: The decline and revival of Darwinism in American social thought.* Oxford: Oxford University Press.
Dissanayake, E. (this volume). What art is and what art does: An overview of contemporary evolutionary hypotheses. In C. Martindale, P. Locher, & V. Petrov (Eds.), *Evolutionary and neurocognitive approaches to aesthetics, creativity, and the arts* (pp. 1-14). Amityville, NY: Baywood.
Dunbar, R. I. M. (1993). *Grooming, gossip, and the evolution of language.* London: Faber & Faber.
Foley, R. A. (1996). The adaptive legacy of human evolution: A search for the environment of evolutionary adaptedness. *Evolutionary Anthropology, 4,* 194-203.

Frank, R. (1988). *Passions within reason: The strategic role of the emotions.* New York: W. W. Norton.

Hogan, R. (1983). A socioanalytic theory of personality. In M. M. Page (Ed.), *Nebraska symposium on motivation: Personality—Current theory and research* (pp. 55-90). Lincoln: University of Nebraska Press.

Irons, W. (1998). Adaptively relevant environments versus the environment of evolutionary adaptedness. *Evolutionary Anthropology, 6,* 194-204.

John, O. P., & Srivastava, S. (1999). The big five trait taxonomy: History, measurement, and theoretical perspectives. In L. A. Pervin & O. P. John (Eds.), *Handbook of personality* (2nd ed., pp. 102-138). New York: Guilford Press.

MacDonald, K. B. (1995). Evolution, the five-factor model, and levels of personality. *Journal of Personality, 63,* 525-567.

MacDonald, K. B., & Hershberger, S. L. (2004). Theoretical issues in the study of evolution and development. In R. Burgess & K. MacDonald (Eds.), *Evolutionary perspectives on human development* (2nd ed.). Thousand Oaks, CA: Sage.

Mellars, P. (1996). Symbolism, language, and the Neanderthal mind. In P. Mellars & K. Gibson (Eds.), *Modelling the early human mind* (pp. 15-32). Cambridge: MacDonald Institute for Archaeological Research.

Miller, G. (2000). *The mating mind: How sexual choice shaped the evolution of human nature.* New York: Doubleday.

Mithen, S. (1998). A creative explosion? Theory of mind, language, and the disembodied mind of the Upper Palaeolithic. In S. Mithen (Ed.), *Creativity in human evolution and prehistory* (pp. 164-191). London: Routledge.

Panksepp, J., & Panksepp, J. B. (2000). The seven sins of evolutionary psychology. *Evolution and Cognition, 6,* 108-131.

Pinker, S. (1997). *How the mind works.* New York: W. W. Norton.

Potts, R. (1998). Variability selection in hominid evolution. *Evolutionary Anthropology, 7,* 81-96.

Saucier, G., & Goldberg, L. R. (1996). The language of personality: Lexical perspectives on the five-factor model. In J. S. Wiggins (Ed.), *The five-factor model of personality: Theoretical perspectives* (pp. 21-50). New York: Guilford Press.

Stringer, C., & Gamble, C. (1993). *In search of the Neanderthals.* London: Thames & Hudson.

Sugiyama, M. S. (2001). Narrative theory and function: Why evolution matters. *Philosophy and Literature, 25,* 233-250.

Turner, M. (1996). *The literary mind.* New York: Oxford University Press.

Wilson, E. O. (1998). *Consilience: The unity of knowledge.* New York: Alfred A. Knopf.

Wilson, J. Q. (1993). *The moral sense.* New York: Macmillan.

CHAPTER 4

Does Reading Literature Make People Happy?

Willie van Peer, Alexandra Mentjes, and Jan Auracher

1. INTRODUCTION

It is a fact of considerable importance that no human societies have been discovered by anthropologists and ethnographers that do not have some kind of "literature." Even those human groups that have the simplest of social structure, where hardly any division of labor exists, and which possess no form of technology whatsoever, have at their disposal a repertoire of myths, legends, tales, or songs. True, this kind of literature is often not written, but functions orally in such groups; but that does not make it structurally different from its written or printed counterparts in technologically more complex cultures. Many of these oral literary forms are no match for *Anna Karenina* or *The Divine Comedy* in evaluative terms, but are instead much simpler in content and structure. Nevertheless, as Karl Popper once remarked, it is worth reflecting on the fact that even societies that do not have sticks (to help them cut fruit from the trees), are not without literature. While it is not the explicit aim of the present chapter to fathom the reasons for this state of affairs, we think it is vital to reflect on the issue. Could literature have survival value in evolutionary terms? Could it be that some groups in the early history of humanity did *not* have some kind of literature at their disposal, but that such groups have died out? We do not know, but the very fact of literature's ubiquity across the globe seems to point to some kind of survival value inherent in literature. As Seabright (2004) has recently argued, the infinitely elaborate division of labor (with over 250,000 types of jobs in postindustrial societies), the sprawl of ever more specialized institutions, and the awesome productivity of the global economy, are simply too staggering things to have been brought about by mere chance in the evolutionary short time span of about 100,000 years. Other, psychological and cultural factors must have been at work. Far from claiming that literature spawned these remarkable achievements, we will nevertheless claim that literature may have contributed to them in part—by making people happy! Happiness, as we will define it, fulfills an important evolutionary function, contributing to health and cooperation, and thus, to greater chances of survival. This will be part of the conceptual analysis that makes up section 3 of the chapter. A significant link in the chain of argumentation therefore is the question whether literature does indeed make people "happy." Since this is an empirical question, we will subject it to an empirical investigation, to be described in sections 5 and 6. But first we will present some historical background to the question at hand.

2. HISTORY

The position of literature in human society is not a self-evident one, in spite of its ubiquitous presence. As is well-known, at the very dawn of literary studies in the Western world, an opposition against literature was already in place. It will be remembered that Plato condemned literature for its emotional content and effects. As we read in *The Republic*, Plato recognizes the power that literature may exert: "you know how even the best of us enjoy it and let ourselves be carried away by our feelings" (605d). And precisely this ability of poetry to affect us is seen as a source of evil: "We are therefore quite right to refuse to admit him [the poet] to a properly run state, because he weakens and encourages and strengthens the lower elements in the mind to the detriment of reason" (605b). Thus, the function of literature as seen by Plato is to provide some sentimental entertainment with outspoken negative effects: it mollifies men, and thus weakens society. There is no place for such literature in an ideal state, requiring battleproof soldiers for its safety.

Aristotle, Plato's student, praised poetry for partly the same reason. He agreed with his teacher's analysis of the power of literature, but drew the opposite conclusion. According to him, literature contributes to the elevation of mankind, to *paideia*. Readers and spectators are drawn into the passage of tragic events, "incidents arousing pity and fear, wherewith to accomplish its catharsis of such emotions" (Aristotle, *Poetics* 1449b, pp. 27-28), a process that purifies us of megalomania (*hybris*), safeguarding democratic government and protecting us from unrestrained tyranny. Thus, while agreeing that literature exerts an effect on its readers (extrapolating from what he said about theater spectators), Aristotle saw this effect as beneficial, psychologically purifying men's souls, thus making society "healthier." To summarize the issue along the lines we wish to investigate in the current chapter, one could say—simplifying matters somewhat—that Plato's view induces us to see literature as creating unhappiness, while Aristotle's position entails a function of literature leading to happiness.

The views proposed by Plato and Aristotle were not wholly speculative, but based on empirical observations. Both had the opportunity to carry out such observations during theatrical performances common in many Greek city states at the time, and certainly frequently in Athens, the then culturally leading city. However, the method of collecting empirical data was at that time insufficient to allow unequivocal support for one or the other theory. As a consequence, the debate between the Platonic and Aristotelian positions became largely philosophical, with little real progress emerging from it for a long time. To settle the issue, we argue here, demands the fulfillment of two requirements: (1) a more thorough conceptual analysis of what is meant by "happiness"; and (2) a more rigorous method to collect and analyze data. Aristotle developed an interesting approach to (1) in his concept of *eudaimonia* (happiness), a concept that is still discussed in philosophy. Empirical methods necessary to fulfill requirement (2) were not, however, available at the time of the Greek philosophers in the fourth century B.C.E., nor indeed for a very long time in Western history. There is no reason, however, why these methods cannot be at least partially made use of nowadays.

3. A CONCEPTUAL ANALYSIS

Conceptual analysis is the predominant mode in analytic philosophy nowadays. It consists of a systematic and detailed analysis of the thought content associated with linguistic expressions we use when we describe, discuss, and explain the world. To apply this method to the problem at hand, a conceptual analysis asks what it means when we say that someone is "happy," what the concept of "happiness" is associated with, or what the necessary and sufficient conditions are to employ the word "happiness" in a given situation. That this is important is already seen in the fact that we must question whether the concept of happiness is itself universal across cultures and languages, or whether it is specific to English and some other related languages. This is an issue we will come back to shortly.

It seems as if at least three dimensions are in need of clarification when carrying out such a conceptual analysis. One is volitionality, another is temporality, and a final one is liberty. *Volitionality* is involved in happiness insofar as the question should be raised whether happiness is something given or something achieved. During large parts of antiquity, for instance, it was thought that happiness was distributed by the gods. *Tyche*, or good fortune, was destiny. The notion survived for an extremely long time, up to the Renaissance in Europe, in the figure of the goddess *Fortuna*. In such a situation, happiness coincides with the notion of "good luck." Notice that in some languages this conflation of meaning is still present. In German, for instance, the word *Glück* can refer both to happiness and to good fortune, while the English language uses "luck" for the latter. Any conceptual analysis of the German term *Glück* will have to take this double meaning into account. It will be obvious that in such a world view, where happiness is whimsically distributed by the gods or by fate, there is no place for an individual contribution to one's happiness. This is different in cultures in which one's own responsibility in creating one's happiness is emphasized. One such view in which the individual acts to create his own happiness is precisely Aristotle's notion of *eudaimonia*: happiness as the goal of life. Another is Kant's notion of an ethic of obligation: to do one's duty in society is to be happy.

Although it is unclear to what extent folk theories of happiness are still based on the "destiny view" (and maybe it is more widespread in some groups of society than in others—working-class culture seems to adhere more to it than middle-class culture, for instance), more informed notions of happiness seem to comprise, as did Aristotle's and Kant's, at least a partial contribution of the individual to its own (un)happiness. In the present chapter, we will work on the assumption that individuals can indeed contribute to their own happiness. Whether this can be achieved by reading literature will then be an empirical question to be answered later.

A second dimension of the concept of happiness involves *temporality*: how long must a state of happiness last before I will call myself "happy"? Can I be happy for a microsecond, 5 seconds, 5 minutes? Or are such mental states too brief to be included in the category of happiness? Must they exceed a minimal duration in order to belong to this category? And if so, how long must this duration be: 5 hours, 5 days, 5 weeks? We cannot answer this question here, but wish to raise the issue. Of course the "stability" of happiness is not an issue dissociated from the volitionality discussed above. Without carrying out your duty in society, Kant argues, no stable happiness will ensue. Aristotle even goes so far that he refuses to define happiness as an emotional state.

Instead, it is seen as a goal, as the most important goal of life, and the individual must arrange his life according to virtue (*arête*) in order to achieve this goal. Epicurus, on the other hand, emphasizes the feeling at this singular moment. Happiness, for him, is the feeling itself, evoked by the personal satisfaction of the moment, not by contributing to the order in society, as was the case with Kant and Aristotle. Thus the issue of temporality is intrinsically related to that of one's own responsibility for one's happiness. At stake here is the notion that happiness can only occur when it is minimally stable. And maybe everyday language reflects this in that we have different words to label different time spans relating to happiness, one we could call a happy "mood," while we could call happy the person who has a fulfilled life over longer periods of time. For the practical purposes of our investigation, we will assume that states of mind of several hours can be subsumed under the category of happiness. The empirical question here is whether the activity of reading a novel is something that can contribute to an (albeit temporarily limited) experience of happiness.

As a final dimension of this brief conceptual analysis, consider the issue of *liberty*. Is happiness something that one is free to experience on one's own, or is it fundamentally dependent on the social group one belongs to? In Aristotle's concept, life was governed by the order of a well-structured cosmos. Happiness is the result of a personal decision to contribute to this order and not a hedonistic fulfillment of desires. Real happiness only develops in the surroundings of a well-functioning society, which forms the frame for each action and intention of individuals. This is a view totally opposite than that of many folk theories that postulate that the individual is free to do as he wishes in order to optimize his possibilities for happiness. In other words, can I be happy on my own, irrespective of what people I esteem and love think and value? Or, to reframe it in yet other terms; to what extent does my happiness depend on its recognition (in both senses) by others? The two extremes here seem to be the hyperindividualistic notion of the solitary recluse attaining happiness all by himself, renouncing all human contacts in the middle of the desert, and the hypersocialized being, on the other hand, able to feel happy only when in consonance with one's own immediate or larger social group. Again, it is not the purpose of the present chapter to resolve such a philosophical issue. It is discussed here primarily to make us aware of the underlying dimension at hand in any notion of happiness. For all practical purposes, we will presume that there is some leeway involving at least some degree of liberty in attaining momentary happiness. Whether readers become happy as a result of their reading is therefore at least in considerable part determined by their own reading experience, irrespective of social conventions or group pressures. Also it will be useful to distinguish between general life satisfaction on the one hand and momentary feelings of subjective well-being on the other, making use of such linguistic distinctions as that between English *happiness* and *delight*, French *bonheur* and *joie*, German *Glück* and *Freude*, or Japanese *shiawase* and *ureshii*. Not all of these terms cover exactly the same meanings, but they all contrast a momentary mood with a more extended general life satisfaction.

We assume that these three dimensions, volitionality, temporality, and liberty all resonate in the meaning of happiness, but with different emphases or focus in different situations. This has a clear bearing on the empirical study we are to report on later. For instance, by influencing the actual mood of readers in the experiment, we highlight the temporary aspect in that we foreground their momentary feelings, not their general life satisfaction. This then means that their feelings of happiness must last long enough for them to be able to subjectively recognize them, but not long enough to mediate their lifestyles. At the same time, we can establish only indirect links between their feelings of momentary happiness (while reading) and the wider social context in which they live and act, by having readers rate their living conditions, their relations to their family life, etc. Finally, we assume that readers will partly determine their own feelings during reading and will also be subject to prevailing patterns of cognition and emotion in society and in the subcultural group in which they live.

4. THE CONCEPT OF "FLOW"

As a further operationalization of the concept of happiness, we shall rely on the notion of "flow" as it has been advanced by Mihaly Csikszentmihalyi. In several books over the past decades (Csikszentmihalyi, 1988, 1990, 1993), this concept has been developed both theoretically and empirically. The central claim is that the quality of life does not depend solely on an achieved state of happiness, but on what one does in order to become happy. Without developing goals that give meaning to one's life, or when failing to use our faculties to the fullest, any "good feelings" will remain superficial and fail to contribute to authentic happiness. Referring to Voltaire's *Candide*, Csikszentmihalyi (1990) argues that the person withdrawing from the world to "cultivate his garden" may achieve contentment, but not true happiness. The latter can only be gained if a person entertains dreams—and risks. But both dreams and risks are the stuff that literature is made from.

One of the most direct routes to arrive at such happiness is the state of "flow," defined as an autotelic activity, demanding considerable investment of mental energy, but bringing little or no conventional reward; instead, the activity is its own gratification. It is even the case that the use of flow activities to gain conventional forms of reward (such as money or prestige) is often considered base, in bad taste, or even immoral. Flow, then, is the state of mind that occurs when a person's resources are fully involved in overcoming a challenge that is neither too demanding nor too facile: if the challenge is too high, then anxiety will impede the flow; if the challenge is too low, by contrast, apathy may be the result. Conversely, if my skills are too highly developed for the task at hand, then boredom will soon set in; if my skills are underdeveloped for the task, then, as with an undemanding challenge, I will experience apathy rather than flow. Flow, then, is the experience that sails between those extremes of boredom, anxiety, and apathy.

To investigate the psychological processes involved in flow, Csikszentmihalyi (1988) developed the Experience Sampling Method, or ESM. ESM uses a pager or a programmable watch to signal people (at random times) to fill out two pages in a booklet they carry with them. At the signal, the person writes down where she is, what she is doing, what she is thinking about, who she is with, and rates her state of consciousness at the moment on various numerical scales such as happiness, concentration, self-esteem, how strongly motivated she is, and so on. Interesting results were gained in this way. For instance, virtually all types of people in all cultures throughout the world tend to sleep about one third of their lives, with the rest of their time divided fairly evenly between traveling, finding and eating food (work), and free leisure, or, put another way, cycles of rest, production, consumption, and interaction. It turns out, moreover, that 15% of people never experience flow, 15-20% say they experience it every day (or several times a day), with the rest in between. Finally, there is no apparent correlation between intelligence and flow experience.

Csikszentmihalyi names religion, sports, and the arts as roads often taken to the experience of flow. Reading literature is also mentioned explicitly by him. Being completely submerged in the world of the book, partaking in the lives of its protagonists, losing sense of time and one's own environment are some signs that the reading has become autotelic, indeed, its own gratification. Nell (1988) makes a similar claim when he writes: "Reading changes the focus of attention from self to environment. Because of the heavy demands reading makes on conscious attention, the reader is effectively shielded from other demands, whether internal or external. At the same time, the intense attention brought to bear by the entranced reader may have the effect of transfiguring both book and reader" (Nell, 1988, p. 9). And Noelle-Neumann (1995), on the basis of numerous empirical studies, concludes:

"In every age group, every educational level, in every group we studied we found those who read books happier than those who did not read books" (Noelle-Neumann, 1995, pp. 24-28). Could it be then that through the processes of flow, readers may experience forms of happiness? We carried out two studies that should shed light on the issue.

5. STUDY 1

In a first study, among other things, we examined the relationship between flow experiences on the one hand and reading experiences and general life satisfaction on the other, with the help of a questionnaire (i.e., off-line). Four hypotheses will be tested: $H1$: reading activities provide a relatively good occasion to experience flow; $H2$: readers who experience flow during reading have special reading experiences that distinguish them from those of readers who do not experience flow; $H3$: the more participants experience flow, the more they are satisfied with their lives; $H4$: readers who experience flow during reading are generally more satisfied with their lives compared to readers who experience no flow during reading.

In order to construct a questionnaire on an empirical basis, unstructured interviews were carried out with 10 persons about their reading habits, reading motivation, and reading experiences. The information gained in these interviews was used to construct a questionnaire, using 5-point Likert scales. In order for participants to complement our questionnaire, open-ended questions were added so that they could also propose their own categories.

Questionnaires were distributed to a convenience sample of 150 individuals in the researcher's circle of friends and colleagues, of which 127 were returned, and of which 122 were usable (70 female, 52 male). Participants' age was predominantly between 20 and 40, and their educational level was high (mainly Abitur, the high school diploma at the German *Gymnasium* that gives access to university education). Initial results indicated that reading was of a significantly higher frequency for women ($p < .001$), a finding in accord with many other studies, especially with respect to belle-lettristic reading materials, while men generally scored higher for the frequency with which they read newspapers, journals, and informative books. An interesting finding was that approximately 65% of our respondents said they experienced flow often or regularly—an indication that perhaps our sample is not representative of the whole German population, but only for the group of young urban people with a relatively high education standard. As to the activities most associated with flow experiences, Figure 1 illustrates the overall pattern.

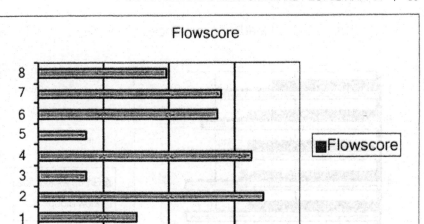

Figure 1. Flow during leisure activities: 8 = health, 7 = sports, 6 = a good conversation, 5 = watching TV, 4 = sex, 3 = drive a car, 2 = reading, 1 = listening to music.

As can be seen, reading scores highest of all activities, even higher than sex! Sports and a good conversation also are scored high by our respondents, while driving a car and watching TV are not really inducive to experiencing flow for our respondents—presumably another indication that our sample may differ from other populations. In Csikszentmihalyi's research, driving a car was one of the most certain categories to elicit flow experiences, presumably a cultural difference concerning car driving between North America and Europe. Hence the conclusion seems clear: in consonance with Csikszentmihalyi's conjecture, reading literature is certainly an activity able to provide flow experiences.

More importantly, of course, is the question whether, as specified by our second hypothesis, readers who report frequent flow activities ($N = 65$) have special reading experiences that distinguish them from readers who report no flow experiences ($N = 42$). Figure 2 shows the results: out of 18 items presented, the following seven show statistically significant differences (at $p < .05$) between both groups. These are the reading experiences that describe flow experiences during reading, which are the ones most promising for further research in studying the experience of flow while reading literature. Moreover, the results are in the predicted direction: the flow group scores systematically higher on all categories compared to the readers who experience no flow. As such, the results provide firm support for the second hypothesis:

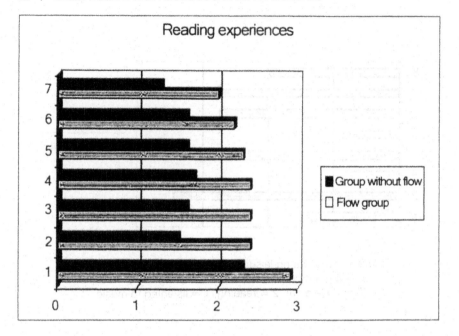

Figure 2. Differences in reading experiences between readers with and without flow experiences during reading: 7 = loss of time experience, 6 = forgetting yourself, 5 = self-determination, 4 = lack of self-perception, 3 = forgetting problems, 2 = free of worries, 1 = not conscious of body.

reading with or without flow makes for different reading experiences, whereby readers with frequent flow systematically experience more intense levels of reading involvement.

Finally, let us inspect the data showing the relation between flow experiences and general life satisfaction. Figure 3 summarizes the results. Again, participants who report flow experiences score systematically higher on all items compared to participants reporting no flow. On four of the nine items, the difference is significant: *leisure* ($p < .05$), *own person* ($p < .05$), *health* ($p < .01$), *life in general* ($p < .05$). The link with perceived health is very convincing, in addition to being highly significant, the effect size is also considerable. The data clearly corroborate the third hypothesis.

Concerning the fourth hypothesis, however, that readers who experience flow during reading are generally more satisfied with their life, no such relation could be established in the data. We found no significant correlations between flow experiences during reading and variables tapping satisfaction with life, with oneself, or with hobbies or

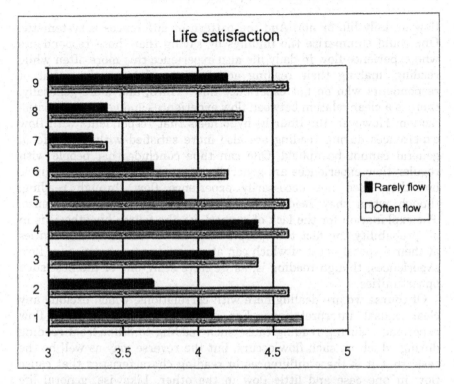

Figure 3. Relation of flow experiences and general life satisfaction:
1 = living conditions, 2 = leisure, 3 = financial situation, 4 = work,
5 = own person, 6 = family, 7 = partnership, 9 = life in general.

leisure time. Hence, the fourth hypothesis, and the one proposed by Csikszentmihalyi, must be rejected.

In sum then, the results provide strong support for a link between flow and reading. First, according to our participants, reading is a good (in fact the best) activity to experience flow. It may be that reading, having a high status in Western societies, may attract socially desirable answers, but other activities, such as music (certainly in a country like Germany, with its strong musical tradition), might elicit socially desirable answers too. Also, the alternative "having a good conversation" and "sports" might do so too. As it is, however, reading attracted the strongest favor of our participants when it comes to optimal flow experiences. Second, readers who reported high flow levels distinguished themselves from readers reporting low such levels in terms of their reading experiences. The activity of reading, in other words, takes on a different quality, depending on whether respondents experience flow in daily life or not. And the pattern of differences is systematic. One could summarize the findings by saying that those respondents who experience flow in daily life also experience this more often while reading, making their reading activity more intense than that of respondents who do not experience flow. Third, and more generally, there is a clear relation between flow experiences and general life satisfaction. However, the (fourth) hypothesis that respondents with flow experiences during reading are also more satisfied with their life in general cannot be upheld. One can thus conclude that people with regular flow experiences are generally more satisfied with their lives, but they need not necessarily experience flow through reading, though when they read, their experiences are also more intense. The explanation for the lack of support for the fourth hypothesis is in all probability the fact that people have many leisure time activities at their disposal, most of which can also provide opportunities for flow experiences, though reading is, as we have seen, one of the best such opportunities.

Of course we are dealing here with correlations, which exclude any clear causal interpretations. For instance, it may be that flow experiences during reading cause such reading to differ from reading during which no such flow occurs, but the reverse may as well be the case: that it is these differences in reading characteristics that cause flow in one case and little flow in the other. Likewise, general life expectancy may be caused by, but also itself cause, flow experiences. And in all cases, the correlation may also be caused by another, invisible variable that causes both other variables, whence they also correlate. Moreover, our study was carried out off-line: participants indicated their reactions in general, without being involved in reading at that moment. To remedy this shortcoming, we carried out a follow-up study online.

6. STUDY 2

In this study, we investigated the relation between flow experiences during reading and the motivation to continue reading. As a general hypothesis, we started from the assumption that the more intensive the flow experienced while reading, the higher the motivation to continue reading will be. It will be appreciated that again this will not allow a strict causal interpretation: the higher motivation to read on may cause flow, or vice versa. But the present study does allow us a look at the reading processes as they unfold *during* reading in time. Secondly, we wished to see whether flow also related to reading delight and other emotions experienced during reading. Summarizing, *H1* says that there is a strong relationship between the flow readers experience while reading and their motivation to continue reading; *H2* that flow is related to the delight readers find in reading and to other emotions, such as happiness or lightheartedness.

As materials, we made use of Bernhard Schlink's novel *The Reader* (original German title *Der Vorleser*). The reasons for this selection were the following: first, the novel is clearly of the best-selling category, which means that it is appealing to large groups of readers, not just to a minority with a specific taste. Second, Schlink writes a simple and straightforward German, making its language and style readily accessible to readers of all levels. Third, its theme (a highly peculiar love relation between a young man and an older woman after the Second World War, but having its roots in the Nazi period in Germany) appeals to both male and female readers. It is also known from many public reactions to it that the novel elicits strong emotions, especially in Germany, and that it boosts a personal positioning. Fourth, since we wished our participants to read the whole novel, it was imperative that it was available in a cheap pocket edition. Finally, and most importantly, Schlink's *Reader* was one of the titles mentioned several times during the 10 interviews held prior to the construction of the questionnaire in Study 1. For all these reasons, we thought the novel would be a good choice. This turned out to be the case; at the end of Study 2, we asked our participants to evaluate the text on a 5-point scale and the average response was 4.0, confirming our choice.

As a method of investigation, we opted for Csikszentmihalyi's ESM, not deployed at random times, but instead after the reading of five segments of the novel, which had been selected for their structural relevance in the plot. After having read each of the sections involved, participants indicated their reading experiences, evaluation of quality and tension, and motivation to keep on reading on 5-point Likert scales. We encouraged them to read the novel in what they themselves felt to be *natural* reading situations.

As participants, we recruited 50 individuals from Study 1, 44 of whom returned our questionnaire, of which 41 could be used. During the experiment, 3 readers gave up, so that we were finally left with 38 respondents. Eight of these readers, however, read the novel for a second time, which is why we separated them from the others. These eight readers provide an excellent opportunity to investigate the question whether flow experiences are different on a second reading. The mean age of respondents was 34.5 years, and the sample was characterized again by a relatively high educational standard and high reading frequencies of its participants. The time required to read Schlink's novels varied from 1 day to 2 months. (We were highly conscious not to put any kind of time pressure on the participants, so as to let the reading process take its natural course for each respondent individually.)

Let us now look at the relationship between flow and the motivation to continue reading after having finished the first 5 sections of the novel, as depicted in Figure 4. As can be seen, except for the development between sections 1 and 2, there is a really good fit between both lines; the overall correlation r is .655 ($p < .001$). Furthermore, for all test times, there is a significant correlation between flow and motivation to continue reading: $r = .40, p < .05$ (section ½); $r = .60, p < .001$ (sections 2/3); $r = .76, p < .001$ (sections ¾); $r = .72, p < .001$ (sections 4/5); $r = .73, p < .001$ (sections 5/6). This means, then, that the first hypothesis is supported by the data: whenever flow is high, readers want to continue reading, and vice versa, thus confirming the first hypothesis of the online study.

An important question here is whether such flow experience also contributes to some kind of happiness on the part of the reader. Although this follows from the theoretical work by Csikszentmihalyi, and certainly sounds plausible, given the descriptions of flow themselves, it is nevertheless good to test this assumption empirically. Fortunately, we are in a situation to do so, as we also asked our participants

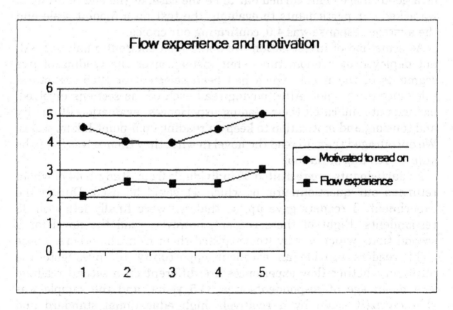

Figure 4. The relation between flow experience and the motivation to continue reading.

to indicate to what extent they experienced *delight* during reading. And yes, flow significantly correlates with reading delight: Pearson correlation over all measures is .673, $p < .000$ (two-tailed). Figure 5 reveals further relations between reading delight and readers' feelings of either being happy or lighthearted, thus in general, corroborating our second hypothesis. As Figure 5 demonstrates, it is *not* the case that reading delight is caused by feelings of happiness or lightheartedness. The graph shows a clear and steady decline of these positive feelings over the six episodes of the novel. This is quite in line with expectations, as the plot becomes more and more grim as it unfolds. And the differences between readers' feelings of happiness and lightheartedness before and after reading the novel show clear effect sizes: .6 points for happiness and .9 points (both on a 5-point scale) for lightheartedness; both differences are significant (as measured by a paired-sample t-test): $t = 2.57, df = 29, p < .016$, and $t = 2.89, df = 29, p < .007$, respectively. Also, the difference between the reading delight is clear: the difference between scores at time interval 2 (after the first episode had been read) and time interval 7 (after having read the sixth episode) is almost a full point on the scale ($t = -3.65, df = 29, p < .001$). So we have here a paradoxical phenomena: one would expect readers to pick a leisure time activity that improves their mood, or at least does not make it worse than it is. Yet, as our results clearly show, this is exactly what

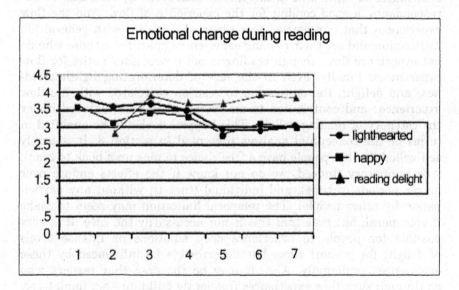

Figure 5. Relation between reading delight, lightheartedness, and happiness during reading.

happened in this case; and those somber feelings that significantly increased during their reading did not affect their reading delight in any negative way. One could even presume that their deteriorating moods boosted the amount of delight they experienced, as the graph for delight goes up each time when the other two lines go down. Hence, the experiences of flow, of reading delight, and the motivation to read on are not triggered by happy events in the story, but must be ascribed to psychological mechanisms involved in the processing of literary artworks. Apparently, readers revel in the somber events unraveling in the story, making the kind of delight experienced a complex one.

7. CONCLUSION

We have come a long way. We started by claiming that the universality of literature in human societies must mean something quite important for the human species. Although at first sight, no clear applications for literature may be perceived, it apparently fulfills functions that are hard to go without. As the discussion between Plato and Aristotle at the dawn of Western science shows, people have reflected on those functions from very early on. It now appears, after having reported the results of our two studies, that the evidence speaks more in favor of Aristotle's than of Plato's view. Apparently literature contributes to some kind of happiness. Literature is, according to our respondents, a good conduit for the experience of flow. And the flow experiences that our participants reported correlate with general life satisfaction and set their reading experiences apart from those who do not experience flow, though reading is not a necessary outlet for flow experiences. Finally, even in the face of deteriorating lightheartedness and delight, the motivation to read on correlated with the flow experiences and contributed to an overall happiness captured under the category of reading delight. This happiness should be qualified in terms of the conceptual analysis presented in section 3. It is partly self-willed (in that people have a free choice to pick up a book to read); it is temporary (indeed, we do not know if the effects endure over longer periods of time), and individual (that is, without any participation by other people). The temporal limitation may seem to make it ephemeral, but note that this is not necessarily the case. It is very possible for people to experience deep emotions or intense levels of delight for a short time, but nevertheless be influenced by these experiences profoundly. Also, it may be the case that readers who go through such flow experiences frequently build up—accumulatively so to speak—a kind of happy fulfillment that makes their reading experiences so special.

REFERENCES

Aristotle. *Poetics*.
Csikszentmihalyi, M. (1988). *Optimal experience: Psychological studies of flow in consciousness*. Cambridge: Cambridge University Press.
Csikszentmihalyi, M. (1990). *Flow. The psychology of optimal experience*. New York: Harper and Row.
Csikszentmihalyi, M. (1993). *The evolving self: A psychology for the third millennium*. New York: HarperCollins.
Nell, V. (1988). *Lost in a book: The psychology of reading for pleasure*. New Haven: Yale University Press.
Noelle-Neumann, E. (1995). Bücherlesen kostet Kraft, erheitert aber das Gemüt. In: *Börsenblatt* 1/ 3, S., 24-28.
Plato. *The Republic*.
Seabright, P. (2004). *The company of strangers*. Princeton, NJ: Princeton University Press.
Schlink, B. (1997). *The Reader*. London: Phoenix.

CHAPTER 5

Cognitive Poetics and Poetry Recital

Reuven Tsur

COGNITIVE AND PHONETIC ASSUMPTIONS

This is an instrumental study of the rhythmical performance of poetry. The recordings discussed in this article are available online at: http://www.tau.ac.il/~tsurxx/KeatsPerformance/Keats.html.

An iambic pentameter line is supposed to consist of regularly alternating unstressed and stressed syllables. In the first 165 lines of *Paradise Lost*, there are only two such lines (Tsur, 1998, p. 24). How do experienced readers of poetry recognize vastly different irregular stress patterns as iambic pentameter? Among the many attempts to answer this question, there is a venerable tradition of instrumental research as well. Since the early 1920s, there has been instrumental research of poetry reading by the so-called sound recorders, in an attempt to discover some regularity. The greatest achievement of these researchers was that they refuted an obstinately persistent myth that there are equal or proportional time intervals between stressed syllables or regions of stress. But they had a naive conception of poetic rhythm: they thought they were measuring relationships that constitute the rhythm of a poem, whereas they were measuring some accidental performance of it. (Their work was summarized by Schramm [1935]; see also Wimsatt & Beardsley [1959]). To avoid this problem, Wellek and Warren (1956, Ch. 13) proposed a model, according to which poetic rhythm has three "dimensions": an abstract versification pattern that consists of verse lines and regularly alternating weak and strong positions; a linguistic pattern that consists of syntactic units and irregularly alternating stressed and unstressed syllables; and a pattern of performance (generative metrists have reinvented the first two of them). Based on this model, I developed a perception-oriented theory of meter, including a theory of rhythmical performance, based on speech research, the limited-channel-capacity hypothesis, and Gestalt theory. What is the psychological meaning of "the rhythmical performance of poetry?" Just as the understanding of a metaphor, it is a problem-solving activity: when the linguistic and versification patterns conflict, they are accommodated in a pattern of performance, such that both are perceptible simultaneously. Thus, the data measured by the instruments stop being accidental; they become functional. They are constrained by the solution of a problem posed by the conflicting patterns of the text on the one hand and by the reciter's (and the audience's) phonetic competence and cognitive system on the other. They give information not about an arbitrary performance, but about the ways in which the conflicting patterns of language and versification can be reconciled and rendered acceptable. In an enjambment, for instance, the performer may convey both the verse line boundary and the run-on sentence as perceptual units, however strained, by having recourse to conflicting phonetic cues: cues of continuity and discontinuity simultaneously.

The versification pattern exists only in the cognitive system as a "metrical set": as an expectation, or a memory trace in short-term memory. Since, according to George Miller (1970), channel-capacity is rigidly limited at the "magical number seven plus or minus two," the vocal material must be manipulated such as to save mental space for the simultaneous processing of the conflicting patterns. Normally, channel-capacity can be saved by recoding: by, for instance, substituting "bad" for "not good." But the words of a poem cannot be changed. Still, processing space can be saved by grouping and clear-cut articulation. When I wanted to test this theory empirically, all the great gurus of instrumental phonetics told me that this was impossible, because the major part of poetic rhythm takes place in the mind, and only a small part of it is detectable in the vocal output. I decided to sidestep this problem by making certain predictions, based on my theory, as to the vocal manipulations required, and see whether performance instances judged rhythmical conform with these predictions. I made predictions in terms of relative stress, clear-cut articulation, gestalt grouping, and certain (musical) pitch intervals. However, again, all the great gurus told me that none of these variables can be read off from the machine's output. It took me over 25 years to find a way to reformulate my research questions in terms that the machine could understand. These terms included continuity and discontinuity. My 1977 hypothesis was that conflicting patterns could be indicated by conflicting vocal cues

(Tsur, 1977, pp. 97, 103, 134). The breakthrough occurred when I found a way to treat a wide range of conflicting phenomena in terms of simultaneous continuity and discontinuity (this happened when I was exposed to the work of Gerry Knowles and Tom Barney at Lancaster University). These conflicting phenomena included run-on sentences, strings of consecutive stressed syllables, and even stress maximum in a weak position.

Continuity is generated by continuous intonation patterns and by the absence of cues for discontinuity, most notably, pauses. I have also found that the alignment of the pitch contour with the syllabic crest may affect grouping. The peak of the pitch contour normally occurs in the middle of the syllabic crest; in some instances, however, it occurs late in the vowel or even at the ensuing sonorant; and sometimes it occurs earlier than the middle (House & Wichmann, 1996; Knowles, 1992; Ladd, 1996, pp. 54, 98, 104). I have found in my corpus that late peaking generates an impetuous forward drive; in fact, the later the peaking, the more impetuous is the forward drive. Early peaking, by contrast, serves as a backward-grouping agent. These effects are also predicted by Gestalt theory and supported by Garrett, Bever, and Fodor's (1966) "click" experiments concerning the psychological reality of linguistic segments. Very little is known about late peaking; but some phoneticians assume that it is quite rare in the speech corpora investigated. As will be observed in our ensuing examples, in the rhythmical performance of poetry, it appears to be quite frequent. Here a device of semantic foregrounding is turned to rhythmic end: "peak delay is said to signal that the utterance is in some way very significant or non-routine" (Ladd, 1996, p. 99).

As to cues of discontinuation, Gerry Knowles (1991) investigated the nature of tone groups. He distinguished internally defined prosodic patterns and external discontinuities at the tone-group boundaries. The former consist in some consistent F_0 pattern ("intonation pattern," in plain English) used in ordinary speech; the latter are temporal discontinuation (pause), pitch discontinuation (a sudden change in F_0), and segmental discontinuation (that is, in normal speech the articulation of adjacent words is overlapping; when there is no overlap, it may count as discontinuity, even if there is no pause). Glottal stops in words beginning with a vowel, or word-final stop releases too, may indicate segmental discontinuation (glottal stop is the speech sound inserted before "aim" when saying "I said 'an aim,' not 'a name'"; stop release is the movement of one or more vocal organs in quitting the position for a speech sound, experienced as a click). Likewise, the prolongation of the final speech sound or the final syllable may be a powerful cue of segmental discontinuation. These would be the most evasive types of

68 / EVOLUTIONARY AND NEUROCOGNITIVE APPROACHES

discontinuity. "The important distinction that seems to be emerging is between boundaries with or without pauses." In my book (Tsur, 1998), I explore how these correlates of tone-group boundaries can be exploited as conflicting cues for the perceptual accommodation of the conflicting patterns of speech and versification regarding three different kinds of conflict: enjambment, strings of consecutive stressed syllables, and stress maximum in a weak position. Here I will explore the first two of these.

Finally, I should point out that when I speak of what we see in a graphic figure and of what we hear in a recording, I am using the indicative mode to perform two different speech acts: in the former, I am using it to make a descriptive statement, whereas in the latter, to make a recommendation what to look for and how to look at it in a delivery instance (that is, I don't deny the possibility that others would look for, and find, different subsets of elements in the same delivery instance).

EXPRESSIVE FUNCTIONS OF VOCAL STYLE

For certain purposes, speakers may deviate from the "ordinary" articulation of phonetic cues: they may, for instance, overarticulate, underarticulate, or distort certain phonemes or phonetic cues. The Hungarian linguist Iván Fónagy is the greatest authority regarding the expressive functions of vocal style. Instead of getting entangled in elaborate expositions, I will briefly present the issue via one of Fónagy's (1971) illuminating examples.

> According to the evidence of facial cinematography, Hungarian or French actresses pronounce /I/ with rounded lips when they mimic a young mother who says tenderly így ("like that") or mais si ("yes, indeed") to her child.
>
> However, subjects who heard the films believed they heard an "I," despite the labialization, which ordinarily transforms [I] into [y] (as in French sure—RT), apparently on the basis of context and situation. Though the speakers deformed the habitual pronunciation of these vowels, their auditors, in decoding the phonological component of the message, re-established the intended phonemes, interpreting the distortion as an expressive manner of pronouncing the phoneme. In the decoding, the sound is broken up into two elements: [y]→[I] + expression of tenderness (Fónagy, 1971, p. 159).

The rounding of the lips can be considered as preparation for a kiss. Fónagy (1971) calls this "phonetic gesture" (p. 160). In this context, Fónagy (1971) speaks of "dual encodedness" (p. 161). I have claimed that in the recitation of metered verse, there is "triple encodedness." As I have elsewhere pointed out at considerable length (Tsur, 2000, 2002), sometimes an overarticulated final stop consonant may be decoded as [p] or [t] or [k] etc. + an assertive, determined, firm attitude + the clear-cut articulation of the end of some prosodic or syntactic unit. One may discern some firm, determined, even authoritarian attitude in the speech of a person who tends to overarticulate the stop consonants. Stop consonants are abrupt, not continuous, and aim at considerable accuracy, at a circumscribed point both in time and in place of articulation. Their overarticulation indicates control, exhibits strict, particular, and complete accordance with a standard, and is marked by thorough consideration of minute details.

Similar triple encodedness may be discerned in the use of intonation contours too. John Ohala (1994) demonstrates, in a well-controlled experiment, a relationship between pitch and affect which, he claims, is deeply rooted in biology. A steep terminal fall is used as a device of auditory punctuation, both in the linguistic and the versification dimension. Ohala's experiment suggests that it may have some inherent emotional potential of dominance too.

Ohala (1994, pp. 327–329) points out that the experimental literature on the F_0 correlates of affect reveals an apparent conflict. Some researchers found that a higher F_0 of voice made a speaker sound "less truthful, less emphatic, and less potent (smaller) and more nervous." Some others found higher maximum F_0 of voice associated with greater confidence in some cases. In an attempt to resolve this conflict, Ohala conducted the following study. Short samples (4 sec) of spontaneous speech were digitally processed in such a way as to remove all spectral details but to retain the original amplitude and F_0 contour, the latter of which was either linearly upshifted or downshifted by varying amounts or left unchanged. These samples of "stripped speech" were presented in pairs to listeners who were asked to judge which voice of each pair sounded more dominant or self-confident. The results indicate that, other things being equal, lower F_0 does make a voice sound more dominant. This is evident, for example, in the judgments for the two samples presented graphically in Figure 1, which are derived from the same speech sample but with one of them upshifted from the original by a factor of 1.25. The sample with the lower F_0 was judged as sounding more dominant than the sample with the higher F_0 by 92% of the listeners. However, when "other things" were not equal, the one feature that contributed most to making a voice dominant was a steep terminal fall in F_0. In Figure 2, the sample shown as a solid line, even though it has a higher-peak F_0, was judged as sounding more dominant (92% of all judgments) than the sample shown as a dotted line, even though the

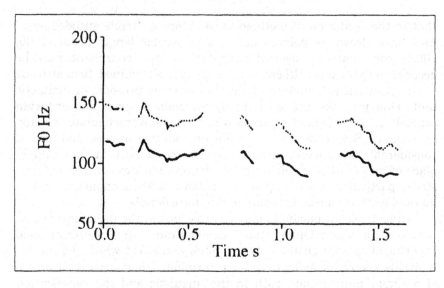

Figure 1. The F_0 contours of two samples of "stripped speech." The lower contour, depicted by the solid line, was judged "more dominant" in 92% of the judgments.

latter is lower in F_0 during most of its duration. "The sharp F_0 terminal fall, lacking in the other sample, seemed to be the determining factor in listeners' evaluations; it suggests that the occasionally higher-peak F_0 in the voices exhibiting greater confidence is there in order to make the terminal fall seem to be even steeper, i.e. by virtue of having fallen from a greater height." Ohala claims that the application of what he calls "the frequency code" to the affective use of low F_0 in human voice for communicating aggression, assertiveness, dominance, etc. and of high F_0 for conveying social subordinacy, politeness, nonthreat, etc. parallels almost exactly the function of F_0 in the nonhuman cries.

To conclude, both a falling pitch contour and an overarticulated final stop consonant may sometimes be construed as a linguistic entity + an assertive, determined, firm attitude + the clear-cut articulation of the end of some prosodic unit.

This conclusion will be consistent with Robert D. Ladd's (1996) observation on final rise of intonation where, by contrast, the "'rising' tune would normally be used to convey doubt, uncertainty, or some other 'questioning' modality" (Ladd, 1996, p. 9). A word must be said about the received view regarding certain supposedly universal perceptual dynamics of intonation. Dwight Bolinger (as summarized by Ladd, 1996, pp. 113-114) claims that intonation has direct links to the

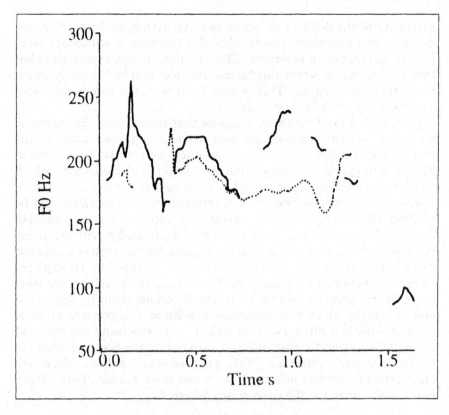

Figure 2. The F_0 contours of two samples of "stripped speech." The contour depicted by the solid line was judged "more dominant" in 92% of the judgments.

prelinguistic use of pitch to signal emotion. Broadly speaking, high or rising pitch signals interest, arousal (active emotions such as anger or surprise), and incompleteness. He points out that the opposition between high and low (or up and down) shows up in the apparently grammaticized uses of pitch—intonation—that turn up in language descriptions again and again. These include the tendency of pitch to drop at the end of an utterance and to rise (or at least not to drop) at major breaks where the utterance remains incomplete; or the use of higher pitch in questions, since in questions the speaker expresses interest and since the exchange is incomplete until the addressee answers. Christine Bartels (1999, p. 34) goes into greater delicacies: "When the fall-rise pattern occurs on statements, it is sometimes referred to as a 'continuation rise' [. . .]. Intuitively, the pattern is a derivative of the declarative fall: it conveys 'statement-hood,' however defined—and something else besides. But the basic illocutionary force [. . .] is still that of an assertion" (Bartels, 1999, p. 35). I will look below into an instance in which this "something else besides" is an openness to further information. This would be thoroughly compatible with "'questioning' modality" or "interest."

Even such a brief summary suggests that rising tones, for instance, may have conflicting potentials, such as doubt and uncertainty on the one hand and active emotions such as anger or surprise on the other. The present approach assumes that it is the other elements with which rising tunes combine (energy level or voice quality, for instance, and, of course, the general context) that determine which potential would be realized. High energy level may activate the "active emotions" potential; doubt and uncertainty, by contrast, would go, typically, with relatively low energy level. As to voice quality, Eugene Morton (1994) points out certain similarities in human and nonhuman vocalization. He explores avian and mammalian sounds used in hostile or friendly, appeasing contexts. He provides two tables in which sounds given by aggressive and appeasing birds and mammals are listed. "Aggressive animals utter low-pitched often harsh sounds [. . .]. Appeasing animals use high-pitched, often tonal sounds" so as to reduce the fear or aggression in the receiver" (Morton, 1994, pp. 350–353). I have elsewhere elucidated the emotive effects of harsh and tonal sounds (Tsur, 2006); here I will not pursue the issue at any length.

Enjambment

Consider the following verse instance from Keats's "Ode on a Grecian Urn" in which the versification unit (the verse line) conflicts with the syntactic unit (the clause), that is, when the phrase or clause runs on from one line to the next one. Versification requires the reciter to stop after "express"; syntax requires to continue. Let us compare two recordings by two leading British actors, Douglas Hodge and Michael Sheen (listen to them online).

> 1. Sylvan historian, who canst thus express
>   A flowery tale more sweetly than our rhyme . . .

The overwhelming majority of listeners made the judgment that Hodge (1995, see Recorded Readings following References) offers an admirably rhythmical solution to the problem by suggesting continuation and discontinuation at the same time at the end of the word "express" (see Figure 3), whereas in Sheen's (1994, see Recorded

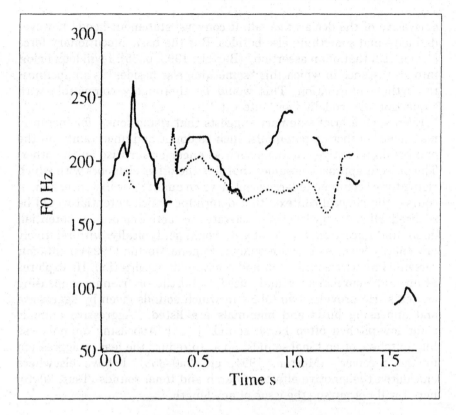

Figure 2. The F_0 contours of two samples of "stripped speech." The contour depicted by the solid line was judged "more dominant" in 92% of the judgments.

prelinguistic use of pitch to signal emotion. Broadly speaking, high or rising pitch signals interest, arousal (active emotions such as anger or surprise), and incompleteness. He points out that the opposition between high and low (or up and down) shows up in the apparently grammaticized uses of pitch—intonation—that turn up in language descriptions again and again. These include the tendency of pitch to drop at the end of an utterance and to rise (or at least not to drop) at major breaks where the utterance remains incomplete; or the use of higher pitch in questions, since in questions the speaker expresses interest and since the exchange is incomplete until the addressee answers. Christine Bartels (1999, p. 34) goes into greater delicacies: "When the fall-rise pattern occurs on statements, it is sometimes referred to as a 'continuation rise' [. . .]. Intuitively, the pattern is a derivative of the declarative fall: it conveys 'statement-hood,' however defined—and something else besides. But the basic illocutionary force [. . .] is still that of an assertion" (Bartels, 1999, p. 35). I will look below into an instance in which this "something else besides" is an openness to further information. This would be thoroughly compatible with "'questioning' modality" or "interest."

Even such a brief summary suggests that rising tones, for instance, may have conflicting potentials, such as doubt and uncertainty on the one hand and active emotions such as anger or surprise on the other. The present approach assumes that it is the other elements with which rising tunes combine (energy level or voice quality, for instance, and, of course, the general context) that determine which potential would be realized. High energy level may activate the "active emotions" potential; doubt and uncertainty, by contrast, would go, typically, with relatively low energy level. As to voice quality, Eugene Morton (1994) points out certain similarities in human and nonhuman vocalization. He explores avian and mammalian sounds used in hostile or friendly, appeasing contexts. He provides two tables in which sounds given by aggressive and appeasing birds and mammals are listed. "Aggressive animals utter low-pitched often harsh sounds [. . .]. Appeasing animals use high-pitched, often tonal sounds" so as to reduce the fear or aggression in the receiver" (Morton, 1994, pp. 350–353). I have elsewhere elucidated the emotive effects of harsh and tonal sounds (Tsur, 2006); here I will not pursue the issue at any length.

Enjambment

Consider the following verse instance from Keats's "Ode on a Grecian Urn" in which the versification unit (the verse line) conflicts with the syntactic unit (the clause), that is, when the phrase or clause runs on from one line to the next one. Versification requires the reciter to stop after "express"; syntax requires to continue. Let us compare two recordings by two leading British actors, Douglas Hodge and Michael Sheen (listen to them online).

>   1. Sylvan historian, who canst thus express
>   A flowery tale more sweetly than our rhyme . . .

The overwhelming majority of listeners made the judgment that Hodge (1995, see Recorded Readings following References) offers an admirably rhythmical solution to the problem by suggesting continuation and discontinuation at the same time at the end of the word "express" (see Figure 3), whereas in Sheen's (1994, see Recorded

Readings following References) reading "A" at the beginning of the next line is irritatingly continuous with "express" (see Figure 4). There is no measurable pause in either of the readings between the two words; and this takes care of syntactic continuity. Two significant differences between the two readings may account for the perceived difference between them. First, in Sheen's reading the [s] of "express" is inseparably run into "A," whereas in Hodge's reading, we may discern a glottal stop that perceptually separates the two words, indicated by a minute "lump" in the waveplot. Second, the syllable "press" in general, and the closing [s] in particular, is considerably longer in Hodge's reading than in Sheen's.

How can we know that these are the variables that determine the effect? This effect of these vocal cues is predicted by the foregoing cognitive model of rhythmical performance. But I have also reproduced, by electronic manipulation, the same perceived effect in Sheen's reading as in Hodge's reading. I copied a section of Sheen's [s] and repeatedly re-pasted it, prolonging the [s]. Then I copied from Hodge's reading the glottal stop and pasted it into Sheen's, before the "A." Again, the majority of listeners judged that in the doctored, but not the original, version, conflicting cues for continuation and discontinuation secure the rhythmic effect of the enjambment.

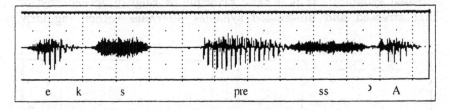

Figure 3. Wave plot of "express A" in Hodge's performance
(ʔ indicates glottal stop).

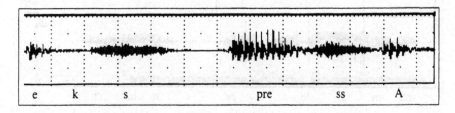

Figure 4. Wave plot of "express A" in Sheen's performance
(no glottal stop).

Strings of Consecutive Stressed Syllables

The iambic meter requires that every even-numbered syllable be stressed and every odd-numbered unstressed. This rarely happens in English poetry, especially in Milton and the Romanticists. Some prosodists would settle for alternation of more and less stressed syllables. But, as delivery instances by outstanding British actors indicate, even this cannot be taken for granted. In the rest of this chapter, I will discuss Hodge's (see Figures 5, 7, and 9) and Sheen's (see Figures 6, 8, and 10) readings of three short lines from Keats's "La Belle Dame Sans Merci." I will not go into the debates about ballad meter. Suffice for my purpose that in the first three lines, for instance, of this ballad, the alternation of unstressed and stressed syllables is exceptionally regular, while the fourth line suddenly deviates from this; and so on, with the necessary changes. Let us consider the following line:

2. And máde swéet móan
   w   s   w   s

The letters w and s under the words indicate the regularly alternating weak and strong positions of the iambic pattern. In the string of words, by contrast, there is one unstressed syllable and three consecutive stressed syllables. "It is a basic principle of English speech rhythm that stressed and unstressed syllables alternate rather regularly.

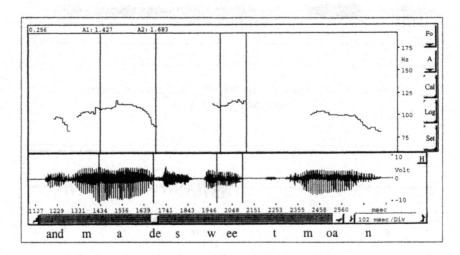

Figure 5. Wave plot and pitch contour of "And made sweet moan" in Hodge's reading.

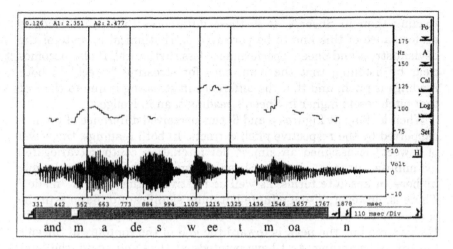

Figure 6. Wave plot and pitch contour of "And made sweet moan" in Sheen's reading.

Consequently, if an utterance contains a succession of, say, three monosyllabic words from stressable word categories, for example, 'big 'black 'bugs, the intermediate stress may be dropped in order to achieve a more regular alternation, e.g., 'big black 'bugs" (Couper-Kuhlen, 1986, p. 37). The stress of "sweet" can, therefore, be demoted, preserving the iambic lilt in the string of three stresses. The present approach, by contrast, predicts the possibility of a reading that will put equally heavy stress on the three consecutive syllables, but will manipulate the vocal material in such a way that the regularly alternating weak and strong positions may be somehow perceived beyond the immediately observable string of stressed syllables.

A characteristic feature of Keats' ballad is that an unusually large proportion of stanzas end with such a sequence of three stressed syllables. When listening to the two readings, one finds that rather than demoting the stress on sweet, both reciters assign to it greater stress than expected in ordinary English, so as to conflict with the versification pattern. Listening to Hodge's recording confirms that it assigns equally heavy stresses to the three consecutive stressed syllables. Listening to Sheen's reading reveals something quite unexpected. Although the three syllables bear heavy stresses, the stress on "sweet" is considerably stronger than on the adjacent syllables, conflicting with the iambic pattern of the sequence of weak and strong positions. As we shall see, there appear to be additional differences between the two readings owing to which the iambic pattern is better discerned in Hodge's reading than in Sheen's. It is these differences that cause Hodge's performance of this line to be perceived as rhythmical in spite of the deviant stress and Sheen's performance less rhythmical. It also becomes clear by listening that the main cues for stressing "sweet" in both readings is pitch; and that the difference in stressing is due to the fact that pitch resets higher in Sheen's reading than in Hodge's.

When looking at Figures 5 and 6, this perceived difference of pitch is supported by the respective pitch extracts. In both readings, the vowel of "sweet" is assigned an almost flat intonation contour (variegated by minute curlings); but in Sheen's reading it resets considerably higher—in absolute terms, as well as relative to the crest of "made." There is, however, also a minute but quite significant difference in the shapes of the pitch curve of this vowel in the two performances: in Hodge's reading the peak is toward the end of the contour, in Sheen's toward its beginning. As I have pointed out time and again, the later the pitch peak of a syllable, the more it "presses" forward; the earlier, the more it "reclines" backward. When a stressed syllable occurs in a weak position, it threatens the integrity of the verse line, inspiring the listener with uncertainty, sometimes even with awe. When the metric structure of the line is reinstated by a stressed syllable in a subsequent strong position (especially when it is the last strong position of the line), the listener experiences relief. In order for this relief to take place, the infringing and the reinstating stresses must be perceptually related, "grouped together." The forward drive exerted by the relatively late peak on "sweet" in Hodge's reading perceptually groups it with the ensuing stress. In Sheen's reading, as we have seen, the infringement of the stress of "sweet" upon meter is stronger; the insignificantly higher peak at its beginning tends to group "sweet" backward, with a much more weakly stressed syllable in a strong position (but certainly not forward), further disturbing the rhythmic impression of the line. Silverman found that a word boundary in combination with "stress clash" (adjacent to another accented syllable) usually increased leftward shift of peak (House & Wichmann, 1996). In my corpus of poetry readings, on the contrary, there is a notable tendency to delay peaking in stressed syllables in weak positions.

This difference is reinforced by another one. To use Gerry Knowles' distinction, the two reciters exploited here for rhythmic purposes an opposition between two types of intonation contour, available for bringing out a semantic contrast (personal communication; cf. Tsur, 1998, p. 253). When we enumerate several items of equal weight, we use just minute humpback intonation contours as Hodge does on "made" in Figure 5. When the speaker wishes to indicate that a later phrase is not just one more item in the list but some additional information about the preceding item, he will "push down" the intonation contour, just as Sheen did on "made" in Figure 6. In this way, Hodge's humpbacks suggest that "made" and "sweet" are of equal weight—in this case, from the rhythmic (rather than the semantic) point of view. Sheen's trough indicates that "made" is semantically subordinated to "sweet moan" (and, by the same token, rhythmically too).

Another prediction of the present approach is that in such an instance of three consecutive heavily stressed syllables that occur in an iambic line, both the phonemes and the syllable boundaries will be overarticulated, so as to save mental processing space, required for the simultaneous processing of the conflicting patterns of stress and meter. Thus, for instance, the [t] of "sweet" is conspicuously overarticulated in both readings, but in different ways. In the waveform of Sheen's reading, one may discern a robust lump indicating the release of the [t]. In Hodge's reading, the [t] is overarticulated in a subtler manner. Here the release is indicated by a much smaller lump which, however, is preceded by a 91-msec-long pause. This longish pause is not perceived as straightforward silence, but as the prolonged closure of the articulatory organs before the release of the stop. The overarticulation of the word-final [t] overarticulates, by the same token, the word boundary.

The most widespread and most effective means, however, for the overarticulation of word or phrase boundaries is a terminal intonation contour. Such a terminal contour is usually a falling curve, with some "rounding out" effect. When we listen to the two performances of this line, we tend to hear something that approximates such a "rounding out" effect in Hodge's, but not in Sheen's, performance, in the utterance of "made" and of "moan." The intonation curves assigned to these words in Sheen's reading tend to sound more "flat." In Figure 6, the intonation contour of "moan" consists of a rising contour assigned to [m], then falling on "-oan." This contour of "-oan" is a very short and moderate "slope," almost flat, falling from 97.137 Hz to 86.133 Hz and then curling up to 89.634 Hz at the end. The corresponding contour in Hodge's reading has a longer fall, from 104.009 Hz to 82.895 Hz (that is, a fall of 11 Hz versus 22 Hz), with a bend, a kind of "curved knee," in the latter contour. A similar difference can be seen in the intonation contours assigned to the vowel of "made" in the two readings. One possible implication of the foregoing discussion is this: the relatively high leap of pitch from "made" to "sweet" in Sheen's reading wrenches the iambic lilt of the line. This should not necessarily undermine poetic rhythm; it could be balanced by a longer-falling intonation contour with a rounded curve on "moan." But Sheen's reading impairs the rhythmic quality of this verse line not only in these obtrusive cues but, as we have seen, in such more elusive ways as grouping "sweet" backward (by an early peak) rather than forward and assigning a short-falling intonation contour with a trough rather than a long-falling contour with a rounded knee to the vowel in "made."

Such divergent strings of heavily stressed syllables in the iambic meter as "made sweet moan" require, in order to arouse a rhythmical impression, conflicting cues for overarticulation and grouping, for continuity and discontinuity, at one and the same time. The lack of pause between the words in both readings takes care of continuity; but in Hodge's reading, there is also the perceptual forward grouping of "sweet" with "moan" by a relatively late peak. The overarticulation of the [t] in "sweet" in both readings also suggests overarticulation of the word boundary. In Hodge's reading, there are two longish pauses in the middle of "sweet": after [s] and before [t]. They are, however, not perceived as silent periods, but as articulatory gestures overarticulating [s] and [t]. This device is more frequent in Hodge's readings than in any other reciter's in my corpus.

We encounter similar problems and solutions in excerpt 3:

3. And nó bírds síng
   w   s w   s

Let us listen to the two readings of excerpt 3. Again, most remarkably, both readings emphasize rather than demote the stress on birds, which is a stressed syllable in a weak position. But the result is again quite different. In Hodge's reading, "no" and "birds" bear roughly equal stress and are perceived as contrapuntal to the alternating weak and strong positions perceived at the same time. In Sheen's reading, "birds" bears much stronger stress, but this time he found a viable solution, generating what I call a "stress slope" (see below). The theory predicts that the boundary of the stressed word in the weak position would be overarticulated; but, at the same time, it would be emphatically grouped with the next (stressed) syllable in a strong position. In Hodge's reading, I would draw attention to the fact that the vowels of "no" and "birds" are perceived as prolonged. Indeed, my measurements show that "birds" is long relative to the adjacent words. Such lengthening is a less obtrusive cue for stress, indicating, by the same token, overarticulation and discontinuation before "sing." But at the same time, some force propelling across it is perceived too. In ordinary speech, such back-to-back [s]s as in "birds sing" almost always overlap; and we frequently find this even throughout my corpus of poetry readings. In both readings discussed here, the two [s]s are run one into the other. In Hodge's reading, however, they are, at the same time, carefully articulated so that two distinct [s]s can be heard. This is most effective as the articulation of a word boundary. In Sheen's reading, by contrast, only one [s] can be heard (the same difference between the two readings we find regarding the back-to-back [s]s in "faery's song"). Compensating for this, the word boundary is overarticulated by an exceptionally long, falling intonation contour in midphrase, which is normally used to indicate sentence ending or, at least, phrase ending. This is quite common in poetry reading, conforming with the predictions of our theory.

Looking at the figures, we get visual support for our auditory impression. In Figure 7, there is a minute "neck" in the waveplot of [s], accounting for the perceptual separation of the back-to-back [s] sounds. The first [s] is further articulated by a 76-msec pause in midword. Again, this longish pause is not perceived as straightforward silence, but as the prolonged closure of the articulatory organs suggesting an overarticulation of [s]. The perceptual force propelling across this overarticulated word boundary is accounted for by the minute "late peak" audible and visible toward the end of "birds." This increases the stress of "birds", and takes care of its grouping with "sing." In Figure 8, the words display a mounting sequence of intonation peaks ("stress slope"), the last two being followed by long-falling terminal contours, clearly articulating the word boundaries. Such a solution (recommended by Wimsatt & Beardsley [1959, p. 594] for highly deviant strings of consecutive stresses) conforms with the iambic pattern: "no" bears considerably stronger stress than "and"; "birds" considerably stronger stress than "no," whereas "sing" bears somewhat

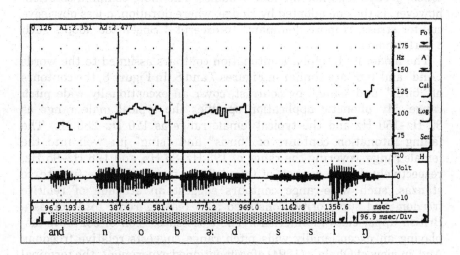

Figure 7. Wave plot and pitch contour of "And no birds sing" in Hodge's reading.

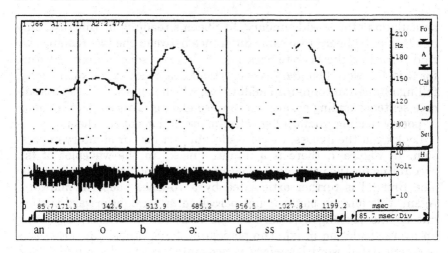

Figure 8. Wave plot and pitch contour of "And no birds sing" in Sheen's reading.

stronger stress than "birds." Thus, the delivery instance foregrounds a group of two consecutive iambic feet. In performing excerpts 1 and 2, Sheen overstressed the last but one syllable (with no linguistic or metric justification). In performing excerpt 3, he accommodated the deviant stress in a rising pattern of pitches which, by the same token, groups together the four syllables. The more common solution, however, is the one adopted by Hodge, where duration, a less obtrusive cue for stress, is more dominant. In excerpt 4 Sheen too adopts such a performance.

The moderate humpback intonation contours assigned to the words "And" and "no" are similar in Figures 7 and 8. In Figure 8, the contours of "birds" and "sing," by contrast, cover an exceptionally wide pitch range. My phonetic application specifies the typical male range as 80 Hz–150 Hz and the typical female range as 120 Hz–280 Hz. The falling intonation contours of "birds" and "sing" jut well into the female range, covering the range of 193 Hz–86 Hz, and 196 Hz–95 Hz, respectively. In the context of this delivery instance of the first three stanzas, such wide-range contours suggest an attitude of relative freedom and superiority, construed as a teasing/ironic tone (or as a British upper-class mannerism). The close succession of contours displaying an exceptionally wide pitch range suggests relative freedom. And, in view of Ohala's (1994) aforementioned experiment, the terminal contours falling from so high a peak to a low baseline may indicate an attitude of superiority.

In Figure 7, by contrast, pitch is restricted to an unusually narrow range. Such reduced pitch movement may be construed in the present context as reduced activity, indicating some "gentle" affect (as compassion, tenderness, sorrow). The utterance ends with a "partial or incomplete fall" (cf. Ladd, 1996, p. 255) followed by a slightly rising intonation contour: at the end of the nasalized portion of "sing," there is a minute, clearly discernible rise of tune, conveying some elusive openness to further information. This may suggest a hesitant descriptive statement plus the question "am I right?" or an attitude of tender concern or both. The late peak on "birds," too, conveys a similar affect. In this way, intonation articulates the end of the syntactic and prosodic units but, at the same time, indicates some inconclusive mood. Thus, in the first three stanzas of the ballad, the speaking voice of the "bard" adopts different, in fact, opposite attitudes in the two readings, indicated by the different intonation contours. This difference may have been reinforced by differences in voice quality; but the theoretical apparatus propounded here cannot handle this issue.

In excerpt 4, the compound-stress rule assigns greater stress to "hill" than to "side." In its first occurrence in particular, Sheen gives, like Hodge, a perfectly level sequence of stressed syllables with overarticulated boundaries and confines himself to a relatively narrow pitch range.

4. On the cóld híll síde
    w   s   w   s

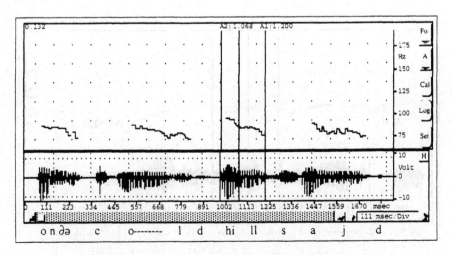

Figure 9. Wave plot and pitch contour of "On the cold hill side" in Hodge's reading.

82 / EVOLUTIONARY AND NEUROCOGNITIVE APPROACHES

The shapes of the pitch contours in the two readings are surprisingly similar. Both reciters separate the three consecutive stressed monosyllables by almost identical intonation contours. Unlike in Figures 6 and 8, the pitch onset of the second stressed monosyllable (in a weak position) is only insignificantly higher than that of the adjacent words, and unlike in Figure 6, the first of the stressed syllables is not subordinated by an intonation trough to the subsequent stress (in a weak position). There is still an interesting difference on "hill." In Figure 9, the contours both on [I] and [l] are more humpback-like than in Figure 10. In Figure 10, by contrast, there is, apparently, a minute trough on [I]. Thus, in Hodge's performance, again equivalence is emphasized by humpback contours. In Sheen's, the following possibility emerges, if I am right: the pitch onset on "hill" is slightly higher than on the adjacent words; but the word is grouped forward, due to the subordinating trough, with the ensuing stressed syllable in a strong position.

In both readings (Figures 9 and 10) the last syllable (in a strong position) is long enough to "break even" with the infringing stress in the preceding weak position. Unlike in Figure 8, the pitch range is exceptionally narrow in both readings, so that the articulation of word boundaries must be done by subtler and more elusive cues. As the waveplot shows, the [k] of "cold" is robust in both readings. The [d] is overarticulated, but by different means: in Figure 10 we see a robust stop release; in Figure 9 a stop release marked by a tiny lump, preceded and followed by minute pauses perceived as closure of the articulatory

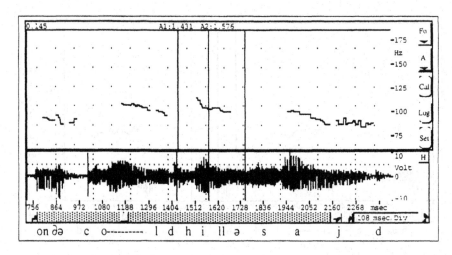

Figure 10. Wave plot and pitch contour of "On the cold hill side" in Sheen's reading.

organs and not as straightforward periods of silence. In Sheen's reading, "hill" is separated from "side" by a very uncommon device (which, however, I have found elsewhere too): a minute schwa intrudes after [l], which cannot be heard outside the artificial computerized conditions (cf. Tsur, 1998, pp. 158-160, 179-181). In Hodge's reading, discontinuity is generated by segmental means: the [l] is exceptionally lengthened relative to [hi]. In this reading, [hi] is 90 msec long; [l] 132 msec long. Compare these proportions to those in Sheen's reading: [hi] is 159 msec long, [l+ə] 97 + 59 = 156 msec long. In the former, [l] is almost one-and-a-half times longer than [hi]; in the latter, [l+ə] is insignificantly shorter than [hi].

Our foregoing discussion may indicate the two artists' attitude toward poetic rhythm: Hodge attempts to strike a delicate perceptual balance between prose rhythm and meter; in Sheen's reading, prose rhythm is dominant. We have also noticed contrasting uses of vocal gestures in the two actors' readings. Sheen displayed relative freedom in his recourse to vocal gestures; Hodge was more "austere." Sheen had recourse to an exceptionally wide pitch range; Hodge to an exceptionally narrow one. They typically resorted to different kinds of vocal gestures. In the speaker's address to the knight, Sheen displayed a greater susceptibility to obtrusive cues both with reference to rhythm and emotions; Hodge displayed a greater sensitivity to subtle and minimal cues. These stylistic characteristics of the two artists are far from thoroughly consistent, but still, fairly typical. In performing "Sylvan historian" (excerpt 1), for instance, Hodge does resort to two successive, affectively loaded falling intonation contours. But as a rule, he has recourse to subtler, minimal cues. Likewise, Sheen too, occasionally has recourse to some of the subtler solutions predicted by the present theory, as in the equal stresses of excerpt 4.

CONCLUSIONS

Wimsatt and Beardsley; (1959, p. 598) claim: "The notion of an accentual spondee (or 'level' foot) in English appears to be illusory, for the reason that it is impossible to pronounce any two successive stresses in English without some rise or fall of stress—and some rise or fall of stress is all that is needed for a metrical ictus." Chatman (1965) collected judgments from a panel of 21 professors of English as to which one in pairs of consecutive syllables is more strongly stressed in 11 recorded readings of Shakespeare's Sonnet 18. The answers indicate that an "accentual spondee" *is* possible in English. Wimsatt and Beardsley's proposal may work fine for excerpts 2-3 above, but not for excerpt 4, where the compound demands a stronger stress in the weak position than in the ensuing strong position. As the foregoing examples suggest, even in instances in which linguistic stress rules would favor the demotion of a stressed syllable in a weak position, some outstanding actors tend rather to overstress it and then find some other solution, predicted by the present theory, to the problem. Notice that while Wimsatt and Beardsley speak in terms of "rise or fall of stress," I am speaking in terms of "rising and falling pitch," "infringing and reinstating stresses," and "breaking even." The two ways of speaking focus on different aspects of meter. The former is part of a campaign to reestablish the authority of meter at a time when most prosodists despaired of it, implying that apparently deviant stresses can be reconciled, in the final resort, with the abstract pattern. The latter too acknowledges the authority of meter, but also implies a conception that pleasure can be derived from a split second of uncertainty or frustration followed by a split second of reassurance.

In a work in progress, I analyze readings of the following line from Shakespeare's Sonnet 73 which, too, ends with a sequence of three stressed syllables:

5. Báre rúin'd choíres, where láte the swéet bírds sáng
   w   sw   s   w   s   w   s   w   s

I have examined four recordings of this sonnet, by Simon Callow, The Marlowe Society, and two by Sir John Gielgud, recorded 14 years apart. According to the principle pointed out by Couper-Kuhlen (1986), the intermediate stress on "birds" may be dropped in order to achieve a more regular alternation; this would conform with the iambic pattern extremely well. Nevertheless, none of the four performances takes advantage of this convenient solution. I don't mean to imply that this is the only way to perform such strings of stressed syllables—merely that such a performance is not only plausible, but even is favored by present-day leading British actors. I have the word of one of these actors that he does this wholly intuitively.

My analysis of the delivery instances of excerpt 2 has been criticized as follows: "Sheen's reading can be refuted in purely phonological terms: it is sufficient to know that in his reading 'sweet' bears stronger stress than either 'made' or 'moan' to account for the failure to preserve the iambic rhythm; why do you need all that phonetic information?" Now this is a rather serious accusation of my argument, since elsewhere I have criticized other researchers for merely multiplying information and obscuring issues by describing the acoustic cues for stress (e.g., Tsur, 1998, pp. 104-105). The present approach, however, does not conceive of poetic rhythm merely in terms of a succession of stressed and unstressed syllables or in terms of the correct mapping of linguistic stress pattern onto the abstract metric pattern; for these, indeed, a phonological description would amply suffice. The present approach conceives of poetic rhythm, rather, in terms of a perceptual solution to a perceptual problem arising from the conflicting patterns of stress and meter. In other words, it places the constraints in the reader's rhythmic competence: a deviant verse line is acceptable provided that the reader is able or willing to perform it rhythmically. Such a conception seems to be required, since all rules hitherto offered that are supposed to generate all metrical lines and no unmetrical ones have been violated by precisely those poets who are usually considered as the greatest masters of musicality in verse: Milton and Shelley.

It was suggested to me in the early seventies that I cannot make such claims, unless I offer a systematic theory of the rhythmical performance of poetry. So, in my 1977 book, I worked out speculatively a psychological model based on Gestalt psychology, speech research, and the properties of short-term memory, which bestows, on the one hand, a psychological meaning upon the phrase "is perceived as rhythmical" and, on the other hand, allows specific and testable predictions as to the vocal manipulations that would render a deviant line rhythmical. At the same time, it allows for the individual reciters' creativity, without impairing the intersubjective foundation of the poem as a "stratified system of norms." It soon became clear, however, that it is not enough to explore the vocal manipulations that generate performances judged rhythmical, but one must compare these to the vocal manipulations that generate performances judged unrhythmical and find systematic differences between them. That is precisely what I have attempted to do in the foregoing discussion. Hodge's reading of excerpt 2 is more rhythmical than Sheen's not only by the criteria of such obtrusive cues as the pitch reset on "sweet," but also of the fine-grained texture of his reading: he deploys, quite consistently, a wide range of minute and elusive vocal devices that help to accommodate the deviant "stressed syllable in a weak position" in a pattern of performance that allows the listener to perceive the conflicting patterns of stress and meter at the same time.

Poetic rhythm can be described in the language of literary criticism; and certain aspects of it in the parallel languages of phonetics and acoustics. We may describe every syllable as stressed or unstressed; and may point out where they confirm or disconfirm the versification pattern. This is the traditional business of literary criticism. But then we may proceed to provide some parallel description in phonetic and acoustic terms. We may describe all the speech sounds and syllables, and provide measurements of duration (in msecs), of fundamental or formant frequencies (in cps), and of the energy envelope (in dbs). We may also provide a detailed description of the articulatory gestures. All this can, no doubt, be perfectly accurate—but futile. Entities should not be multiplied beyond necessity. But just how much is "necessity" that should not be transcended? As I said before, the rhythmical performance of poetry is a problem-solving activity. Performance accommodates the conflicting patterns of language and versification. One should have recourse to no more acoustic, phonetic, and cognitive information than what is necessary to solve the problems. There are sentences that run on from one verse line to another, demanding conflicting intonation contours. Chatman (1965) believes that the performer must choose between them; I claim that the performer may preserve both by having recourse to conflicting phonetic cues. This requires a description of the relevant phonetic cues. Or, consider the question: how is it possible that the same speech sounds (e.g., voiceless plosives) can indicate, at the same time, both determination and contempt; and, in addition, may cue word boundary and line boundary where the sentence keeps running on? To answer such questions, we must know one or two things about the place and manner of articulation and the acoustic structure of the speech sound, as well as one or two things about the body language and vocal gestures characteristic of mental states and so forth. Very recently I came to realize an additional use of going outside literary studies to more "basic" processes. The use of "cognitive" language, "neurological" language, and "phonetic" language may provide a metalanguage where no established metalanguage is available for describing literary effects.

REFERENCES

Bartels, C. (1999). *The intonation of English statements and questions—A compositional interpretation*. New York/London: Garland Publishing, Inc.
Chatman, S. (1965). *A theory of meter*. The Hague: Mouton.
Couper-Kuhlen, E. (1986). *An introduction to English prosody*. London: Edward Arnold.
Fónagy, I. (1971). The functions of vocal style. In S. Chatman (Ed.), *Literary style: A symposium* (pp. 159-174). London: Oxford University Press.
Garrett, M., Bever, T., & Fodor, J. A. (1966). The active use of grammar in speech perception. *Perception and Psychophysics, 1,* 30-32.
House, J., & Wichmann, A. (1996). *Investigating peak timing in naturally-occurring speech: From segmental constraints to discourse structure. speech, hearing and language: Volume 9.* Available online: http://www.phon.ucl.ac.uk/home/shl9/jill/house.htm
Knowles, G. (1991). Prosodic labelling: The problem of tone group boundaries. In S. Johannson & A.-B. Stenström (Eds.), *English computer corpora.*

Selected papers and research guide (pp. 149-163) (Topics in English Linguistics 3). Berlin: Mouton de Gruyter.

Knowles, G. (1992). *Pitch contours and tones in the Lancaster/IBM spoken English corpus.* In G. Leitner (Ed.), *New directions in English language corpora—Methodology, results, software developments* (pp. 289-299). Berlin: Mouton de Gruyter.

Ladd, R. D. (1996). *Intonational phonology.* Cambridge: Cambridge University Press.

Miller, G. A. (1970). The magical number seven, plus or minus two: Some limits on our capacity for processing information. In *The psychology of communication.* Harmondsworth: Pelican.

Morton, E. S. (1994). Sound symbolism and its role in non-human vertebrate communication. In L. Hinton, J. Nichols, & J. J. Ohala (Eds.), *Sound symbolism* (pp. 348-365). Cambridge: Cambridge University Press.

Ohala, J. J. (1994). The frequency code underlies the sound-symbolic use of voice pitch. In L. Hinton, J. Nichols, & J. J. Ohala (Eds.), *Sound symbolism* (pp. 325-347). Cambridge: Cambridge University Press.

Schramm, W. L. (1935). *Approaches to the science of English verse.* Iowa City: Iowa University.

Tsur, R. (1977). *A perception-oriented theory of metre.* Tel Aviv: The Porter Israeli Institute for Poetics and Semiotics.

Tsur, R. (1998). *Poetic rhythm: Structure and performance—An empirical study in cognitive poetics.* Bern: Peter Lang.

Tsur, R. (2000). Phonetic cues and dramatic function—Artistic recitation of metered speech. *Assaph—Studies in the Theatre* (pp. 173-196). Theatre Department of Tel Aviv University.

Tsur, R. (2002). Phonetic cues and dramatic function—Artistic recitation of metered speech (Expanded version). *PSYART: A hyperlink journal for the psychological study of the arts.* http://www.clas.ufl.edu/ipsa/journal/2002_tsur05.shtml.

Tsur, R. (2006). Sound—Size symbolism revisited. *Journal of Pragmatics, 38,* 905-924.

Wellek, R., & Warren, A. (1956). *Theory of literature.* New York: Harcourt, Brace & Co.

Wimsatt, W. K., & Beardsley, M. C. (1959). The concept of metre: An exercise in abstraction. *PMLA, 74,* 585-598.

Recorded Readings

Hodge, Douglas reading *John Keats.* Hodder Headline AudioBooks HH 186. (1995).

Sheen, Michael reading *Great Poets of the Romantic Age.* Naxos AudioBooks NA 20 2112. (1994).

CHAPTER 6

The Alphabet and Creativity: Implications for East Asia

Wm. C. Hannas

ASIAN AND WESTERN CREATIVITY

It is an open secret that East Asia lags behind the West in abstract science. This hard fact, acknowledged by government planners in China, Japan, and Korea and by scholars of East Asian development in general, is swept aside by Western intellectuals because it contradicts the conventional belief that all cultures are adequate in their own ways. The notion that Asia "can't do science" also conflicts with our perception of Asia as a technological powerhouse. How can the region that gave the world paper, movable type, and countless other technical marvels be deficient in basic research?

Yet the evidence that East Asia has problems spawning radically new ideas is compelling. Looking at the contemporary scene, there is a credible body of scholarship suggesting that Asia's competitiveness in high-tech sectors was *and still is* a function of its skill at adapting ideas created elsewhere (Fialka, 1997; Hansen, 1996; Reid & Schriesheim, 1996). Paul Herbig (1995), author of a book on Japanese industrial innovation, argues persuasively that Japan's postwar "miracle" depended almost entirely on imports of foreign technology. This pattern of commercializing ideas culled from abroad remains the country's preferred means of progress.

Things in China are no different. Notwithstanding its rhetoric about a creative past and its present aspiration to lead in selected technology sectors, China's failure to distinguish itself in abstract, concept-driven science is conspicuous. Richard Baum (1982), in a study of Chinese scientific practices, noted a preference for observation, concrete thinking, and induction that contrasts totally with the Western penchant for conceptualization, theory, and deduction. Denis Simon (1989) drew similar conclusions about China's lack of an "ethos associated with scientific investigation—such as skepticism, innovation, and inquiry into the unknown" (Simon, 1989, p. 5). Richard Suttmeir (1989), in another such study, described Chinese scientists' "tendency to be oblivious to the underlying theoretical principles from which the preferred, and often 'right' technological practice is deduced" (Suttmeir, 1989, p. 379).

As a consequence of neglecting underlying theory, Asia, by and large, has been forced to follow the Western lead in most fields of advanced science, including those in which their governments are most interested. While it is commonplace for modifications of existing ideas to be made to product and process technology, paradigm shifts that result in entirely new technologies in East Asia are rare. This fact is apparent on many levels: in explicit statements by Asian policymakers about the need to address a creativity gap; in technical glossaries that are indistinguishable from bilingual Asian language/English dictionaries; and in the multifarious techniques China, Japan, and Korea use to transfer Western wellspring technology, often without the consent of the originator (Hannas, 2003; Schweizer, 1993).

Downplaying the magnitude of this issue inhibits our ability to understand it. Charles Murray (2003), in a book that credits most of the world's scientific progress to the West, is still obliged to reject the "cliché that East Asians are intelligent but lack creative flair." Murray, however, goes on to describe Chinese science as "unsystematic" and lacking in theory (Murray, 2003, pp. 38-39) and ends by restating what historians of China long ago concluded; namely, that the country "never developed the [theoretical] framework that would enable the accumulation of scientific knowledge" (Murray, 2003, p. 235).

The reality of Asian creativity is also obscured by a misinterpretation of Joseph Needham's work, which demonstrated that China once led the world in *applied* science. Needham has been criticized for an overly sympathetic approach and for an antiquarianism that accords more weight to detailed examples than to generalized observations (Nakayama, 1973; Qian, 1985). But it is enough in the present context to note that Needham (1954, 1969) himself was puzzled by Chinese scientists' reluctance to think abstractly and systematically.

Other apologists have suggested political, economic and demographic reasons why Asian countries fall short of the creativity levels shown in the West. But the important fact to be recognized—one that underlies any attempt at identifying causes—is that the region as a whole has not shown an aptitude to create *entirely new* ideas, not now and not in the past, when the structural factors that frustrate radical innovation in East Asia today did not exist, absolutely or relative to the West.

However one feels about Asia's creative achievements, there is no disagreement about the different *forms* of creativity favored by East and West. This affords us the possibility of resolving by recourse to a convention used in cognitive science, without prejudice to the principals or the facts, the issue of whether East Asians, raised and working in Asia, are scientifically creative. Clarifying the matter in this way moves us closer to determining the fundamental cause of Asia's preference for incremental progress and the West's inclination toward wholesale restructuring.

Creativity researchers distinguish two types of creativity based on the cognitive processes involved and the end states of those processes. The first type focuses on improving existing rules as instruments for attaining particular goals (Holland, Holyoak, Nisbett, & Thagard, 1986). Elements of a problem are stretched and shuffled, but are not modified by recourse to external data. All reinterpretation is done within a given context (Brick, 1997). While broadly creative, the process does not lead to radical changes.

A second type of creativity depends on abstract patterns imported from domains outside the area under study. Elements of the target set are reordered or completed by analogy with a source pattern originally thought to be unrelated to the issue at hand. To perform this act, the thinker must be able to recognize and validate "out-of-the box" propositions that redefine the problem itself, a feat that is made possible only if the target and source patterns are cast in a sufficiently abstract way to expose their commonalties.

While it is clear that East Asians excel at this first type of step-by-step (Japanese: *ippo ippo*) creativity, scientific breakthroughs of the sort idealized in the West presuppose a culture that promotes abstract thinking as a matter of course. This abstract or "theoretic" cognitive style (Donald, 1991) is not and never was characteristic of East Asian culture partly, in the present author's view, because of the orthographies used there, which are nonanalytic in their design or execution. Lacking a general model of analysis and abstraction, such as that provided by Western alphabets, East Asians are less apt to reconsider the foundations for existing ideas, which impacts Asian science and creative style.

THE ALPHABET AS A COGNITIVE MODEL

As intimated above, abstract thinking is indispensable for the creativity associated with scientific breakthroughs because the information needed to resolve intractable problems is often unavailable at the concrete level. Prototypes distilled from experience, integrated and stored in a "vertical abstractive hierarchy" (Koestler, 1964), are used as models to reconfigure problematic data that conflict with existing paradigms. Solutions are achieved when problems are viewed as instances of established patterns from more general (more abstract) domains.

This "right-track" skill (Taylor, 1988) of applying by analogy abstract patterns found in one cognitive domain to another is preceded and followed in a creative act by the left-track skill of analysis. These "sweaty" stages are generally ignored in popular accounts of creativity but figure prominently in standard theories of the process (Abra, 1988; Csikszentmihalyi & Sawyer, 1995; Martindale, 1995; Ward, 1995). For analogical transfers to work, the elements of a problem must be stripped of their concrete context in a preparatory stage of analysis to visualize the essence of a problem, or simply because smaller pieces are easier to reorder than larger ones (Hofstadter, 1995). A final stage attempts to validate the hypothesized right-track solutions with more left-track analysis.

Alphabetic literacy supports creativity by serving as an early and pervasive model of both types of cognitive skills. On the one hand, the learner is made to recognize practically, if not consciously, that speech and language are not synonyms and that underlying the familiar speech act is an abstract body of rules separable from their concrete representation. What was once considered a unitary process is found to be composed of discrete systems that interact on an abstract plane. Shifting between these cognitive levels in the routine exercise of linguistic skills conditions one to abstraction in general, as evidenced by studies showing a propensity among literates to engage in abstract forms of cognition uncommonly observed among nonliterates (Goody & Watt, 1968; Luria, 1976; Olson, 1994; Ong, 1982).

A second task facing those learning to read an alphabetic orthography, which has a bearing on the cognitive skills used in creative acts, concerns the need to split concrete syllables into abstract phonemes (Gleitman & Rozin, 1973). This highly unnatural task, one of the main obstacles to literacy in the West, requires one to *analyze* the units of sound that humans are naturally equipped to perceive (syllables) into their hypothetical parts (phonemes). These abstract elements are, at best, a compromise between psychological units and conventional constructs, whose links with the concrete world are far from obvious.

Their abstractness is further evidenced by the historical tendency for writing systems, in the absence of a foreign model, to end their development at the depiction of syllables. And it is apparent in sound spectographs that show no clear division between these hypothesized subsyllabic elements or, for that matter, any stable substance identifiable with phonemic "units" as such, whose realization varies with the phonetic environment. Learning phonemes thus constitutes for individuals in an alphabetic culture their first and most significant venture into the world of abstraction.

Several scholars have alluded to the link between phoneme recognition and creative skills. Robert Logan (1986) stated, "It is our claim that the constant repetition of phoneme analysis, every time it is written in an alphabetical form, subliminally promotes the skills of analysis and matching that are critical for the development of scientific and logical thinking" (Logan, 1986, p. 109). Leonard Shlain (1999) argued that unlike images, which are perceived as wholes, alphabets require one to think linearly and analyze "each word down into its component letters" (Shlain, 1999, p. 5). Derrick de Kerckhove's (1988) thinking is closest to the present author's.

> Regarding discovery, there is an inversely proportional ratio between the extent to which data is contextualized and the ability to recombine it, that is, to discover and create.... Western cultures ... accustomed as they are by their coding systems to break down information into its smallest components, and to recombine and reorder raw data into properly aligned and classified arrays, have a permanent access to the possibility of recombining individual units (de Kerckhove, 1988, p. 108).

Just as phoneme analysis mimics the preparatory stage of creativity by forcing a thinker to deconstruct concrete wholes (syllables) into abstract, fragmentary components (phonemes), so does the alphabet's synthetic operation model the right-track stages of a creative act by acclimating its users to *re*constructing wholes from defined parts. This synthesis of words and higher linguistic units is governed by rules constraining legal outcomes (phonology and grammar), which parallels the requirement that creative propositions manifest plausibility. In neither the linguistic realm nor the domain of creativity are combinatory processes random.

Finally, alphabetic writing facilitates creative processes by helping thinkers distance their thoughts from the words that bind them together. Creativity (and creative) scientists agree on the need to transfer control over a problem from language-based cognition to an evolutionary earlier state in which images, or abstractions of images, dominate (Brown, 1997; Findlay & Lumsden, 1988; Koestler, 1964; Schooler & Melcher, 1995). The phrase "tyranny of words" describes this conflict between our customary use of language to fix concepts, so that they have common currency and can be manipulated as units, and our need to be rid of these linguistic symbols so that dissociating and integrating processes can operate on the concepts themselves. But how does one suspend the link between language and thought, particularly in science, where the need for language to tag concepts is most compelling?

The feat is managed as a by-product of literacy. Words (and the morphemes that make up words) act as the conventional interface between meaning and one or more sets of extrinsic signs. Legal phonological, graphic, or signed sequences without meaning are pseudowords. Meaning without some kind of systemic marker is ambiguous, transient, and incapable of precise manipulation. Given this tight, functional relationship between language and thought, speakers of language do not easily distinguish signs from their meanings—not consciously, as measured by the confounding of inner speech with thought by early psychologists, and not subconsciously, where the most prominent part of the package is the linguistic marker.

Writing gives speakers an opportunity to distinguish linguistic form and cognitive substance by drawing attention to the existence of a sign apart from its meaning. If a concept is marked by a single sign (speech), there is nothing to set it apart from what the sign is signifying. By adding a second (written) marker, the unity of sign and concept is subverted by the contrast set up between the two signs. This draws attention to their existence per se and by extension to meaning *as a separate entity*. The bond between language and thought is more readily dissolved. Cast on their own, concepts become open to creative reordering.

The difficulty nonliterates have distinguishing sign from concept is the most compelling reason for the conservatism of oral societies. By the same token, the ease with which this distinction is achieved by literates varies with the accessibility of the sign. When linguistic signs are displayed discretely as letters, words, and sentences, which is the case now for nearly all alphabetic orthographies, and when their components are perceived as having no necessary connection with meaning, the linguistic block to creativity is less daunting.

THE IMPACT OF ASIAN ORTHOGRAPHY ON CREATIVITY

Any system of writing, from a narrow phonetic transcription to systems that depict sound holistically as syllables, will support creativity by drawing attention to the externalized text apart from its meaning (Olson, 1994). By objectifying language, writing distances it from the ideas it embodies, exposing those ideas to creative manipulation. That said, there are significant differences in the level of abstraction embodied by writing systems that influence the creative habits of their users. We have seen how alphabets emulate creativity's abstract and analytic processes. How does East Asian writing fare in this regard?

Given the myths associated with Asian orthography, and Chinese character-based writing especially, it will be helpful to describe how these systems are structured before addressing their impact on creativity. The salient fact that will emerge is that although Asian writing spans a range of orthographic types from morphemic (Chinese) to phonemic (Vietnamese) representation, all are focused to a greater or lesser degree on syllables.

Chinese characters began life as pictographs of natural phenomena. The symbol for "tree" looked like a tree, "moon" followed the shape of a crescent moon, and so on. These basic symbols were extended semantically by combining them to represent words (*not* "ideas") that shared the sense of the two elements. For example, the symbol for "sun" and "moon" were written together as a single symbol for the word "bright." More commonly, the inventory was expanded by using an existing character for a (near) homonym, or by combining a character whose phonetic association had become fixed with another character that depicted a general category of meaning—each becoming a component of the new character.

This last class of characters now makes up some 85%–90% of the inventory. In the three millennia that they have been in use, their meanings and shapes have evolved so much that the semantic components are useful today only as an *ad hoc* indexing device in lexicography. A character's phonetic element does provide useful clues to its sound. But the representation is holistic and variable. Sound is not depicted discretely. Instead, whole syllables are associated with graphic complexes—hundreds of them—in a loose and inconsistent manner that provides enough regularity for the system to operate but not enough for prediction either from symbol to sound or vice versa. Chinese characters thus are properly categorized as a large and rough syllabary (DeFrancis, 1984), although one in which morphemic representation plays a role.

Japanese, for its part, adopted Chinese characters *in toto* to represent borrowed Chinese vocabulary (most of its literary lexicon) and native Japanese words. Beyond this, Japanese also adapted Chinese characters to depict sounds independently of their meaning. There are two such sets of 47 *kana* today, each symbol representing a basic Japanese syllable (*mora*). One set, *hiragana*, is used for inflections and other grammatical indicators and is mixed into the same text with *kanji*, which represent most content words. *Katakana* depict Western loanwords and onomatopoeia. The orthography is almost entirely syllable based.

Korean was originally written in Chinese characters. It continues to use them as an aid to understanding phonetic *hangul* writing by mixing them into the text, where they represent Chinese loanwords, and by sensitizing users to the Sinitic morphemes on which the language heavily depends. Unlike Japanese, Koreans have the option of writing entirely in phonetic *hangul*, not serially like Western alphabets but in syllabic blocks, which is how *hangul* is taught and perceived. Even where only a single letter is intended, for example, on license plates or serialized text headers, Koreans write a formatted syllable.

Vietnamese, which adopted a Western-style alphabet, also clings to a Chinese-like syllabic paradigm. Instead of dividing text at the word level, Vietnamese puts a space between each orthographic syllable, reinforcing the syllable's psychological importance and the language's monosyllabic morphology. Indeed, viewed at a distance, both Korean and Vietnamese texts resemble the block-like forms of Chinese characters—a function of orthographic typology and a political need to emulate the region's dominant culture.

The syllable's centrality in East Asian writing parallels a strong tendency for the spoken languages to use canonically simple syllable types. There are no clusters of the CCV or VCC variety in any of these languages. Although (C)VC forms exist, the final consonants are restricted in number and perceptually indistinct. Whether speaking or writing, East Asians are focused on basic syllables to a degree unimaginable to speakers of European languages, who are acclimated to complex consonant clusters and well-articulated word division in writing.

Although the full psychological import of these differences has yet to be explored, one can judge the effect of Asian syllabic writing on creativity by extrapolating from the alphabet's impact in this area. By choosing concrete, naturally occurring syllables instead of abstract phonemes and words as orthographic units, East Asians forego the cognitive tutorial forced on users of alphabets that helps build creative skills. Committed to syllabaries, and systems that act *like* syllabaries, Asians do not divide sounds into parts, relate these parts to abstract classes, and resynthesize them deliberately into larger linguistic wholes. Instead, they map opaque units of meaning (morphemes) onto holistic lumps of sound (syllables) and tag them with graphic units that have no discrete relationship to meaning or sound.

This is not to imply that East Asians use language differently than speakers anywhere else in the world. Rather, the point is that they are not *aware* of these abstract processes because the orthography does not require it. The alien nature of phonemic analysis to literate East Asian speakers, known to Western linguists who have struggled with this gap in their field studies, was verified by Read, Zhang, Nie, and Ding (1986) in a study that showed character-literate Chinese no better able to identify linguistic abstractions than nonliterate Westerners. By the same token, Asians have trouble identifying words, and even the concept of "word," because their writing systems do not require it (Korean is an exception).

An inability to grasp linguistic abstraction was documented by Scribner and Cole (1981) in their study of the Vai, a West African people who use an indigenous syllabary. The authors, who tested the claim that literacy induces abstract thinking, found no evidence of a predicted cognitive shift by those Vai literate in the syllabary, but did find traces of the shift among Vai schooled in alphabetic writing. These findings pertain to a group that owes nothing culturally or linguistically to Asia, which strongly suggests a general relationship between orthographic type and abstract thought. As expected, Tibetans, who are steeped in Chinese traditions but have been using an alphabet for centuries, boast a legacy of logic and abstract thinking that has no counterpart in the surrounding Sinitic culture (Nakamura, 1964).

Syllabic writing not only fails to encourage abstract thinking, it also does little to help users distinguish language from concepts as a condition for their creative reordering, and may even exacerbate this universal problem by tightening the bond between the two. The holistic mapping of symbol to meaning betrays no hint of its conventionality. And with no principled connection between graphic symbol and sound, East Asians are more likely than Westerners to retrieve meaning from print directly (Tzeng & Hung, 1988). Asian writing and speech thus lead to concepts semi-independently, minimizing the opportunity for a contrast between signs that would support awareness of their existence apart from meaning.

Beyond these purely cognitive issues, Asian orthography's negative impact on creativity can be inferred from the need to master a system whose units number in the thousands and from the psychological effect that this rote memorization has on learners. Knowledge in East Asia is perceived less as a result of active exploration and more as an exercise in absorbing past truths. Obsession with form over substance, which is hardly conducive to creative thinking, is another effect of an orthography that requires a heavy investment in the mechanism itself.

Given the costs associated with traditional Asian orthography—in terms of time needed to master the systems, their inefficiency for most modern tasks, and their ill effects on creative thinking—one wonders how long East Asians will accept this cultural burden, particularly as alphabets gain popularity through computerized applications and are perceived as viable alternatives.

REFERENCES

Abra, J. (1988). *Assaulting Parnassus: Theoretical views of creativity*. Lanham, Md.: University Press of America.
Baum, R. (1982, December). Science and culture in contemporary China. *Asian Survey*.
Brick, I. (1997). The gist of creativity. In A. Andersson & N. Sahlin (Eds.), *The complexity of creativity*. Dordrecht: Kluwer Academic.
Brown, J. (1997). Process and creation. In A. Andersson & N. Sahlin (Eds.), *The complexity of creativity*. Dordrecht: Kluwer Academic.
Csikszentmihalyi, M., & Sawyer, K. (1995). Creative insight: The social dimension of a solitary moment. In R. Sternberg & J. Davidson (Eds.), *The nature of insight*. Cambridge, MA: MIT Press.
DeFrancis, J. (1984). *The Chinese language: Fact and fantasy*. Honolulu: University of Hawaii Press.
de Kerckhove, D. (1988). Inventio. In C. Findlay & C. Lumsden (Eds.), *The creative mind*. London: Academic Press.
Donald, M. (1991). *Origins of the modern mind*. Cambridge, MA: Harvard University Press.
Fialka, J. (1997). *War by other means: Economic espionage in America*. New York: W. W. Norton.
Findlay, C., & Lumsden, C. (1988). *The creative mind*. London: Academic Press.
Gleitman, L., & Rozin, P. (1973). Teaching reading by use of a syllabary. *Reading Research Quarterly, 8*(3), 494-500.
Goody, J., & Watt, I. (1968). The consequences of literacy. In J. Goody (Ed.), *Literacy in traditional societies*. Cambridge: Cambridge University Press.
Hannas, W. (2003). *The writing on the wall: How Asian orthography curbs creativity*. Philadelphia: University of Pennsylvania Press.
Hansen, J. (1996). *Japanese intelligence—The competitive edge*. Dexter, MI: Thomas-Shore.
Herbig, P. (1995). *Innovation Japanese style*. Westport, CT: Quorom Books.
Hofstadter, D., & FARG. (1995). *Fluid concepts and creative analogies*. New York: Basic Books.
Holland, J., Holyoak, K., Nisbett, R., & Thagard, P. (1986). *Induction: Processes of inference, learning, and discovery*. Cambridge, MA: MIT Press.
Koestler, A. (1964). *The act of creation*. New York: Macmillan.
Logan, R. (1986). *The alphabet effect*. New York: William Morrow and Co.
Luria, A. (1976). *Cognitive development: Its cultural and social foundations*. Cambridge MA: Harvard University Press.
Martindale, C. (1995). Creativity and connectionism. In S. Smith, T. Ward, & R. Finke (Eds.), *The creative cognitive approach*. Cambridge, MA: MIT Press.
Murray, C. (2003). *Human accomplishment: The pursuit of excellence in the arts and sciences, 800 B.C. to 1950*. New York: HarperCollins.
Nakamura, H. (1964). *Ways of thinking of Eastern peoples*. Honolulu: East-West Center Press.

Nakayama, S. (1973). Joseph Needham: Organic philosopher. In S. Nakayama & N. Sivin (Eds.), *Chinese science: Explorations of an ancient tradition*. Cambridge, MA: MIT Press.

Needham, J. (1954). *Science and civilisation in China*. Cambridge: Cambridge University Press.

Needham, J. (1969). *The grand titration: Science and society in east and west*. Toronto: University of Toronto Press.

Olson, D. (1994). *The world on paper: The conceptual and cognitive implications of writing and reading*. Cambridge: Cambridge University Press.

Ong, W. (1982). *Orality and literacy: The technologizing of the word*. London: Methuen.

Qian, W. (1985). *The great inertia: Scientific stagnation in traditional China*. London: Croom Helm.

Read, C. A., Zhang, Y., Nie, H., & Ding, B. (1986). The ability to manipulate speech sounds depends on knowing alphabetic reading. *Cognition, 24*, 31-44.

Reid, P., & Schriesheim, A. (1996). *Foreign participation in U.S. research and development: Asset or liability?* Washington, DC: National Academy Press.

Schweizer, P. (1993). *Friendly spies*. New York: Atlantic Monthly Press.

Schooler J., & Melcher, J. (1995). The ineffability of insight. In S. Smith, T. Ward, & R. Finke (Eds.), *The creative cognitive approach*. Cambridge, MA: MIT Press.

Scribner, S., & Cole, M. (1981). *The psychology of literacy*. Cambridge, MA: Harvard University Press.

Shlain, L. (1999). *The alphabet versus the goddess*. New York: Penguin Putnam.

Simon, D. (1989). Technology transfer and China's emerging role in the world economy. In D. Simon & M. Goldman (Eds.), *Science and technology in post-Mao China*. Cambridge, MA: Council on East Asian Studies, Harvard University.

Suttmeir, R. (1989). Science, technology, and China's political future—A framework for analysis. In D. Simon & M. Goldman (Eds.), *Science and technology in post-Mao China*. Cambridge, MA Council on East Asian Studies, Harvard University.

Taylor, M. (1988). The bilateral cooperative model of reading. In D. de Kerckhove & C. Lumsden (Eds.), *The alphabet and the brain: The lateralization of writing*. Berlin: Springer-Verlag.

Tzeng, O., & Hung, D. (1988). Orthography, reading, and cerebral functions. In D. de Kerckhove & C. Lumsden (Eds.), *The alphabet and the brain: The lateralization of writing*. Berlin: Springer-Verlag.

Ward, T. (1995). What's old about new ideas. In S. Smith, T. Ward, & R. Finke (Eds.), *The creative cognitive approach*. Cambridge, MA: MIT Press.

CHAPTER 7

Creativity, Gender, History, and Authors of Fantasy for Children

Ravenna Helson

In 1965 I was helping my children adjust to life in a foreign country. Among the books I read to them were works of fantasy, including *The Hobbit* by J. R. R. Tolkien (1937) and *The Children of Green Knowe* by L. M. Boston (1954). It seemed to me that such books treated questions of self and identity and aspects of inner life with a wonderful richness of symbols, and that they should be thought of primarily in relation to the adult author and only secondarily in relation to the child reader. In fact, the adult author might be particularly undefensive under the cover of writing "for children." Furthermore, the books were relatively short. Might it not be possible to devise a rating form for describing the nature and motives of the characters and the stylistic features of the book? One could pick a sample of books and have experts rate their creativity. Because the genre was relatively small, one could include all of the most creative works. Because men and women wrote these books in about equal numbers, one could study gender differences. Perhaps one could go on to study the authors, how their characteristics were related to features of the book.

I went ahead with these ideas. I selected a sample of creative products (stories), obtained ratings of their creativity, and devised materials to provide a systematic quantitative description of them across gender of author and date of publication. Later I studied the personality, self-described work style, and personal history of most of the living English-speaking authors. In addition to the primary sample of stories published between 1930 and 1972, I also studied a sample of works published between 1800 and 1910.

There were several guiding ideas in the shaping of the study. One was that fantasy allows the expression of the inner processes of the author, and that fantasy for children was a genre especially appropriate for authors who were engaging in processes of self-discovery or midlife renewal. Jung (1969) said that the archetype of the child was often activated when there was a potential for personality growth or development, and a number of outstanding works in the genre are known to have been written after crises in the authors' lives (e.g., Elms, 1994, on L. Frank Baum; Helson, 1984, on E. Nesbit).

Another guiding idea was that creative fantasy would show a more serious and convincing kind of irreality than the less creative, because it would have been written by an author more motivated and more able to work with the emotional and unconscious. A third guiding idea, taken from Neumann (1954a), was that creative individuals differ in the relation between the ego and unconscious. The ego of some individuals is more differentiated from the unconscious and more likely to take an assertive role in the creative process than that of other individuals, which works to sum up and express unconscious contents. Though Neumann described men as generally more assertive in their creative processes than women, there were also expected to be men who took an unassertive role in the creative process and women who took an assertive role. These ideas about creative style had been supported in a previous study of men and women mathematicians (Helson, 1967).

THE STUDY OF TWENTIETH-CENTURY STORIES

Selecting a Sample

Works of fantasy (stories with unreal content) that were directed at children 8 to 12 years old, published since 1930, and mentioned at least twice in seven British and American guides to children's literature between 1956 and 1968 or, in a few cases, recommended by consultants, composed the original sample of 72 books. This sample provided the basis for the first publication (Helson, 1970). It was expanded over the next 10 years to 98 books, 49 by men and 49 by women. No author was represented by more than one book. For authors of multiple works, the first well-known book that was clearly a fantasy was selected.

Measuring Creativity

Thirteen judges rated the books on creative excellence, defined as "originality, depth, and charm." The judges were chosen to represent different roles and points of view within the field of children's literature in the United States and England. Because of the large number of books, the judging task was carried out in several stages. The average ratings of a first group of 8 judges were correlated .92 with ratings acceptable to a second group of 5 judges.

Describing the Books

A descriptive inventory was constructed with several sections. The first section asked for a ranking of the emphasis of the book on five formal dimensions: setting, relationship between characters, plot, verbal or imaginative play, and analysis of parts (devices, maps, etc.). The second section asked for ratings of emphasis on each of 10 motives, such as aggression, achievement, exploration or discovery, having wishes gratified, tender emotion or intimacy, and contact with the irreal. A third section consisted of ratings of 8 types of interpersonal relationship, such as alliance with a magical woman, alliance with a wise and powerful male, a peer group, and two children of opposite sex. Another section consisted of 16 stylistic evaluations, such as high aspiration level, innovative in plot, skillful use of small details, and leisurely in manner. Another section consisted of 100 adjectives, and still other sections inquired into respects in which the story was a fantasy, ways the fantasy world differed from the real world, and types of setting.

The goal was to obtain a thorough description of the books that included material relevant to the guiding ideas behind the study. The section on relationships between characters was derived from Perry's (1962) schema of the development of the archetype of the self, and some of the stylistic characteristics were adapted from previous work on sex differences in creative style in mathematicians (Helson, 1967), derived from Neumann's (1954a, 1954b) work on patriarchal and matriarchal style.

The descriptive inventory was used by two rater/analysts who were professionals in children's literature. The reliability of their ratings was .79, which was reasonable in view of the complexity and global nature of the task. Their ratings were averaged for the description of each book.

The quantitative findings to be described in this chapter are based on t tests, ANOVAs, or chi squares significant at the .05 level or beyond. Where the findings have not previously been published, statistics are provided.

Characteristics of Creative Books

A study of creative and sex-specific patterns in the original sample of 72 stories (Helson, 1970) found that creative books (rated in the upper half of the sample on creativity) emphasized the formal dimension of setting more than comparison books and put relatively less emphasis on plot and analysis of parts. They received higher ratings on the motives of tender emotion and contact with the irreal, and on the theme of opposition to conventional values or to evil and restrictive trends within society. Thus, whether by men or women, creative books showed more embodiment of feeling and the nonrational and less conventionality.

No formal dimension, need, theme, or characteristic of style showed a difference between books by all male and female authors which reached the .05 level of significance. However, creative books by men differed significantly in many ways from all other books. For example, they received higher ratings on the motive of aggression and on being complicated in structure; having many characters, places, and events; and showing much cleverness and virtuosity. Creative books by women were rated higher on setting and lower on analysis of parts when compared with all other books. They were rated higher on the motives of tender emotion and attaining order by bringing things into the right relationship, on having a leisurely tempo, and on not being marred by false attitudes, self-consciousness, pomposity, or antagonisms. Thus, creative books by men showed assertive skills, whereas creative books by women showed emotional sensitivity with a lower level of assertiveness and a lack of defensiveness.

Identifying Dimensions of Fantasy

The 5 formal dimensions of style and 10 motives were included in a cluster analysis undertaken to identify dimensions of fantasy. As described in Helson (1977), three clusters emerged. The first cluster had to do with purposeful action against resistance. Four motives loaded on it: aggression, order (overcoming dissident elements), achievement (individual exploit), and accomplishment (achieving a satisfactory state by cooperative endeavor). The second cluster contrasted feeling and relationship with plot and an analytical attitude. Tender emotion, setting, relations between characters and order (bringing things into the right relationship) were positively loaded and analysis of parts and plot were negatively loaded. The third cluster was positively correlated with cluster 1 and negatively correlated with cluster 2. Verbal play and humor, achievement (individual exploit), and wish-fulfillment comprised it. The three cluster dimensions were labeled heroic, tender, and comic.

Identifying Stylistic/Motive Patterns

To place books into categories, one needed to know how the heroic, tender, and comic cluster dimensions patterned together. When the cluster scores for the 98 books were plotted on a radial graph, four areas of books were evident: (1) high on the heroic cluster and medium or low on the comic; (2) high on the tender cluster and low on the heroic and comic; (3) high on the comic and low on the tender; and (4) moderate or low on all clusters but somewhat higher on the comic. Books from these areas were described as having stylistic/motive patterns that were labeled heroic, tender, high comic, and pleasant comic, respectively.

Relationships of Stylistic/Motive Pattern, Creativity, and Sex of Author

Let us imagine the 98 books in a bookcase, the 49 books by women on one shelf and 49 books by men directly beneath, both ordered from low to high on creativity. The books are bound distinctively, so that from the covers one can identify the stylistic motive pattern. Although one notices a predominance of pleasant comic at the extreme left (least creative end) of each shelf, what is most conspicuous is the run of heroic books near the middle of the shelf of books by women, with many tender books to the right, where for men there is a massing of tender books in the middle with heroic and high comic works to the right.

Let us assume that the heroic and high comic are traditionally masculine and the tender traditionally feminine. Then we can classify all of the books as pleasant/traditional, counter sex/traditional, or sex/traditional. Table 1 shows that the least creative books include most of the pleasant comic. Most books rated near the middle on creativity tend to be written in the counter sex/traditional mode, and highly creative books tend to be written in a sex/traditional mode, though with

Table 1. Distribution of Books by Mode of Fantasy and Level of Creativity

	Creativity rating		
	Low	Middle	High
Pleasant comic	10	5	3
Counter sex/traditional	6	19	15
Sex/traditional	9	3	28

$\chi^2 (4) = 28.68$. $p < .001$.

a strong representation of books in a counter sex/traditional mode also. If one binds the books with blue covers for pleasant comic, green for counter sex/traditional and red for sex/traditional and puts them into one long bookcase, one can envisage a spectrum of creativity, that is, an array in which stylistic motive pattern in gender context changes discontinuously as creativity increases continuously.

WRITERS: CREATIVITY, PERSONALITY, AND WORK STYLE

Of the works of fantasy we had studied, 83% of the living English-speaking authors agreed to participate in a study of their personality and work style. These 57 authors, 34 from the United States and 23 from Canada, England, or Scandinavia, were sent a packet containing several inventories and questionnaires. The California Psychological Inventory (Gough, 1969) was used to study personality characteristics and the Writers Q Sort, developed for this occasion, was used to study work style. There were also open-ended questions about personal and professional background, including how the author came to write the book included in the study.

The 57 authors were assigned to one of three groups on the basis of the placement of their book on the creative spectrum (Helson, 1977). Authors of 14 pleasant comic or sex/traditional books in the lower third of the creativity distribution constituted one group; authors of 17 counter sex/traditional books found mainly in the middle of the creativity distribution composed the second group; and authors of the 26 highest-rated books (both sex/traditional and counter sex/traditional) composed the third group.

On the California Psychological Inventory, authors of pleasant/traditional fantasy scored higher than other authors on two measures of social skills (Capacity for Status and Sociability) and on seven measures of conventional adjustment (Responsibility, Socialization, Self-control, Tolerance, Good Impression, Achievement via Conformance, and Sense of Well-being). On all of these scales, scores of authors in the middle counter sex/traditional and high creative groups were much lower and almost identical.

The Writers Q Sort consisted of 56 items. The items described many aspects of work style, including statements about the degree of interest in the creative process itself versus external rewards, and statements about the level of conscious control and direction of the creative process. The authors placed each item in a category according to how well it described their way of working. Four clusters of items were identified in these data.

The first cluster contrasted extrinsic vs. intrinsic motivation. Items with positive weights included "Would welcome adaptation by mass media," "Desire for money is an important motivating factor," and "Writes for the reader rather than for self." Negatively loaded items were "Places literary goals above all others" and "Is aware of personality changes that seem related to developments in writing." The authors of pleasant/traditional fantasy scored the highest on this cluster, the authors of middle-rated counter sex/traditional fantasy next, and the authors of the most creative fantasy lowest (that is, in the intrinsic direction). The authors of pleasant/traditional fantasy also scored highest on cluster 3, labeled Order and Efficiency (e.g., has an active, efficient, well-organized mind; is orderly in work habits).

Another set of analyses was confined to authors in groups 2 and 3 and to characteristics associated with writing tender vs. heroic fantasy. (Five of six authors of the high comic were assigned to the heroic category, the other to the tender category, on the basis of their scores on the radial graph of cluster scores.) On the California Psychological Inventory, authors of tender fantasy scored lower on the Communality and Achievement via Conformance scales, indicating inner absorption and an ear for a "different drummer" on the part of these authors. On the Writers Q Sort authors of tender fantasy scored lower on both clusters 3, Order and Efficiency, and cluster 4, Productive Orientation. Thus, the authors of tender fantasy were less likely to describe themselves as having an active, efficient, well-organized mind, as organized in work habits, flexible in thinking, and inventive and ingenious than the authors of heroic fantasy, and more likely to describe themselves as having fluctuating moods, being easily distracted, and as having cyclical variations in productivity.

Finally, on both the California Psychological Inventory and Writers Q Sort, there were significant interactions between level of creativity and writing heroic or tender stories, all involving crossovers by the middle-rated counter sex/traditional groups. For example, cluster 2 of the Writers Q Sort, Literary Ambition, contains items such as "Has a keen desire for fame and immortality in literature" and "Has an inner conviction of the worth and validity of one's efforts." The authors of highly creative heroic fantasy, male and female, scored high on this cluster and the authors of highly creative tender fantasy, male or female, scored low. However, authors of middle-rated heroic fantasy, who were all women, scored low and authors of middle-rated tender fantasy, who were all male, scored high. These findings suggest that the personality and work style of the authors of the middle-rated books were less well integrated than they were in the authors of the highest-rated books. For example, in the writing of a tender fantasy, a surge of ambition or a shift of orientation outwards can lead to an overly dramatic or grandiose ending that seems unconvincing or false.

These findings supported the expectation that differences in the creative product would be associated with different personality characteristics and ways of working in the authors. Accounts from individual authors about how the stories in the study had been written supplied illustration and amplification of the findings (Helson, 1978a). Authors of pleasant/traditional fantasy were much more externally oriented than authors of groups 2 and 3. For example, one began by saying "I wanted to prove I wasn't a one-book author, and yet I didn't want to be typed by doing another book of the same kind." Authors of creative heroic fantasy gave detailed accounts of the interplay of craft and inspiration and impassioned accounts of their experiences in writing the book we had studied. Here is an excerpt from Russell Hoban about how he wrote *The Mouse and His Child*.

"That book nearly killed me, literally. In the two years I was trying to live on four or five hours of sleep and commuting to New York, I wore myself down so that when I went into the hospital for gall bladder surgery, I almost didn't make it back. . . . But writing that book was the most living I'd done up to that time, and I got hooked on that level of being alive, that degree of being in over one's head in a piece of work that mattered more than anything else."

On the other hand, authors of tender fantasy rarely gave articulate accounts: they usually said they couldn't remember or that it was unwise to probe or that it was a special time or that the book wrote itself. E. B. White (author of *Charlotte's Web*, one of the highest-rated tender fantasies) did not participate in the study, but in a review of a book by Kenneth Roberts (author of *Northwest Passage*) on why authors want to write, White (1954) contrasted Roberts' state of mind and his own. Writing seems to prompt Roberts, he said, "to sit upright at a desk, put in requests to libraries, write friends, examine sources, and generally raise hell throughout the daylight hours and far into the night." But for writers like himself, "The thought of writing hangs over our mind like an ugly cloud, making us apprehensive and depressed, as before a summer storm . . ." (White, 1954, pp. 162-163). But not even lying down and closing the blinds, he said, could stop him from writing. Rejecting the possibility that he was not a writer at all but a "bright clerk" crowding his destiny, White concludes that it is a foolish undertaking to try to understand how writers write. An alternative conclusion is that authors of tender fantasy engage in the creative process with a less focused consciousness than authors of heroic works.

In sum, authors of pleasant/traditional fantasy tend to be well-adjusted people who want to give pleasure and gain external rewards and often succeed. Authors of heroic and tender fantasy are immersed in their inner worlds from which they bring deeper and more original works. Authors of highly creative fantasy have a personality and work style that is consistent with the nature of the work they are writing, which is ambitious and assertive in the case of heroic fantasy, passive and "pregnant" in the case of tender fantasy. Authors of works intermediate in creativity are similar to the authors of highly creative works but seem less well integrated. For other studies of the authors, their creative processes (where Martindale, 1969, was an inspiration), their backgrounds, and how they compare with critics and gatekeepers in children's literature, see Helson (1973a, 1973b, 1978b).

COMPARING FANTASY WRITTEN IN DIFFERENT HISTORICAL PERIODS

The preceding sections have described how fantasy for children that was published between 1930 and 1972 was related to the creativity of the book and to the gender, personality, and work style of the author. How do culture and social climate affect fantasy? The genre of fantasy for a child readership developed in England in the nineteenth century. It reached its first flowering in the mid-Victorian period and its second around the turn of the century, in the Edwardian period. Accepted values changed considerably between these two periods and between the nineteenth and twentieth centuries. According to Jung (1966), the unconscious presses in a direction to compensate the accepted values of society. If so, it might be possible to understand changes in the fantasy of different historical eras in these terms.

I undertook to draw a sample of imaginative literature for children published between 1800 and 1910. Stories were listed on the basis of their favorable mention in histories of children's literature. All of these available in libraries or bookstores in the San Francisco Bay Area were included in what will be called the nineteenth-century sample. As in the study of twentieth-century stories, only one work was allowed per author. All of the 31 stories, 21 by men and 10 by women, were considered creative. They were described with the same inventory used in the 20th-century study and by the same rater-analysts. Most were British, but 8 were by Americans or writers of other nationalities.

Preliminary t tests were conducted to compare all nineteenth-century stories with 49 stories rated as above average on creativity in the twentieth-century sample. For men (Helson, 1972) and for men and women combined, these comparisons showed no significant differences in stylistic emphases (setting, plot, etc.) and little difference in motives, such as aggression or achievement. However, there were large differences in two areas. One was the evaluation of literary quality. Children's literature became a highly competitive field in the middle of the twentieth century, and writing for children became less casual. It is thus not surprising that the twentieth-century stories were described more favorably in terms such as being well-told tales, being inventive in plot, and showing high aspiration (t tests, $df = 75$, ranging for variables cited from 4.30 to 5.72, $p < .01$).

The other area of large differences was the nature of characters and their relationships. In the nineteenth-century stories, an alliance with a magical woman, young people of the opposite sex, and human/animal relationships were more salient than in the twentieth-century sample, in which an alliance with a wise and powerful male and relationships with peers and between children and adults of the same sex were more salient (t tests, $df = 75$, ranging for variables cited from 2.47 to 3.18, $p < .05$). These differences became even sharper and clearer when nineteenth-century works were divided into periods labeled as Victorian (up to 1880) and Edwardian (after 1880). A multivariate $F(10, 142)$ of 3.67, $p < .001$ showed that the association between types of relationships between characters and the three historical periods was highly significant. Degree of emphasis on a magical woman and on a wise and powerful male contributed the most to this multivariate pattern. Figure 1 shows how the salience of these two characters varied over the Victorian, Edwardian, and modern periods for men and for women.

Closer comparison of Victorian and Edwardian stories shows that 11 of 13 stories in which an alliance with a magical woman was important were written by Victorians, whereas Edwardians wrote all 7 stories in which a band of peers without alliance to a magical female or wise male was salient. Chi square (2), including an "other" category, was 13.30, $p < .01$. Men and women alike showed the characteristics distinctive to the era. Whether Victorians wrote serious fantasy, as George MacDonald, Dinah Mulock, Charles Kingsley, and Louisa Molesworth did, or comic fantasy, as Dickens and Thackeray did, most of them had magical women in their stories. Whether Edwardians wrote about groups of animals, as Kenneth Grahame, Rudyward Kipling, and Beatrix Potter did, or of children, as James Barrie and Edith Nesbit did, most of them wrote about characters whose adventures took place without adult human or superhuman guidance.

Do these findings support Jung's view that fantasy expresses needs that are being suppressed by the dominant values of the culture? The mid-nineteenth century in England was a period in which independence, self-reliance, and materialistic values were emphasized, relationships with the opposite sex were constrained, faith in religion and patriarchal authority were strong, and the artist and intellectual

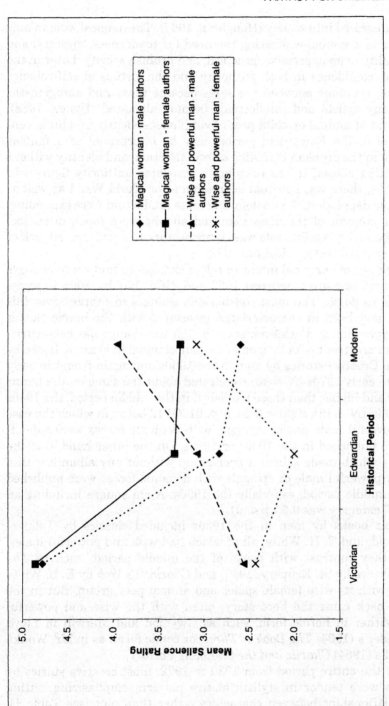

Figure 1. Change in salience of important characters from Victorian to Edwardian and modern periods.

were integrated into society (Houghton, 1957). The magical woman may be seen as a symbol expressing the need for tenderness, mystery, and spirituality in an aggressive, practical, and prudish society. Later in the century, confidence in both authority and the virtues of self-reliance declined, relations between the sexes became tense and antagonistic, and many artists and intellectuals became alienated (Hynes, 1968). The band of animal or child peers living independently of adults, conspicuous in the Edwardian period, may be interpreted as a fantasy solution to the problem of finding safety, affection, and identity without committing oneself to sex roles or to derogated authority figures. In the 1930s, there was spiritual depression after World War I as well as economic depression. Technology and mass production were expanding, and the concept of the mass man and anomie were much discussed. The wise and powerful male was compensatory to a widespread lack of meaning and direction (Helson, 1972).

It was not my original intent to relate changes in fantasy to changes in cultural pressures between 1930 and 1972, but by 2004 it seems possible to do so. The most conspicuous changes in fantasy over this period have been in characteristics associated with the heroic cluster (e.g., aggression and achievement), though the change has been curvilinear in creative books by men and unidirectional in creative books by women. Creative stories by men in the 1930s and again from the early 1960s to early 1970s ($N = 13$) were rated about the same on the heroic cluster and higher than those published in the middle period, the 1940s and 1950s ($N = 12$), $t(23) = 3.26, p < .01$. Of 12 books in which the wise and powerful male and/or struggle with demonic forces were salient, 10 were published in the 1930s or 1960s. On the other hand, 6 of the 7 books which made salient a peer group without any alliance with a wise or powerful male or struggle with demonic forces were published in the middle period, especially the 1950s. A chi square including an "other" category was $9.55, p < .01$.

Heroic books by men in the 1930s included classics by Tolkien, Masefield, and T. H. White, all of which had wise and powerful males. Thus, they contrast with books of the middle period, such as *The Little Prince* by St. Exupery (1943) and *Charlotte's Web* by E. B. White (1952) with its wise female spider and animal peer group. But in the 1960s, back came the hero story, often with the wise and powerful male, either in heroic form, such as Gwydion and Merwin in Lloyd Alexander's (1964) *The Book of Three*, or comic form, as in Mr. Wonka of Dahl's (1964) *Charlie and the Chocolate Factory*.

Over the entire period from 1930 to 1972, most creative stories by women were tender in stylistic/motive pattern, emphasizing setting and relationships between characters rather than plot (see Table 1).

However, the number of creative stories by women with peak scores on the heroic cluster increased from 0 of 11 between 1930 and 1955 to 7 of 14 between 1956 and 1972, $\chi(1) = 7.64, p < .01$. Books from the later period were described as more concerned with aggression, going out on one's own, and adventure and companionship than those from the earlier period. They were also described as less leisurely and more frightening. Ts (20) ranged from 2.74, $p < .05$, to 3.70, $p < .01$, for variables cited. Some of the earlier heroic stories by women emphasized the band of peers operating against authority (e.g., *The Gammage Cup* by Kendall, 1959), but a later story concerned the development of a wise and powerful male (*The Wizard of Earthsea* by LeGuin, 1968), suggesting that the wizard archetype was no longer inaccessible to women writers.

Cultural changes in the twentieth century included strong honoring of male heroism in the 1940s and unprecedent gender role conformity in the 1950s (e.g., Skolnick, 1991). The authors of creative fantasy went counter to this cultural pressure. Male authors avoided the hero story and women authors began to increase their expression of aggressive and agentic themes in the 1950s (before the beginning of the Women's Movement). Perhaps the crisis of disbelief in patriarchal and civic authority in the 1960s influenced both male and female authors to turn to the wise and powerful male or at least to heroic themes in their fantasy. In the 1970s, fantasy declined in popularity in children's literature, being superseded by real-life stories.

CONCLUSION

This study has limitations. For example, it would have been stronger with a larger sample and with each author represented by more than one work. The findings address many issues in creativity research, but one wonders whether they would generalize to other areas of literature and to other areas of creativity, where the creative product is more opaque to the expression of personality. The genre of fantasy is particularly valuable to study because it allows the expression of aspects of psychological organization that are obscured by concerns with external situations and constraints. Nevertheless, the findings tend to be supported by creativity theory and research. For example, the distinction between individuals who work for extrinsic versus intrinsic rewards is familiar in the literature. Gender differences in creative style similar to those identified in authors of fantasy were previously demonstrated in mathematicians (Helson, 1967). A pattern of findings similar to the creative spectrum of authors of fantasy was reported in the classic study of male architects by MacKinnon (1965). However, further research is needed to show whether the creative spectrum reflects important aspects of inner life in the middle half of the twentieth century that would no longer be found today, when sexuality and gender roles are less constricted. Fantasy for children is again a flourishing genre and would repay renewed study. Here I have had space only to describe my main quantitative findings, but many other comparisons and analyses testify to the richness of symbolization in these stories and their relevance to our deepest concerns (Naranjo, 1999).

REFERENCES

Alexander, L. (1964). *The book of three.* New York: Holt.

Boston, L. M. (1954). *The children of Green Knowe.* London: Faber.

Dahl, R. (1964). *Charlie and the chocolate factory.* New York: Knopf.

Elms, A. C. (1994). *Uncovering lives: The uneasy alliance of biography and psychology.* New York: Oxford University Press.

Gough, H. G. (1969). *Manual for the California Psychological Inventory.* Palo Alto: Consulting Psychologists Press.

Helson, R. (1967). Sex differences in creative style. *Journal of Personality, 35,* 214-233.

Helson, R. (1970). Sex-specific patterns in creative literary fantasy. *Journal of Personality, 38,* 344-363.

Helson, R. (1972). From magical woman to wizard: Comparisons of literary fantasy in the nineteenth and twentieth centuries. *Proceedings, XVIIth International Congress of Applied Psychology, Liege, Belgium, 1971, Vol. II,* pp. 1515-1519.

Helson, R. (1973a). The heroic, the tender, and the comic: Patterns of literary fantasy and their authors. *Journal of Personality, 41,* 163-184.

Helson, R. (1973b). Heroic and tender modes in women authors of fantasy. *Journal of Personality, 41,* 493-512.

Helson, R. (1977). The creative spectrum of authors of fantasy. *Journal of Personality, 45,* 310-326.

Helson, R. (1978a). Experiences of authors in writing fantasy: Two relationships between creative process and product. *Journal of Altered States of Consciousness,* 3, pp. 235-248.

Helson, R. (1978b). Writers and critics: Two types of vocational consciousness in the art system. *Journal of Vocational Behavior,* 12, 351-363.

Helson, R. (1984). E. Nesbit's 41st year: Her life, times, and symbolizations of personality growth. *Imagination, Cognition, and Personality,* 4, 53-68.

Houghton, W. E. (1957). *The Victorian frame of mind, 1930-1970.* New Haven: Yale University Press.

Hynes, S. (1968). *The Edwardian turn of mind.* Princeton, NJ: Princeton University Press.

Jung, C. G. (1966). On the relation of analytical psychology to poetry. In *Collected Works, Vol. 15.* Princeton, NJ: Princeton University Press.

Jung, C. G. (1969). The psychology of the child archetype. In *Collected Works, Vol. 15.* Princeton, NJ: Princeton University Press.
Kendall, C. (1959). *The gammage cup.* New York: Harcourt.
LeGuin, U. (1968). *The wizard of Earthsea.* Berkeley: Parnassus.
MacKinnon, D. W. (1965). Personality and the realization of creative potential. *American Psychologist, 20,* 273-281.
Martindale, C. E. (1969). *The psychology of literary change.* Unpublished dissertation, Harvard University.
Naranjo, C. (1999). *The divine child and the hero: Inner meaning in children's literature.* Nevada City, CA: Gateways/IDHHB.
Neumann, E. (1954a). On the moon and matriarchal consciousness. *Spring,* 83-100 (Analytical Psychology Club of New York).
Neumann, E. (1954b). *The origins and history of consciousness.* New York: Bollingen Foundation.
Perry, J. W. (1962). Reconstitutive process in the psychopathology of the self. *Annals of New York Academy of Sciences, 96,* 853-876.
Skolnick, A. (1991). *Embattled paradise: The American family in an age of uncertainty.* New York: Basic Books.
St. Exupery, A. de (1943). *The little prince.* New York: Reynal & Hitchcock.
Tolkien, J. R. R. (1937). *The Hobbit.* London: Allen & Unwin.
White, E. B. (1954). *The second tree from the corner.* New York: Harper & Row.
White, E. B. (1952). *Charlotte's web.* New York: Harper.

CHAPTER 8

Trends in the Creative Content of Scientific Journals: Good, But Not as Good!

Robert Hogenraad

How fitting the first entry in John Ayto's (1999) *Twentieth Century Words* is the word "accelerator"! Acceleration, rate, forward, advance are cliché images often associated with progress of science. The late Christopher Lasch (1991) opens *The True and Only Heaven* with the delusory simple question "How does it happen that serious people continue to believe in progress?" (Lasch, 1991, p. 13). To add, three lines later, "in a century full of calamities." If the notion of progress in science is not innocent, that of creativity is above suspicion. The focus of this study is on creativity in social and behavioral science.

The most solid single achievement of this study is in setting up whether social and behavioral science journals are getting more creative or not with the passage of time. We may be unable to analyze fully a domain of science. But we may still opt for controlling the material drawing from the textual status of a domain of science and look into this material for indicators of the degree of change undergone. With science, you begin and end with words. After all, only facts mentioned in a text can be known. Titles are a valid representation of the reality of a scientific field (Bernard, 1995; Lindauer, 1988; Whittaker, 1989). They are also quickly available and definite time savers. By analyzing the titles of scientific journal articles, one puts scholars' communications to the same empirical treatment they habitually apply to the subjects of their studies. What makes the analysis of written communication so sure-fire is that all the varied facts contained in journal articles become homogenized into a single class of equivalence through the language used by scientists to communicate the facts of their discipline to others.

In literature, Martindale (1990) shows that novelists and poets use ever more vivid images and strong metaphors in response to pressure toward novelty. The unity of this chapter stems from taking scientific writing as literature while using pressure toward novelty as a formidable potential for change in literature and science. Novelists and scientists are aware of the high capacity of novelty as a source of arousal and of the ghastly capacity of boredom to destroy significance. Another rule in science requires it to become ever more symbolic. Two centuries ago, Schopenhauer (1958) argued that a science of the concrete is a contradiction in terms. The rule to rise ever more above particulars is achieved by the constant accretion of generalizations of the various inputs into chunks representing increasing degrees of conceptualization. In psychological jargon, images and metaphors are dubbed primary or primordial thought contents (Kris, 1952). The opposite processes that represent degrees of conceptualizations, such as law and order, abstract thinking, temporal references, and moral imperatives, are dubbed secondary or symbolic thought contents.

A work of science should find a knowledge niche where it copes with its forerunners while progressing by proposing refreshing changes. Pressure toward novelty is not the major constraint on science, but it is a constant one. Under pressure toward novelty, which breed symbolic thought content, scientists normally offer new theories and altered frames of reference that make facts appear under a different light. Scientists achieve their goal by moving toward more abstract ideas. Scientists also seek to correct the weaknesses of their theories. Either they offer new theories, or tweak older ones, or bring in new facts that are usually more complex (Weber, 1968). These new facts and theories correct the failures of the existing theory while also refining it. This sequence is repeated many times until anomalies and unintelligibility are so overwhelming that a reversal—a scientific revolution—is preferable to repairing the failures of old theories (Kuhn, 1970). Each time this is put into action, science becomes more abstract and complex (Hayes, 1992): the cure for uncertain science is always more science. In this sense, the pressure toward novelty leads to more general theories because it often "brings several special theories together" (Alexander, 1987, p. 3).

So much for a model of scientific change. Martindale (1990) set up the primordial and symbolic thought contents into a measuring instrument for content analysis, the Regressive Imagery Dictionary. The difference between primordial and symbolic thought contents is that between the sensate and ideational systems of culture (Sorokin, 1985). In sensate systems, reality is that which is presented to the sense organs; in ideational systems, one considers that it is the inner meaning that gives value to the world. Sensate contents are "found in the world" (*love, sex, food, chaos, dream, flying,* for example). Ideational contents are "built into the world" (*money, work, discipline, police, time, justice, law,* to name a few).

An innocent notion can lead one occasionally to deep waters. Sorokin (1985, pp. 93, 214) has shown how sensate systems of culture are necessarily associated with individualism. Sensate words *love, sex, food, chaos, dream, flying,* for example, are ever-changing sensate values that are the exclusive concern of the individual. At the other end, words *money, work, discipline, police, time, justice, law* represent durable ideational values that concern collectivities and their conventions. The possibility to connect creativity in science with morals comes as an interesting surprise. Increases in creativity could be associated with increases in the interest in other people, at least for what concerns the products of creativity. "Interest in other people" closely defines McClelland's (1987) notion of "need for affiliation." One can test the truth of this insight using one of the modules of the Motive Dictionary (more anon). Evidence is needed. For while the products of scientific creativity can be associated with interest in other people, creative people are sometimes associated with madness: "A great soul . . . alternates between the highest height and the lowest depth" (Carlyle, 2004, lecture I, section II; Martindale, 1971).

The general expectation from the prior studies reviewed here was that sciences would become ever more symbolic and abstract. The creative content of the titles of articles in *Psychological Review* and the French *L'Année Psychologique* increased over the years 1894–1988 (Hogenraad, Bestgen, & Durieux, 1992). In a later study (Hogenraad, McKenzie, Morval, & Ducharme, 1995), the creative content of the titles of the *Journal of Applied Psychology* increased too, from 1917 to 1994, while that of *Harvard Business Review* decreased between 1923 and 1993. Also in 1995, Hogenraad, Kaminski, and McKenzie showed how much the creativity of the *Journal of Criminal Law and Criminology* was damaged by memorable political events such as when capital punishment was reinstated in some American states. Elsewhere (Hogenraad, Boulard, & McKenzie, 1994; Hogenraad, Boulard, McKenzie, & Basch, 1997), the titles of five industrial relations journals were analyzed for signs of trends in their creativity. Industrial relations showed a serious inability to imagine new ways of representing the industrial and management reality. Finally, the analysis of the titles of *Empirical Studies of the Arts* (1983–1998) (Hogenraad & Martindale, 2001) revealed a downward trend followed by a modest upward movement. These analyses are revisited here with data updated to 2004 for four of these journals, *Psychological Review, Journal of Applied Psychology, Industrial and Labor Relations Review,* and *Empirical Studies of the Arts.* Now is an opportunity to reflect on these previous studies. Is the history of science written in advance, as if sealed in aspic? How much change did occur, or not, during the last decade, and what part of these studies do we need to unsay?

METHOD

Data

The textual data include the titles of articles in 10 scientific journals see Table 1). These are two century-old American journals, *Psychological Review* (4,009 titles) and the *Journal of Applied Psychology* (7,060 titles). The American Psychological Association publishes both journals, and both data sets are updated to 2004. Next come the 4,694 titles of *Harvard Business Review* over 72 years, from its start in 1923 to 1994. For industrial relations, data sets include the titles of *Industrial and Labor Relations Review* (1,680 titles), *Industrial Relations* (944 titles), the *British Journal of Industrial Relations* (766 titles), *Journal of Industrial Relations* (896 titles), and *Relations Industrielles/ Industrial Relations* (1,342 titles). The 3,591 titles of the *Journal of Criminal Law and Criminology* run over 81 years from 1910 to 1990. Finally, *Empirical Studies of the Arts,* the official journal of the International Association of Empirical Aesthetics, contains 273 titles for the period 1983–2003.

Content Analysis

Many imagine they have explained a text when all they have done is told a story. Two qualities in particular serve to distinguish content analysis from even the best literary criticism: theory testing and quantifying. In part 10 of the play "*Frogs,*" Aristophanes (1978) has the character Aeacus scoff at Euripides, "Levels they'll bring, and measuring-tapes for words," and later, "Euripides vows that he'll test the dramas, word by word." Yet this is what we do here. *Pace* Aristophanes, content analysis is insistent on the need to express facts through numbers. I analyzed the data with the help of the PROTAN procedure of computer-aided content analysis (Hogenraad, Daubies, Bestgen, & Mahau, 1995) and two computer-readable semantic dictionaries, the Regressive Imagery Dictionary (Martindale, 1990) and the Motive Dictionary (Hogenraad, 2003). PROTAN allows one using a

Table 1. Statistical Summary of the Titles Corpus

Journal	Years	Number of words	Number of different words
Psychological Review	111 (1894-2004) (updated)	30,832	4,808
Journal of Applied Psychology	88 (1917-2004) (updated)	72,551	7,167
Harvard Business Review	72 (1922-1994)	25,786	4,566
Industrial and Labor Relations Review	57 (1947-2004) (updated)	14,926	2,680
Industrial Relations	33 (1962-1995)	6,474	1,553
British Journal of Industrial Relations	33 (1963-1995)	7,309	1,568
Journal of Industrial Relations	37 (1959-1995)	7,439	1,660
Relations Industrielles/ Industrial Relations	50 (1946-1995)	9,629	1,976
Journal of Criminal Law and Criminology	81 (1910-1990)	11,693	3,334
Empirical Studies of the Arts	21 (1983-2003) (updated)	2,598	993
Total		777,131	

procedure of classification for analyzing the content of a text. This procedure rests on semantic dictionaries; that is, lists of words that have been proved to assess a particular word meaning. Having selected a list of relevant words, such as a list of abstract words, one compares all the words of the text to all the words of the list. A dictionary in textual analysis, is no more than a list of words organized into categories; that is, words with a role in a hierarchy. When one applies a dictionary to a text, one looks for matches between a word in a dictionary and a word in a text. One shoves the text words into the categories, counts the number of word matches in each category and takes the percentage of the number of word matches.

The Regressive Imagery Dictionary contains 2,484 entries (29 categories of primordial thought and 7 categories of symbolic thought). The indicator of creativity is the difference between words tagged in symbolic content and words tagged in primordial content. The "need for affiliation" (nAff) is part of the Motive Dictionary, beside the "need for achievement" and the "need for power." Only the nAff (777 entries) interests us here. Intimacy, friendship, and positive emotional ties with a person, as well as liking and wanting to be liked, define the "need for affiliation." A word from the dictionary assigned to a category cannot be present in another one except in its superordinate category.

RESULTS

The indicator of creativity for *Psychological Review* (Figure 1) increases cubically over the 111 years of existence of the journal, $R^2 = .61$, $F(3, 107) = 55.0$, $p < .0001$. For the same journal, nAff increases too, but linearly, $R^2 = .27$, $F(1, 109) = 40.9$, $p < .0001$. In this and the remaining cases, autocorrelations—correlations between observations— have been removed using the SAS/AUTOREG procedure (Hogenraad, McKenzie, & Martindale, 1997). The correlation between nAff and creativity for *Psychological Review* amounts to .28 ($n = 111, p < .01$). In the *Journal of Applied Psychology* (Figure 2), both creativity and nAff, $r = .32$, $n = 88$, $p < .01$, increase linearly, $R^2 = .09$, $F(1, 86) = 8.3$, $p < .01$, for creativity, and $R^2 = .65$, $F(1, 86) = 163.1, p < .0001$, for nAff.

In *Relations Industrielles/Industrial Relations* (Figure 3), creativity follows a negative trend, $R^2 = .12$, $F(1, 48) = 6.3$, $p < .05$, while the course of nAff is not significant, $R^2 = .07$, $F(1, 48) = 3.8, p < .10$. The correlation between creative and nAff is .34, $n = 50, p < .05$.

In summary, creativity and need for affiliation follow a positive course in two cases, *Psychological Review* and *Journal of Applied Psychology*. The course of creativity is negative in the other journals. That of the need for affiliation is still positive in *British Journal of Industrial Relations, Harvard Business Review,* and *Empirical Studies of the Arts,* but negative in criminology and most industrial relations journals. What happens in the latter journals is precisely the individualism exposed by Sorokin (1985) and specifically by Piore (1995). Table 2 is a summary of the results.

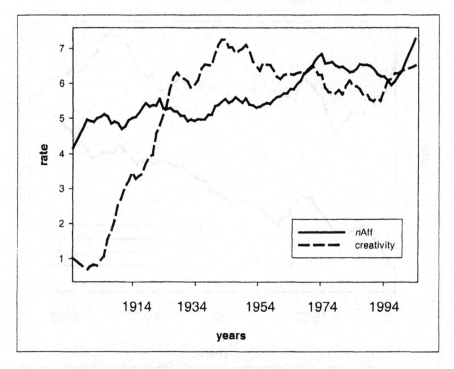

Figure 1. Creativity and need for affiliation in 111 years of *Psychological Review* (1894-2004)—smoothed data.

Applied Social Science: "Last one out switch off the light"? (Motto on an East Berliner's T-shirt during the westward passage of the Berlin Wall in November 1989 (Stern, 1992, p. 290).

(1) In a perfect world, the connection between creativity and need for affiliation in works of science might be systematic. In reality, this association exists in only two journals (*Psychological Review* and *Journal of Applied Psychology*). This association confirms Sorokin's (1985) theory and observations about the connection between individualism and sensate literature. That creativity and need for affiliation are declining or stagnant in the remaining journals reminds us of Schlesinger's (1999) comment that the intellectual effect of individualism is stagnation.

(2) What we see has all the appearances of a stagnation, and sometimes decline, of modeling in applied social sciences. Industrial relations, management sciences, and criminology prosper in their own intellectual cul-de-sacs and sensate words are doing all the work. These

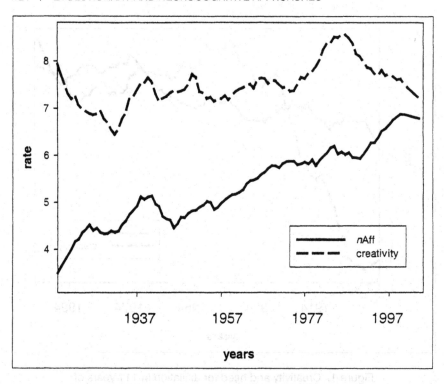

Figure 2. Creativity and need for affiliation in 88 years of the *Journal of Applied Psychology* (1917-2004)—smoothed data.

results confirm the findings of the earlier studies described at the beginning of this chapter. With variations of detail, the data updated to 2004 (*Psychological Review, Journal of Applied Psychology, Industrial and Labor Relations Review,* and *Empirical Studies of the Arts*) show little change compared to the former analyses. Meanwhile, science-minded disciplines (experimental psychologies) show an increase in conceptual thought. Martindale (1990, ch. 10) analyzed excerpts for every fifth year of the *American Journal of Psychology* (1887-1987), *Psychological Review* (1895-1985), and the *Journal of the Experimental Analysis of Behavior* (1958-1986). His results are similar to those culled from the analysis of the titles of *Psychological Review*.

And yet, there is perhaps no need for anyone in applied social science to desert the field and ask the last one out to switch off the light. In his commentary of Gustave Flaubert's (1993) "*L'éducation sentimental,*" David Trotter argues that Flaubert had "set aside the doctrine of psychological determinism (...) to emphasize the part played (...) by

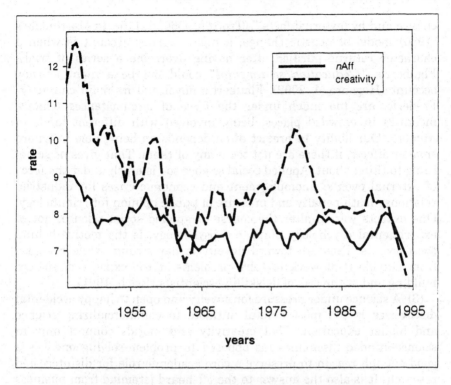

Figure 3. Creativity and need for affiliation in 50 years of *Relations Industrielles/Industrial Relations* (1946-1995)—smoothed data.

Table 2.

	nAFF+	nAFF−
creativity+	*Psych. Rev.*	
	J. Appl. Psychol.	
creativity−	*Brit. J. Industr. Rel.*	*Rel. Industr./Industr. Rel.*
	Harvard B. Review	*Industr. Labor Rel. Rev.*
	Emp. Studies Arts	*J. Industr. Rel.*
		J. Crim. Law Criminology

chance and by 'external facts'" (Trotter, 2000, p. 115). In Martindale's (1990) model of artistic change, a night journey account is when a character returns purified after having overcome a series of trials. Flaubert's *"L'éducation sentimental"* could not be a night journey account (Hogenraad, 2002). Flaubert's novel and its main character, Frédéric, are too much under the force of circumstances (chance meetings in crowded places, being involved with different kinds of women). Our ability to predict often depends on being able to ignore smaller effects, if there are not too many of them. That gives us something to think about. Applied social science too is much under the force of external events: unemployment and economic crises for industrial relations, death penalty and pressure of public opinion for criminology. One expects war to alter the course of applied social science, not of experimental psychology. Fate, not psychology, is the motive behind these events. Pressure toward novelty is hamstrung, while pressure from outside is at work to solve problems at the expense of science building and at the risk of de-skilling scientists (Reich, 1991).

(3) A science under pressure for novelty and open to happy accidental discoveries is the most helpful antidote to commercializing science and higher education. That creativity and morals connect only in science-minded disciplines (as opposed to problem-solving ones) is a good enough reason to preserve a core academic role for disinterested research. It is also the answer to the oft-heard jeremiad from business people, "science for what?" (and do they love that question!). Besides, connecting creativity with morals may make you see a work of social science with new eyes when you next meet one.

REFERENCES

Alexander, J. C. (1987). What is theory? In J. C. Alexander (Ed.), *Twenty lectures: Sociological theory since World War II* (pp. 1-21). New York: Columbia University Press.

Aristophanes. (1978). *Frogs*. Oxford: Oxford University Press. (Original work published 405 B.C.E.)

Ayto, J. (1999). *Twentieth century words*. Oxford: Oxford University Press.

Bernard, M. (1995). A juste titre: A lexicometric approach to the study of titles. *Literary and Linguistic Computing, 10,* 135-141.

Carlyle, T. (2004). *On heroes and hero-worship and the heroic in history*. North Charleston, NC: BookSurge Classics. (Original work published 1897.)

Flaubert, G. (1993). *L'éducation sentimentale*. Paris: Seuil. (Original work published 1869.)

Hayes, D. P. (1992). The growing inaccessibility of science. *Nature, 356,* 739-740.

Hogenraad, R. (2002). Moving targets: The making and molding of a theme. In M. M. Louwerse & W. van Peer (Eds.), *Thematics: Interdisciplinary studies* (pp. 353-376). Amsterdam: Benjamins.
Hogenraad, R. (2003). The words that predict the outbreak of wars. *Empirical Studies of the Arts, 21,* 5-20.
Hogenraad, R., Bestgen, Y., & Durieux, J. F. (1992). Psychology as literature. *Genetic, Social, and General Psychology Monographs, 118,* 455-478.
Hogenraad, R., Boulard, R., & McKenzie, D. P. (1994). *Les mots qui ont fait les relations industrielles.* Quebec: Presses de l'Université Laval.
Hogenraad, R., Boulard, R., McKenzie, D. P., & Basch, J. (1997). Management science in space and time: Strategic intelligence servicing an early warning system of scientific creativity. In D. Caseby (Ed.), *Between tradition and innovation: Time in a managerial perspective* (pp. 115-129). Palermo: ISIDA.
Hogenraad, R., Daubies, C., Bestgen, Y., & Mahau, P. (1995). Une théorie et une méthode générale d'analyse textuelle assistée par ordinateur. Le système PROTAN (PROTocol ANalyzer)' (Version 32-bits du 22 novembre 2003 par Pierre Mahau, service informatique de la Faculté de Psychologie) [A general theory and method of computer-aided text analysis: The PROTAN system (PROTocol ANalyzer), 32-bits Version of November 22, 2003 by Pierre Mahau, computer services, Psych. Dep.]. Louvain-la-Neuve, Psych. Department, Catholic University of Louvain. www.psor.ucl.ac.be/protan/protanae.html.
Hogenraad, R., Kaminski, D., & McKenzie, D. P. (1995). Trails of social science: The visibility of scientific change in criminological journals. *Social Science Information, 34,* 663-685.
Hogenraad, R., & Martindale, C. (2001). Self-referential aesthetics: The style of '*Empirical Studies of the Arts.*' In V. Ryzhov (Ed.), *Information approach in the human science* (pp. 104-115). Taganrog, Russia: Taganrog State University of Radio Engineering.
Hogenraad, R., McKenzie, D. P., & Martindale, C. (1997). The enemy within: Autocorrelation bias in content analysis of narratives. *Computers and the Humanities, 30,* 433-439.
Hogenraad, R., McKenzie, D. P., Morval, J., & Ducharme, F. A. (1995). Paper trails of psychology: The words that made applied behavioral sciences. *Journal of Social Behavior and Personality, 10,* 491-516.
Kris, E. (1952). *Psychoanalytic explorations in art.* New York: International Universities Press.
Kuhn, T. S. (1970). Logic of discovery or psychology of research. In I. Lakatos & A. Musgrave (Eds.), *Criticism and the growth of knowledge* (pp. 1-23). London: Cambridge University Press.
Lasch, C. (1991). *The true and only heaven: Progress and its critics.* New York: W. W. Norton.
Lindauer, M. S. (1988). Physiognomic meanings in the titles of short stories. In C. Martindale (Ed.), *Psychological approaches to the study of literary narratives* (pp. 74-95). Hamburg: Buske.

Martindale, C. (1971). Degeneration, disinhibition, and genius. *Journal of the History of the Behavioral Sciences, 7,* 177-182.
Martindale, C. (1990). *The clockwork muse: The predictability of artistic change.* New York: Basic Books.
McClelland, D. C. (1987). *Human motivation.* Cambridge, England: Cambridge University Press.
Piore, M. J. (1995). *Beyond individualism.* Cambridge, MA: Harvard University Press.
Reich, R. B. (1991). *The work of nations. Preparing ourselves for 21st-century capitalism.* London: Simon & Schuster.
Schlesinger, A. M., Jr. (1999). *The cycles of American history.* Boston: Houghton Mifflin.(Original work published 1986.)
Schopenhauer, A. (1958). *The world as will and representation* (Vol. 1) (E. F. J. Payne, Trans.). Indian Hills, CO: The Falcon's Wing Press. (Original work published 1818.)
Sorokin, P. (1985). *Social and cultural dynamics. A study of change in major systems of art, truth, ethics, law, and social relationships.* (Revised and abridged in one volume by the author. With a new introduction by Michel P. Richard, ed.). London: Transaction Publishers. (Original work published 1957.)
Stem, J. P. (1992). *The heart of Europe: Essays on literature and ideology.* Oxford, England: Blackwell.
Trotter, D. (2000). *Cooking with mud. The idea of mess in nineteenth-century art and fiction.* Oxford: Oxford University Press.
Weber, M. (1968). Science as a vocation. In M. Weber (Ed.), *On charisma and institution building. Selected papers* (Edited and with an introduction by S. N. Eisenstadt, pp. 294-309). Chicago: The University of Chicago Press. (Original work published 1919.)
Whittaker, J. (1989). Creativity and conformity in science: Titles, keywords and co-word analysis. *Social Studies of Science, 19,* 473-496.

CHAPTER 9

The Information Approach to Human Sciences, Especially Aesthetics

Vladimir M. Petrov

Two features are now inherent in humanitarian studies, especially aesthetic ones.

First, these studies exist in *"isolation"* from the realm of *natural and exact sciences*: physics, biology, mathematics, etc. C. P. Snow (1959) wrote of the dangerous "gap" between the "Two Cultures": science and the humanities. Such a gap did not exist until the Renaissance. (Leonardo da Vinci combined the highest achievements in both cultures.) This "breach" was formed during the last three centuries, mainly due to the specialization of different branches of our intellectual life. Because of this "splitting," the entire system of knowledge is incapable of being harmonious. Contemporary intellectuals should be able to deal with various regularities when turning from one field of activity to another (e.g., from physics to everyday psychology, perception of art, history, etc.). However, for intellectuals' consciousness, such transitions are sometimes rather painful. Because of this splitting, the effectiveness of knowledge in the humanities seems to be very low.

Second, within the sphere of humanities studies, we see a *great diversity of approaches*, most of them having nothing in common with each other. This diversity sharply increased in the last two decades, during the so-called post-structuralist era. Moreover, the *incompatibility* of different approaches became almost a slogan of this era. Some theorists even treat the originality of each approach as its most esteemed feature, as if this approach were a work of art. Nevertheless, the main goal of studies in the humanities is not to provide aesthetic pleasure, but to search for knowledge.

In total, the "flourishing diversity" of humanitarian approaches is like the situation which took place in medieval alchemy. It was marked by a chaos of paradigms; each alchemist was proud that he possessed his own approach, which should be the only "true path" to create gold! This era lasted until the arrival of scientific chemistry at the beginning of the eighteenth century with its general paradigm, which dealt with discrete chemical elements and atoms. (Modern chemistry uses practically the same paradigm.) But alchemists had certain practical goals, and on this point they differed from most contemporary researchers who proclaim "discourse" (i.e., the very fact of consideration) to be the most valuable thing in the activity of researchers!

What are the *results* of the two features mentioned? The "retribution" for both kinds of researchers' independence is very *low effectiveness* of knowledge in the humanities. The situation in this field was characterized by G. Golitsyn: "One of the main dangers of modern development is the strikingly low effectiveness of human knowledge.... Now we can control a space ship at the distance of millions of kilometers from the Earth; but we cannot control our own behavior. And the ability to control is the main criterion for the effectiveness of knowledge.... We cannot overcome our own weaknesses—laziness, envy, jealousy.... In all these cases we try to control, but do it badly. And we so wish we could do it well. It seems to us that some experience of the exact sciences could help us in this situation" (Golitsyn & Petrov, 1995, p. IX).

The incompatibility of different co-existing approaches in the humanities also contributes to this low effectiveness. Let us imagine a more or less complex technical project which is to be realized by scientists and engineers representing several fields of science. I think its realization would be impossible if each of these persons used his or her own paradigm, having nothing in common with the paradigm of his or her neighbors!

In the humanities (and especially in aesthetics), we have a circumstance recalling that of chemistry at the end of the era of alchemy. The era of brilliant flourishing diversity was coming to its end. In later years, something like a crystal will start growing, forming the *basic paradigm* for various branches of investigations. Of course, in each branch, some peculiarities will remain, but the *core* of their paradigms will contain some *common features*. Moreover, I think some of these features will also be common to *natural sciences*. Due to this, the *effectiveness* of knowledge in the humanities will hopefully increase sharply! I believe this will happen very soon, and the core of this new paradigm will be nothing other than the *information theory* in its new version: the so-called principle of the information maximum (based on the concept of "mutual information" introduced by Fano, 1951; for a description of this principle see: Golitsyn & Petrov, 1995; the foundations of this approach one can find in the Appendix). Of course, among various branches of the humanities, *aesthetics* will be the field in which the most impressive achievements of this new approach will be felt.

PATHS TO A NEW PARADIGM: LEVELS OF ANALYSIS

Though the *information approach* has numerous achievements in such fields as biology (including the evolution of living matter), physiology, psychology (from psychophysics to studies of sensation and perception) and sociology, history, art studies, linguistics (including perception of speech flux and phonetic structures), semiotics, and so on, it is desirable to build a scientific forecast of its future as a *basis for a new paradigm*. So I should try:

1. to prove that the long-range *vector of paradigmatic evolution* of knowledge in the humanities possesses a quite *definite orientation*, irrespective of the peculiarities of each branch;
2. to find some *features of the paradigm* that will dominate the humanities *in the future* (i.e., to prove that the core of this paradigm is the information theory in its final version).

Our analysis will proceed from the concept of *hierarchy of systems* "embracing" each other: each system functions in the framework of a more broad system, and is subdued to some of its requirements. Such a hierarchy is similar to *matreshka*: a Russian wooden doll in peasant dress, with successive smaller dolls fitted into it. We can single out *three systems* of such a kind:

A. The *entire sphere of practical human activity*, including its biological foundations, economics, international relations, etc. Evidently this sphere is rather "mighty"; it is capable of influencing all of its constituents, including the mental life of the society.

B. The *sphere of mental life*, including its various branches: religion, art, science, humanities, etc. These branches are capable of influencing each other. But what is much more important is that the "spirit" of this sphere as a totality can influence the spirit of the humanities. (At least, a rather strong correlation between this "common spirit" and the style of thinking dominating each of the above branches was shown empirically (e.g., Maslov, 1983.)

C. Finally, the *sphere of humanitarian knowledge* itself. This sphere consists of different branches (sociology, psychology, aesthetics, art studies, etc.). They are capable of influencing each other, but evidently a certain common sociopsychological "climate" can be also formed within this sphere, influencing the spirit dominating each branch.

Our task is to study the evolution of paradigms dominating each of these spheres. Then we shall extrapolate into the future the evolutionary tendencies found (of course, having proved their mutual compatibility). But *how many* regularities should we look for in each sphere?

It seems reasonable to restrict our consideration by quite a small number of tendencies in order to facilitate my "combinatorial" analysis. We shall look for *two principal tendencies* characterizing each of the above three spheres. What should be the type of these two tendencies to be singled out? The first tendency to be looked for should be of rather general character, whereas the second tendency should concretize the nature of this general tendency.

Our investigation will be based on the so-called *deductive method*: evolution is "constructed" in a purely *logical way*: being based on rather abstract postulates which are consequently unfolded in order to come to the *empirical reality;* that is, the concrete historical facts and regularities observed. We shall use these *empirical data* to illustrate our theoretical conclusions deduced for each sphere, as well as to concretize them and to build a forecast for each sphere studied. Then we shall prove their compatibility and combine them with each other. As a result, we shall come to a rather objective and versatile *forecast* of the paradigmatic evolution.

THE ENTIRE SPHERE OF PRACTICAL HUMAN ACTIVITY: THE GROWING IMPORTANCE OF THE INFORMATION AND REFLEXIVE PROCESSES FORMING HIERARCHICAL STRUCTURES

We shall start our consideration from the first system (A), which embraces the two other systems (B, C). As it was mentioned above, first we shall single out *two principal tendencies* inherent in the evolution of this sphere. The logic of our narration is illustrated in Table 1.

1) Here the question about the *general tendency* is evident: as soon as *information* is the most interesting "personage" of our consideration, we should clear up the *dynamics of* its *role* in the *development of sociocultural systems*. To determine this role, we shall resort to the help of the above-mentioned-information approach. In the framework of this approach, a rather fundamental long-range evolutionary regularity was deduced for any complex developing system: a constantly *growing role of information* in comparison with the role of resources. The nature of

Table 1. Principal Evolutionary Regularities Inherent in the Spheres Considered

Quantitative tendencies	Qualitative tendencies
Sphere of practical human activity	
THEORETICAL RESULT: GROWING ROLE OF INFORMATION in comparison with matter and energy.	GROWTH OF REFLEXIVE PROCESSES, forming MULTILEVEL HIERARCHICAL STRUCTURES
EMPIRICAL OBSERVATIONS: Decreasing importance of natural resources in comparison with technology and culture, e.g., in the fields of *economics, technology,* and *international relations.*	Development of reflexive processes and hierarchical structures, e.g., in the fields of *biological evolution, technology, human being,* and *cultural life.*
Sphere of mental life	
THEORETICAL RESULT: INCLINATION TO CENTRALIZATION, the need to have a "CENTRAL CORE."	NATURE OF THE "CORE": INFORMATION form of the "core": OPTIMALITY PRINCIPLE
EMPIRICAL OBSERVATIONS: CENTRALIZATION in various fields, e.g., *technical systems,* system of *commerce, "genuine intellectual" systems* (religion, physics).	"CORE" constantly moving toward INFORMATION and OPTIMALITY PRINCIPLES in various systems: *natural sciences* and the *humanities.*
Sphere of humanitarian studies	
THEORETICAL RESULT: TRANSITION from simple and non-reflexive objects—TO CONCEPTUAL AND REFLEXIVE ones, concerning each branch of the humanities and its entire system	"FACES" of CHANGING STYLE OF THINKING: model of ASYMMETRY OF COGNITIVE PROCESSES and appropriate PERIODICAL STYLISTIC WAVES.
EMPIRICAL OBSERVATIONS: ATTENTION TO THE HUMANITIES, their complicated and reflexive branches, and LATENT VARIABLES, e.g., in the fields of *psychology, sociology,* and *art studies.*	COINCIDENCE OF FOUR MAIN DIRECTIONS in the humanities of the twentieth century with L- and R-HEMISPHERICAL WAVES in *sociopsychological climate.*

resources can vary, but usually it is nothing other than the matter or energy available. Of course, such a regularity is not surprising. To become more independent of the environment and the resources available is the goal of any system. In the case of sociocultural systems, this tendency assumes the aspect of the *growing role of culture*. This was specified by Lotman and Uspensky (1971) as "non-genetic information," which is generated and stored by various human collectives.

2) Let us turn to the *second principal tendency* inherent in any complex developing system. Obviously, this tendency should concern the character of *using* this growing information. As was shown by Golitsyn and Petrov (1995), in every system sooner or later a specific "informational device" should appear, which is called "*reflexion*" (in a broad sense of this term). This device consists of the "transformation of the *conditions* of the control ("means") into the *aim* of the control ("end"), as the transfer of the control from the *effect* to the *cause*" (Golitsyn & Petrov, 1995, p. 35).

Due to reflexion, any system becomes a *multilevel hierarchical structure*, where each level is working to prepare the conditions for its functioning. The "substances" of these levels may be different: it can be, for instance, various kinds of matter or energy or information. If all the levels deal with information, such a structure becomes a multilevel structure for information processing, which is inherent in each living organism. Each level processes the information received and transmits its part upward, to the higher level. As well, each level controls its own conditions: it "descends" its criteria of the information choice to the lower level (Golitsyn & Petrov, 1995, p. 117). Such structures (based on reflexive processes) penetrate all the spheres of life and all kinds of human activity.

To corroborate both of these tendencies, let us turn to appropriate *empirical observations*.

1) The *growing importance of the information* in comparison with the role of resources in various fields of human activity is evident. For instance, in *economics* we see (especially during the second half of the twentieth century) the decreasing importance of natural resources. Moreover, in some countries, the absence of natural resources (coal, iron, and rich soil) had a positive influence on their economic development by stimulating informational activity: elaboration of new technologies, education, etc. Some countries started to use natural resources, but preferred to develop informational *technologies* (e.g., nuclear energy instead of oil). In general, it was only several decades ago that most of the *energy* existed in the form of food (i.e., provided mainly by genetic information). Now the share of food in our energy supply is sharply decreasing.

At last, an appropriate shift is observed in *international relations*. In former times, there were numerous wars connected with the struggle for natural resources, such as land and mineral wealth. Now such conflicts take place only at the periphery of the civilized world. They are impossible in Europe, because natural resources have lost their importance. The same reason caused the *disintegration of colonial systems* in the twentieth century: now colonialism is simply senseless.

2) As for the second tendency, we see everywhere various *hierarchical structures* penetrated by *reflexive processes*. The very existence of life, occurred possibly due to numerous reflexive steps, each consisting in a certain transformation of means (of a given level) into goals (for another level). Such were the main mechanisms both of *biological evolution* and *technological* evolution. Examples of this kind were observed many times in the course of evolution. For instance, in the early stage of evolution living beings could use *hydrolysis* of natural phosphates from the surrounding environment as a source of energy. Soon there was a deficit of natural phosphates. Organisms began to produce phosphates using the process of *glycolysis* with glucose as a source of energy. Hence phosphates are transformed from the end into the means. Furthermore, when glucose became deficient, organisms shifted to the production of glucose through the process of *photosynthesis* using CO_2 as a resource and the sunlight as a source of energy. . . . In human history we also find many examples of similar transformations. First iron was used primarily as a raw natural material, but later when the need for iron increased, man switched to artificial production of iron. In a similar manner, hunting was replaced by cattle-breeding, collection of wild vegetables and cereals, and agriculture (Golitsyn & Petrov, 1995, p. 37). A brilliant example of such hierarchical structure was realized in the personal *multilevel system of information processing* inherent in *human beings* (Golitsyn & Petrov, 1995, p. 117). This system fully coincides with the above features.

In the *realm of art,* we also see quite similar processes of "building superstructures," which become more and more important. Here we can enumerate such phenomena as

1. Increasing impact of *art criticism, aesthetics, art theory*, etc. In contemporary artistic life, theoretical documents or manifests are sometimes more important than works of art themselves. Moreover, sometimes certain "conceptual" (theoretical) opuses replace works of art.
2. Increasing reflexive processes in the *creativity* in different kinds of art. Besides, against the background of this long-range trend, we observe some sharp peaks of high reflexivity, each of them being

connected with a transition to a new cultural epoch. Of course, *parody* (which is a structure superimposed over its objects) becomes more and more widespread because of this trend. Moreover, in the second half of the twentieth century the phenomenon of so-called *meta-arts* appeared; for example, metatheater, which is theater devoted to the language of theater; metapainting, which is painting devoted to the language of painting (Lotman, 1977).
3. Finally, recently a special direction of creativity appeared dealing both with *aesthetic theory and art itself*: "Constructive Conceptualism" (Gribkov & Petrov, 1997); each oeuvre combines the strict ("immediate") impact of its structure with definite theoretical reflexion.

Summarizing these results, we can make a conclusion about the *growing role of information and reflexion-based hierarchical structures* in the entire sphere of practical human activity.

THE SPHERE OF MENTAL LIFE: THE INCLINATION TO CENTRALIZED STRUCTURES, WITH INFORMATION AS THEIR CORE

The sphere of intellectual life (B) comprises various branches: religion, science, humanities, etc. We shall try to find the principal evolutionary tendencies common for them.

1) The first tendency to be singled out should concern the *general contours of any mental evolutionary trajectory*. And we do see such a general evolutionary tendency. This tendency is inherent in any system dealing with information processing. It is the *inclination to centralization*, which is caused by the *economy* (both of resources and information). The resulting increase of effectivity can be illustrated by Newton about the effectiveness of scientific theories: To explain the maximum of facts by using the minimum of initial assumptions (postulates).

In turn, to realize centralization, it is necessary to make the system *hierarchical*: links between elements may require substance that differs from the substance of elements themselves; that is, different levels for their functioning. The system becomes "two-storyed" (at least), which coincides with the above inclination toward hierarchies. To illustrate such structures, one can consider some advanced systems of scientific knowledge like theoretical physics: their first story deals with primary observations and concrete regularities concerning reality, whereas the function of the second story is to connect the links of the first story, i.e., "to explain the empirical reality as logical necessity" (A. Einstein). So the system possesses a *central "core."*

2) The second tendency relates to the *nature of* this *"core."* With which *category* (substance) should we deal when speaking of links "centered" by the core? In natural sciences, there exist *three main categories* capable of competing for this role: matter, energy, and information or its "shadow," namely, entropy. Both information and entropy describe the degree of disorder within the system. These categories can be *ranked* to form a hierarchy on their ability to transformations: matter is the "weakest" category, and information is the most "powerful" one, energy being placed between them. In fact, if we have any amount of matter, we can get neither energy nor information (i.e., "due" ordering of the substance). But having energy, we can get matter, but not information. Having information, we are capable of getting both matter and energy.

Hence, it seems natural for any mental system to show the "enhancing" evolution of the category involved in its central core: it should move from matter to energy and then to information. Besides, *information* has a specific gnosiological meaning, because the concept of information connects the regularities observed with the very fact of observation. That is why information should become the "final" category common for different branches of intellectual activity. So, information-based methodology can be successfully used to remove the "unbridgeable gap" between the "two cultures" mentioned by C. P. Snow (1959).

Further, we can tell something about the *form* in which this category should be used. We can single out three main gradations of this form: simple (naive) observation, conservation, and optimization (i.e., maximization or minimization). Of course, the last gradation is the most advanced form of the core, because optimization is capable of determining the dynamics of the system, not only its static states, as happens in the case of using conservation. That is why the *optimality principles* are very "powerful" (see, e.g., Rosen, 1967): they *predict* the behavior of the system. For instance, the law of the energy conservation can predict only a set of possible states of the system studied. Meanwhile such an optimality principle as the law of the extremal optical way (Fermat's principle) can predict the path which will be chosen by light in a certain medium. Hence, the evolution of the core of any centralized mental system should be directed from matter to information—with information presented in the form of the optimality principle.

These theoretical conclusions are corroborated by due *empirical data*.

1) *Inclination to centralization* can be illustrated with numerous phenomena. For instance, at the dawn of their development, such

technical systems as telephone nets, connected subscribers to each other directly by wire; so the total number of links needed to connect N subscribers with each other, was equal to $L = N(-1)/2$. So if there are 5 subscribers, $L = 5(5-1)/2 = 10$, if there are 100 subscribers, $L = 4950$. Afterwards, a central telephone exchange appeared, connected with each subscriber; so the number of links needed diminished: $L = N$. If there are 100 subscribers, $L = 100$, i.e., 49.5 times less, which responds to a giant advantage! Hence, centralization results in a rather large economy of the resource (wire).

The *system of commerce* "also evolved towards centralization. At first one product was exchanged for another one directly. But with the growth of the number of commodity, one of the products stood out among others (usually it was gold) and became the "means of exchange." Each product was exchanged for gold and then gold—for any other product. The system of exchange thus became simplified" (Golitsyn & Petrov, 1995, p. X).

One can find similar examples in many fields of *"genuine mental" systems*. All religious systems show the evolution from polytheism to monotheism: Abraham searched for a single God controlling the multifarious natural and spiritual phenomena. Newton searched for a single Law of Universal Gravitation which explains the fall of apples, the motion of the moon and the planets. Such a regularity is also inherent to the development of scientific theories. At the end of the evolution of a scientific theory usually only one central postulate remains. As a rule it has the form of an optimality principle (or variational principle)—like the principle of the least action in mechanics or the principle of the entropy maximum in thermodynamics and so on (Golitsyn & Petrov, 1995).

In the field of *art and culture* the phenomenon of centralization reveals itself in that within each culture, we can find one subculture which functions as a "means of exchange" for other subcultures. Usually it is the so-called elite subculture determining the development of the entire cultural system. As well in the world system of culture such a "central subsystem" is West European culture, which connects all other regional cultural systems with each other (Golitsyn, 2001).

2) And what about evolutionary (empirical) observations concerning the *nature of the core* of such centralized intellectual systems? Here we also see full agreement with our theoretical predictions, especially in the case of *scientific theories*. Three centuries ago the main "personage" of physics and chemistry was matter, which was subdued to the law of conservation (M. Lomonossov, 1748; A. Lavoisier, 1789). Then, in the first half of the nineteenth century, almost all the attention of physicists turned to the second category; energy, and the law of its conservation

was theoretically established by J. R. Mayer (1842) and empirically proved by J. Joule.

But soon the attention of physicists turned to the *dynamics* of energy; that is, to the direction of its transformations. In 1865, Clausius introduced the concept of entropy, which is common both for thermodynamics and information theory. All the development of physics in the twentieth century was focused on entropy and information. In quantum mechanics, the "principle of uncertainty" deals with information, describing interaction between a researcher and the object studied. In general, all contemporary natural sciences (and such, their derivatives as synergetics) are focused on the structural properties of objects, on their ordering (the information). At the same time, there was a movement toward *principles of optimality*. The above mentioned Fermat's principle was established around 1660. Since that time, such principles appeared in various models (e.g., in electrodynamics).

In the *humanities,* we also see the "core" in question, which evolves in "due" direction. For instance, some social and economic theories in the nineteenth century dealt mainly with "energetic" concepts. For example, K. Marx tried to deduce all the regularities of social and economic life, proceeding from such purely energetic categories as the "quantity of necessary labor". But in the beginning of the twentieth century M. Weber turned to "purely mental" socio-psychological changes, which means a movement toward information-oriented categories. As well at the same time psychoanalysis appeared, which also tried to deduce all the regularities of mental life, proceeding from some general postulates. Afterwards G. Zipf (1949) proposed another kind of optimization: the "principle of least effort" dealing with many kinds of human behavior.

Hence, all mental systems are *moving toward centralized structures*, with certain *optimality principles* in their core, besides, "switching" over to *information-oriented categories*.

THE SPHERE OF HUMANITARIAN STUDIES: MOVEMENT TOWARD MORE COMPLICATED AND REFLEXIVE OBJECTS, AND THE "INFORMATIONAL COLORING" OF STUDIES

Here our analysis should be focused on the evolutionary logic of scientific research.

The first long-range tendency deals with specific features of the sphere of humanitarian knowledge. *Two principal peculiarities* of this sphere are to be taken into account:

1) The very *complicated* character of the phenomena studied. For instance, some works of art are so "multifaced" that different researchers describe the same oeuvre with the help of quite different sets of terms or categories. And each of such sets usually contains a large number of parameters.

2) The proximity of the phenomena studied to the internal (intellectual) world of a researcher. For example, psychology deals with human mental life, which is investigated by means of the mentality of a researcher. In other words, the "instrument" of investigation is very close to its object (i.e., subject). As well we discuss the problems of language and literature, using this very language and literary means. Researchers studying social life are living in quite definite social conditions and so forth. Hence, the effect of *reflexion* (in its usual, "narrow" meaning of this term) plays a great role in such processes, as if one mirror reflected another mirror. That is why our understanding of our own mental life is connected with great obstacles. As a result, we know about human mentality, language, art, and other "close" phenomena less than we know about remote planets and stars.

These two peculiarities determine the direction of our consideration concerning the humanities. How can our knowledge master the sphere of such specific phenomena? It is necessary to clear up an appropriate *strategy of humanitarian knowledge;* that is, its evolutionary regularities. In principle, these regularities should be inherent in any branch of knowledge. Nevertheless, in the humanities, these regularities should be much more pronounced.

The strategy in question is evident: studies should proceed from simple objects and then turn to more difficult phenomena, which baffle all investigation. So the *first stage* of this evolution recalls an old joke: "If you lost your watch at night, you should look for it under a street lamp, because the light is better there." Such an attitude seems to be quite natural. In application to researchers, we should speak of an "instrumental lamp," permitting us to "light up" some fragments of reality or its properties. However, the most interesting fact is that this "lamp" is not so much "instrumental" as "mental," responding to the researcher's thinking. Two features relating to the above two peculiarities characterize this "mental lamp" and the fragments of reality seen in its light:

1. The *simplicity* of the objects to be examined. In fact, it is easier to study those objects that function more or less "independently," being "isolated" from other ones. As well, those properties that are not "interwoven" with other ones are evidently more convenient for investigations.

2. The *"passive"* character of objects. In fact, it would be very difficult to study those objects, which change their parameters even under the influence of the observation.

However, because of such restrictions, this first stage cannot be very fruitful. Hence, *movement* should take place along the lines of the above features:

1) Movement toward *more complicated*, not obvious objects and properties studied. It means that the objects chosen for investigations can become "interwoven" with each other, as well as the properties studied. Besides, both objects and properties investigated become more and more *"abstract,"* far from immediate observations.

2) Movement toward more *"active"* objects and properties studied. In other words, those objects become subject to investigations, which change their parameters because of observation, for example, *"reflexive"* phenomena that switch their parameters while being investigated.

Both movements describe the tendency that should be inherent in the *evolution* of each field of investigations embracing both science and the humanities. Though in the humanities this tendency is much more pronounced, especially in aesthetics. As well, this trajectory should reveal itself in the evolution of the sphere of knowledge *as a totality*.

The second tendency concretizes the *"faces"* of this movement. Here it seems reasonable to use a model elaborated in the framework of our information method: the so-called *model of asymmetry of cognitive mechanisms* (see, e.g., Maslov, 1983; Petrov, 1992, 2001). This model is based on the above-mentioned representation of human mental activity as a *multilevel hierarchical structure* of information processing. All the processes can be divided into *two types*:

1. Information processing at a given level, organized according to definite rules (paradigm). Small portions of the information received are processed in a serial order. This type of activity is characterized by analytical, rational features with an important role for logic.
2. Information transmittal from one level to a higher one. This activity is characterized by a change in the rules of information processing. Rather large amounts of information are processed parallel to each other. This activity may be described as synthetic, emotional, and intuitive.

A significant difference thus exists between these types: the first is primarily *analytical,* and the second is mainly *synthetic*. These two types may be correlated respectively with the *left- and right-hemispherical activity* of the brain. At any given moment, each society should possess a quite definite *degree of prevalence* of one of these two types. This prevalence should embrace all branches of the sociopsychological sphere, including the sociopolitical "climate," style of music, painting, literature, etc.

This prevalence should show *periodical "swithes"* from one type to another, against the background of a *long-range monotonic trend*. The duration of these cycles should be about 50 years because each generation can dominate the sociopsychological sphere for about 20–25 years. So the epoch of left-hemispheric prevalence (L-wave) should last about 20–25 years, as well as the epoch of right-hemispheric prevalence (R-wave). Exactly such waves were observed *empirically* by means of *measurements* concerning the above-mentioned cultural branches on materials of the evolution both of Russia and Western European countries during the fifteenth through twentieth centuries.

As for the direction of the *monotonic trend*, it depends on the nature of each branch. For the *entire sociopsychological sphere*, this trend is directed toward the *increase of analytical features*, which corresponds to the above-mentioned growth of nongenetic information—our *information approach*, having an inclination to rationality, corresponds with this trend.

Both tendencies (deduced theoretically) were corroborated by appropriate *empirical data*.

1) The first tendency, the *evolution* from studies of simple and nonreflexive phenomena *to more complicated and reflexive* ones and to more and more *abstract concepts*, was observed in the sphere of the humanities, as well as in the entire sphere of knowledge. Thus we do see *increasing attention to the humanities* especially in the nineteenth and twentieth centuries, because the humanities deal exactly with phenomena marked both by complicated features and reflexivity. Moreover, *within the humanities,* we see a trend toward studies of more and more complicated and reflexive phenomena: linguistics, semiotics, psychology, and works of art (including literature), processes of their creation and perception. This trend is especially well-pronounced in the field of *methods of humanitarian investigations*.

In *psychology*, Martindale (1990) measured the relations between the "conceptual" and "primordial" content in publications in psychological journals of the nineteenth and twentieth centuries. "Conceptual" content showed temporal increases (in contrast with art, which shows long-range decreases in its "conceptual" content). In other words, publications in the field of psychology become more and more remote from "primordial," matters which can be "touched with the fingers." We can draw various examples of inclination toward such abstract categories, and first of all toward numerous "latent" variables: "libido" in psychoanalysis, "three principal components" in Osgood's semantic differential techniques, Eysenck's IQ, etc.

Quite similar movement is found in quantitative *sociology*, with the same movement toward abstract categories such as various latent variables (especially after 1950, when Lazarsfeld introduced the first latent variable, "ethnocentrism"). In *art studies*, we see the arrival of various rather complicated methods of structural investigations and *empirical aesthetics*. Analogous movement is seen in linguistics, literary studies, anthropology, ethnography, and so on.

The movement toward *reflexivity* in the humanities is now only at its early stage. But a high degree of reflexivity responds to rather advanced stages of the development of any system. As an example of movement toward reflexive structures, we can present the appearance of the concept of so-called *discourse*, which became so fashionable in last several decades, especially in aesthetics.

In the natural sciences similar tendencies have occurred. We see evolution from studies of "isolated" and "passive" objects (planets in ancient astronomy) to more complicated phenomena. Following this way, sciences started to use rather abstract categories: phlogiston, ether, energy, and entropy. The last one requires very deliberate thinking that is quite remote from "primordial" thought. As for the path toward reflexivity, it revealed itself in the movement of the scale of objects studied: from macro-objects at early stages (because such objects cannot be influenced by the observer) to the contemporary stage, with micro-objects investigated, their parameters being commensurate with those ones of the interaction in question. As well, researchers' attention turned to the phenomena of mental life, which are close to the researcher's mental "instrument." Starting from relativistic models derived by A. Einstein, and quantum mechanics, the observer became an "indigenous inhabitant" of theories. Hence, information became the "genuine substratum" of models.

2) Turning to the second tendency, we see the *alteration of styles* dominating the humanities, quite synchronous with the waves in other branches of the sociopsychological sphere. In the twentieth century, there were *four main directions* in aesthetics: formalism (1920–30); existentialism (1940–50); structuralism (1960–70); post-structuralism (1980–90).

If we use our opposition of two "polar" types of information processes, then we see a *regular alteration* of these two types. Formalism and structuralism should be considered as belonging to the analytical L-pole, while existentialism and poststructuralism belong to the synthetical R-pole. The peaks of these directions coincide with appropriate peaks of the evolution of the sociopsychological "climate" both in Russia and Western Europe (see, e.g., Maslov, 1983). So the appropriate *traditions* are observed in each of these lines. It was not without reason that structuralism borrowed most of its ideas and categories from Russian formalists, whereas the existentialist world view is followed by contemporary poststructuralism.

So, the *forthcoming stage* will be again of the *L-type;* it should follow the structuralist line. Hence, it is possible to *deduce* its *features*, which are to be the result of a certain *progress* within this line; overcoming the shortcomings of structuralism. Structuralism possesses two *Achilles' heels* relating to the "top" of the hierarchy of scientific knowledge and to its "bottom."

The *"top heel"* is the *arbitrariness* in the choice of the basic parameters of theoretical models. Such parameters are, for example, those binary oppositions that are used in aesthetic analysis. A way to eliminate this arbitrariness is to *deduce* the parameters from the general model of the phenomena studied, and evidently the information approach would enable us to do so.

As for the *"lower heel"* of structuralism, it is the *lack of quantitative verification* of the hypotheses used, including their basic parameters. And here the information approach proposes a whole set of quantitative methods for such empirical verification.

Hence, both Achilles' heels of structuralism can be "cured" in the framework of the information approach. Besides, it follows the analytical line. In general, the extrapolation of both tendencies revealed in the sphere of humanitarian studies predicts the *growing interest* in this sphere as a whole, as well as its *inclination to information models and categories*.

So the results obtained for *all six tendencies* belonging to three spheres are in agreement with each other. Hence, the next stage in the humanities (including aesthetics) will be based on the *information paradigm*, with the core consisting in the "principle of the information maximum." It is necessary not to confuse this approach with some early versions of the information approach (e.g., Bense, 1969; Moles, 1958, 1967), which were rather eclectic and possessed no fundamental theoretical basis. This approach is *not a metaphoric* one (like some other fashionable approaches); on the contrary, it deals with quite concrete functions and parameters of the phenomena studied, using *quantitative methods*. Even now, the results obtained in the framework of this approach embrace a rather broad circle of phenomena, for instance such *aesthetic* ones as

1. features of means and devices of art; various concrete expressive devices used in painting, architecture, poetry, prose, music, etc.: rhyme, meter, the golden section, musical consonance, and so forth were deduced, together with their parameters (see, e.g., Golitsyn & Petrov, 1995);
2. optimal frequency of different devices, both in separate works of art (e.g., a novel) and a set of oeuvres, e.g., a given kind of art (such as a given national school of painting (see Petrov, 2002);
3. features of erotic (sexual) attractivity, especially parameters of woman's beauty, together with their evolution (see Mazhul & Petrov, 1999; Petrov, 1999);
4. national peculiarities of some kinds of art (e.g., painting) (see Gribkov & Petrov, 1996);
5. general regularities of cultural evolution, including "horizontal" expansion (interrelations of kinds of art) and "vertical" ones ("high" against "low"), development of national cultures along their "Common Path," etc. (see Petrov & Majoul, 2001; Petrov & Gribkov, 2003);
6. periodical waves both in style of different kinds of art (music, architecture, poetry, painting, etc.) and the intensity of artistic life (see Maslov, 1983; Petrov, 1992, 2001, 2003);
7. middle-range and long-range forecasts of the development of different cultural systems, including various kinds of art (see Gribkov & Petrov, 1997; Petrov & Majoul, 2002);
8. methods of measurement for the level of aesthetic development of personality that were used in various sociological and psychological investigations and were applied in the practice of cultural politics and can be used in cross-cultural studies (see Golitysn & Petrov, 1997).

Of course, the information paradigm is rather prospective for humanitarian studies and mainly aesthetic ones. As well, the new paradigm will permit a removal of the "unbridgeable gap" between the "Two Cultures," paving a path toward the "Integral Culture" of the future.

APPENDIX:
Foundations of the "Principle of the Information Maximum"

The principle uses the concept of *mutual information* between two variables (Fano, 1951):

$$I(x, y) = \log \frac{p(x, y)}{p(x)\, p(y)}, \quad (1)$$

where *p(x)*, *p(y)* are the probabilities of the values *x* and *y*, and *p(x, y)* is the joint probability of the combination of *x* and *y*.

Starting position: The *mutual information* between the *conditions* of the environment and the *responses* (parameters, traits) of the system is the most suitable *measure of* its *adaptation* (Golitsyn & Petrov, 1995).

The principle of the information maximum: In the processes of evolution, behavior, and problem solving, the system chooses such reactions *r*, which provide maximization of average mutual information between the system and environmental conditions ("stimuli") *x*:

$$I(X, R) = \sum_x p(x) \sum_r p(r/x) \log [p(r/x) / p(r)] = H(R) - H(R/X) = max, \quad (2)$$

where *p(x)*, *p(r)* – probabilities of *x* and *r*; *p(r/x)* – conditional probability of *r* when *x* occurred; *H (R)* – unconditional entropy of reactions; *H (R/X)* – conditional entropy of reactions.

Usually there exist some *restrictions* that prevent the system from reaching the absolute (unconditional) maximum of information. Then the system has to be satisfied with the *conditional maximum*. A very typical condition is the restriction of the average resource *E (X,R)*, e.g., energy:

$$\sum_{x,r} p(x,r)\, e(x,r) = E(X,R), \quad (3)$$

where *e(x,r)* is a resource expense in the state *(x,r)*.

Hence, it is possible to come to the *main equation*:

$$L = H(R) - H(R/X) - \lambda - \beta E(X,R) = max, \quad (4)$$

where λ and β are the Lagrange multipliers. A physical sense of the multiplier β is a *deficit of resources*.

So *three principal tendencies* relating to appropriate three free members of equation (4), should be inherent in the *behavior and development* of any system:

1. *Expansion* – aspiration to increase the number and the variety of the system responses (reactions) $H\ (R)$: "search behavior."

2. *Idealization* – aspiration to increase the "exactness" of the responses, i.e., to decrease the entropy of the errors $H(R/X)$: "conservative behavior."

3. *Economy* of resources: on the one hand, to choose situations (x,r) with minimal resource expense $e(x,r)$; on the other hand, the aspiration to decrease the deficit of resource β, i.e., to increase the resource supply.

REFERENCES

Bense, M. (1969). *Einfuerung in die informationstheoretische Aesthetik [Introduction to informational aesthetics]*. Hamburg: Rohwolts Deutsche Enzyklopaedie.

Fano, R. M. (1951). *Transmission of information*. New York: Wiley.

Golitsyn, G. A. (2001). "High" art and "low" art: On the systemic role of an elite subculture. *Journal of Russian and East European Psychology, 38,* 28-44.

Golitsyn, G. A., & Petrov, V. M. (1995). *Information and creation: Integrating the "two cultures"*. Basel: Birkhauser Verlag.

Golitsyn, G. A., & Petrov, V. M. (1997). The principle of the information maximum, Zipf's law, and the measurement of individual cultural development. In L. Dorfman, C. Martindale, D. Leontiev, G. Cupchik, V. Petrov, & P. Machotka (Eds.), *Emotion, creativity, and art* (vol. 1, pp. 179-221). Perm: Perm State Institute of Arts and Culture.

Gribkov, V. S., & Petrov, V. M. (1996). Color elements in national schools of painting: A statistical investigation. *Empirical Studies of the Arts, 14,* 165-181.

Gribkov, V. S., & Petrov, V. M. (1997). Constructive Conceptualism as a means to integrate emotional and rational components of perception. In L. Dorfman, C. Martindale, D. Leontiev, G. Cupchik, V. Petrov, & P. Machotka (Eds.), *Emotion, creativity, and art* (vol. 1, pp. 117-133). Perm: Perm State Institute of Arts and Culture.

Lotman, Yu. M. (1977). Art of cinema in the mechanism of culture (in Russian). *Works on Semiotics* (Vol. 8, pp. 138-150). Tartu: Tartu State University.

Lotman, Yu. M., & Uspensky, B. A. (1971). About semiotical mechanism of culture (in Russian). *Works on Semiotics* (Vol. 5, pp. 144-166). Tartu: Tartu State University.

Martindale, C. (1990). *The clockwork muse: The predictability of artistic change*. New York: Basic Books.

Maslov, S. Yu. (1983). Asymmetry of cognitive mechanisms and its consequences (in Russian). *Semiotika I Informatika, 20,* 3-34.

Mazhul, L. A., & Petrov, V. M. (1999). The roots of sexuality and sexual choice: From nature to culture, and within the latter (information approach to evolution). *Semiotische Berichte, 23,* 231-249.

Moles, A. (1958). *Theorie de l'information et perception esthetique*. Paris: Flammarion.

Moles, A. (1967). *Sociodynamique de la culture*. La Haye: Mouton.
Petrov, V. M. (1992). Evolution of art and brain asymmetry: A review of empirical investigations. In G. C. Cupchik & J. Laszlo (Eds.), *Emerging visions of the aesthetic process: Psychology, semiology, and philosophy* (pp. 255-268). Cambridge University Press.
Petrov, V. M. (1999). Social signs of woman's attractiveness (information approach). *Semiotische Berichte, 23*, 287-305.
Petrov, V. M. (2001). Creativity in art: Stylistic waves and monotonous evolutionary trends (information approach). *Bulletin of Psychology and the Arts, 2*, 30-33.
Petrov, V. M. (2002). Devices of art: Optimal frequency of occurrence (information approach). In R. Tomassoni (Ed.), *La psicologia delle arti oggi* (pp. 43-48). Milano: Franco Angeli.
Petrov, V. M. (2003). Cyclic cultural evolution against the background of long-range progressive trends: Information approach. *Journal of Cultural and Evolutionary Psychology, 1*, 85-107.
Petrov, V. M., & Gribkov, V. S. (2003). Leading national schools of European painting: Psychology and geography of evolutionary shifts. *Rivista di Psicologia dell'Arte, 14*, 47-60.
Petrov, V. M., & Majoul, L. A. (2001). Divergent cultural universe: 'Horizontal' and 'vertical' expansion in the light of the information approach. *Quale Psicologia, 17*, 37-41.
Petrov, V. M., & Majoul, L. A. (2002). Art of the future: Elements of a middle-range forecast. In T. Kato (Ed.), *Art and environment. Proceedings of the 17th Congress of the International Association of Empirical Aesthetics* (pp. 319-322). Takarazuka, Japan.
Rosen, R. (1967). *Optimality principles in biology*. London: Butterworth.
Snow, C. P. (1959). *The two cultures and the scientific revolution*. Cambridge: Cambridge University Press.
Zipf, G. K. (1949). *Human behaviour and the principle of least effort*. Cambridge: Addison-Wesley.

CHAPTER 10

Art and Cognition: Cognitive Processes in Art Appreciation

Helmut Leder and Benno Belke

INTRODUCTION

In the present chapter, aesthetics and art appreciation are discussed from an information-processing viewpoint. We describe a cognitive model of aesthetic experience recently proposed by Leder, Belke, Oeberst, and Augustin (2004). Moreover, we give a short historical overview on cognition in empirical aesthetics and particularly focus on processes involved in aesthetic appreciation that are concerned with artists' style and expertise of the beholder.

Aesthetic experiences for many people are fundamental to human experience. As Ramachandran and Hirstein (1999) pointed out, aesthetic behavior is not just a domain of human behavior but seems to be a typical or even exclusive domain of humanity. They state that *"our propensity to create and enjoy painting and sculpture—would be among the most puzzling"* (Ramachandran & Hirstein, 1999, p. 16) aspects of human nature. Not only is it puzzling, but we do not even know of explicit aesthetic behavior in any other species. Nowadays we are facing a world of "aesthetization" in which exposure to art is a frequent experience for large numbers of people. Art is no longer the exclusive domain of the rich and privileged. Exhibitions such as the contemporary art show *Documenta* in the German city of Kassel have more than half a million visitors, and the Louvre in Paris attracts about five million visitors a year. The possibility of having access to art has never been broader in human history. However, the reason people produce or appreciate art, and what is the function of art (and particularly modern art), is not apparent at first sight. The permanence of art production and consumption in all known human cultures has led psychologists to assume that something exclusive has to be discovered in art. This in turn would then explain why humans produce and appreciate it. Recently, Aiken and Coe (2004) have proposed an approach based on social functions that states that art might have served a purpose in the evolutionary past and still affects our behavior. For example, they assume that basic forms of cultural activities might support the bonding between family members. However, they also claim that responsiveness to color, pattern, and form are essential to aesthetic experiences.

In the present chapter, we propose an approach that further tries to enlighten essential cognitive and emotional processes that occur in the perceiver during an aesthetic experience. We shall describe a model of cognitive processing stages involved in art appreciation that considers affordances that artworks and particularly contemporary artworks pose. In many respects, the attempt is in the tradition of empirical aesthetics. In psychology, empirical aesthetics already has a long history, and as background, we present a very brief survey of aesthetics in modern psychology with special emphasis on cognitive aspects.

A BRIEF HISTORY OF COGNITION IN EMPIRICAL AESTHETICS

Historically, empirical aesthetics is among the most traditional fields in experimental psychology. The founders of academic empirical psychology, Fechner and Wundt, were interested both in perception and sensation as well as aesthetic responses (see Fechner, 1871, Vorschule der Ästhetik or Wundt, 1874, Grundzüge der physiologischen Psychologe for more details). When empirical psychology was established in the last quarter of the nineteenth century, the important questions that "psychologists" dealt with were closely related to the philosophical questions of their times. Baumgarten (who lived from 1714–1762) had already coined the term "aesthetics" in the eighteenth century. His seminal lectures focused on the possibility that through aesthetic experience, the human mind has a way of cognition that is mainly based on "sensory validity." In modern terms, this relates to the "validity" of beauty, which is apparent to the perceiver and related to the quality of an artwork. In short, the philosophical importance of aesthetics is related to the possibility that the beautiful is the good, or even stronger, that beauty reveals truth.

Baumgarten's (1988) position is different from Kant's (1968) understanding of aesthetics, which referred to variables within the beholder. In modern terms, Kant's (1968) position is related to what we would call "taste," while Baumgarten's (1988) position is related to an object's beauty. When Fechner (1871) and Wundt (1874) made aesthetics a question of empirical research, they were interested in empirical studies of stimulus qualities and their psychophysical relation to responses of pleasantness and apparent beauty. Thus, they in a way tested predictions in the tradition of Baumgarten. Importantly, from today's perspective, the nineteenth century offered a much more stable standard of what constitutes good artwork for Fechner (1871) and Wundt (1874) to refer to.

It was particularly Fechner (1871) who started his empirical investigations on aesthetics in close relation to his psychophysics paradigms. For example, Fechner's experiments concerning the beauty of the golden section, as a relation of beautiful harmony, revealed a preference for rectangles that corresponded to this relation (see Höge, 1995, for a discussion of recent views on the golden section). However, even Fechner already knew that the processing of art depends on higher-order cognitive processing, much in the tradition of Kant's approach. In his seminal *Vorschule der Ästhetik,* Fechner (1871) distinguished two forms of aesthetics, one from below and one from above. The former is concerned with stimulus properties, such as the proportion, complexity and other stimulus-inherent, often perceptual, features. The latter refers to top-down influences of knowledge, education, and taste. These two forms of "aesthetic variables" have often been considered since then, but the majority of empirical psychological research has been concerned with the aesthetics "from below."

At least three major movements that saw a larger number of empirical aesthetics publications in the twentieth century should be mentioned. Following the Gestalt psychologists approach, it was mainly Rudolf Arnheim (1954) who analyzed Gestalt laws in artworks. Following a comprehensive analyses of visual properties and their physical qualities, he also proposed principles of aesthetic experience such as entropy, structure, order, and complexity (Arnheim, 1971). Beyond the perception of stimulus properties, Arnheim also stressed dimensions of higher-order vividness when he wrote "A high level of structural order is a necessary but not sufficient prerequisite of art. What is ultimately required is that this order reflect a genuine, true, profound view of life" (Arnheim, 1971, p. 2).

Berlyne (1974) conducted an influential program of *"a new experimental aesthetics"* in which he analyzed aesthetics as serving fundamental needs of arousal and excitement that are closely related to a drive for exploration and curiosity. According to his approach, aesthetic responses are optimal at a certain medium level of activation. Berlyne distinguished three types of stimulus factors that are important for the aesthetic qualities of a stimulus (and which contribute to its hedonic value): psychophysical, ecological, and collative qualities.

Psychophysical qualities consist of color, intensity, or contrast. Ecological variables describe aspects of meaning of a stimulus and are learned through experience. Berlyne's empirical works with visual pattern revealed the importance of variables such as complexity, novelty, or ambiguity, which he termed "collative" (Berlyne, 1970).

However, results from investigations with real artworks were not always clear (Berlyne, 1974). Berlyne produced valuable efforts concerning the characteristics that may be common to all works of art. Moreover, although Berlyne referred to the state of activation of the perceiver, higher order processes such as extraction of meaning and interpretation go beyond the scope of his psychobiological approach. Later, Berlyne's approach was criticized because of its exclusive focusing on activation in terms of arousal, which according to Martindale (1984), cannot account for aesthetic experiences as it neither considers semantic aspects of artworks nor distinguishes aesthetic from nonaesthetic experiences.

In a somewhat mixed approach, Kreitler and Kreitler (1972) proposed a psychodynamical approach, including elements of psychoanalyses and elements of cognitive psychology. Kreitler and Kreitler developed a theory of "meaning" in psychology, an aspect that any theory of higher-order effects on art appreciation has to consider. Their empirical work (Kreitler & Kreitler, 1984) tested hypotheses concerning the time dimension of extraction of meaning and found that the longer a stimulus is perceived, the more elements of meaning might be activated. An explicit cognitive orientation is essential in the Kreitler's approach. This cognitive orientation is supposed to follow a need for successful understanding or extraction of meaning from an artwork and leads to a pleasurable experience of homeostasis. The approach explicitly states that aesthetic appreciation cannot be understood without consideration of the perceiver's knowledge and other interindividual variables such as self-understanding. Kreitler and Kreitler (1972) are prominent examples of early cognitive approaches to aesthetics and art, which still link cognitive processing with a concept of psychodynamical states of homeostasis.

Cognitive psychology since Broadbent (1958) has been the leading approach in empirical psychology over the last 40 years. The main source of research about cognition and art comes from studies in which basic mechanisms of cognitive processing have been applied to aesthetic phenomena, mainly to preference and perceptual phenomena of art (Solso, 1994). It is often assumed that measurements of preference are the most basic aesthetic judgments. The cognitive approach produced a number of insights in variables affecting experimental aesthetics (Berlyne, 1974; Ramachandran & Hirstein, 1999; Zeki, 1999). These are often concerned with visual features used by artists. For example, it seems that most people prefer prototypical stimuli (Martindale & Moore, 1988), perceptually sharp (Reber, Winkielman & Schwarz, 1998), and familiar (Zajonc, 1968) objects. Martindale (1984) has introduced a theory of hedonic experience that proposed that hedonic experiences are stronger when more associated units are activated. For example, successful classification of an artwork increases pleasure because more related objects are associated, while a misclassification produces inhibition and prevents associations with related objects.

In the last decade, cognitive psychology has provided a number of studies where perceptual and cognitive features in respect to aesthetic experience were tested. However the field lacks a comprehensive theory of processing stages that are involved in aesthetic experiences. Consequently, as a first step, we proposed a model of aesthetic experiences that incorporates a number of these findings. The model aims to provide a framework for future research and is mainly concerned with aesthetic appreciation of visual arts.

A COGNITIVE MODEL OF AESTHETIC EXPERIENCE

Our approach intends to explain what levels of processing are involved in art appreciation. The model identifies features of aesthetic experience that make it psychologically important in that it describes processing stages of a perceiver of an artwork. It seems that aesthetic appreciation is a somehow self-rewarding process because it challenges our mind in a specific way. The model endeavors to discover what these challenges are, how the cognitive system is equipped to deal with them, and how they motivate the perceiver to search further experiences of art.

From an evolutionary perspective, our brain has developed as an efficient adaptation tool to solve problems of survival. The evolutionary link between cognitive skills and their function is now widespread. What is a likely explanation for the adaptive value of art and aesthetics? Baumgarten (1988), in the eighteenth century, was convinced that perception allows direct access to the truth value of perceived objects. Thus, in modern terminology, he assumed that sensory processing reveals higher-order evaluation of the intellectual qualities of objects. Aiken and Coe (2004) discussed the social functions of art, such as bonding between children and parents, and kin relationships in general. Our view of the function of art states that the information processing that underlies aesthetic experience somehow must produce positive, self-rewarding experiences (Leder et al., 2004). This does not exclude the widely accepted view that art serves the purpose of gaining knowledge about the world (Zeki, 1999). However, in our view, cognitive and affective experiences during an aesthetic episode might be the essential psychological part of gaining knowledge through art.

As our model is concerned with appreciation of visual art, we first describe those features that make art, and particularly modern art, interesting and offer experiences that are somehow art specific. Artists were liberated from academic institutions since the beginning of what is called the "Modern" period of art at the end of the nineteenth century. As a result, they were unfettered from traditional topics such as portraiture, but were no longer guaranteed the stable source of income that portraits afforded. Together with the development of photography as a medium of depiction, artists gained more and more freedom in topics.

Artists, such as van Gogh, Gauguin, or Cézanne, developed individually distinct approaches to depiction: style rather than content as the way to depict (Leder, 1994). In some cases, for example Cézanne, the relation of an individual style was accompanied by theoretically based approaches to art (Shiff, 1986). There were also developments in the marketing of "modern art," which also encouraged the individualization of single artists due to their style (Grasskamp, 1989). In the twentieth century, there was a rapid development of numerous artistic approaches, sometimes organized in movements such as the Expressionism, Dadaism, or Surrealism.

In the second half of the last century, even the binding labeling of art schools was mostly abandoned in favor of a completely individualized production of art mainly associated with single artists. Moreover, since 1910, with the advance of abstract art, the modernist era developed a dominance of style over content. Tyler (1999) has pointed to the psychological consequence of this development toward abstraction. While representational art often is perceived effortlessly, abstraction of depiction requires far more effort to solve the problem of understanding and meaning.

These distinctive features of modern art come along with a specific basic market mechanism (Grasskamp, 1989). Commercial success of artists is mainly due to a distinctive artistic style, which perceivers recognize and appreciate. This need for individually distinctive styles produced a large number of innovations in twentieth-century art.

The variety of styles and innovations in artworks also has had dramatic effects for the perceiver. Art is classified according to style, and features that define individual art styles often exceed the border between art and nonart. Duchamps' use of everyday objects as artworks or the introduction of temporary performances since Dadaism sometimes make it difficult to recognize that one is exposed to art. In contemporary art, nearly every conceivable kind of object has been used as art, such as the recent presentation of body fat or water from dead bodies washings by Teresa Margolles as an extreme.

Due to its experimental nature, twentieth-century art has developed a larger need for interpretation than any art before. Concerning the psychological understanding of aesthetic experience, presumably, the better the understanding of an artwork, the more it produces an aesthetic experience. This is no trivial matter as the understanding is no longer achieved with a visual representation of "what is depicted." Conceptual ideas, abstract concepts, and reflection no longer become apparent from the appearance of the artwork. Such features are more and more essential in contemporary art. This aspect explains the importance of top-down influences for aesthetic experiences, as specific declarative knowledge enables the viewer to derive meaning through an alternative search in concepts (Zeki, 1999).

In order to understand how modern art provides aesthetic experiences and what cognitive processing stages are involved, we have presented an information-processing model of aesthetic appreciation (Leder et al., 2004). Figure 1 shows a simplified version of the model where we particularly focus on higher-order influences.

The model identifies a number of processing stages. Input is an artwork, and outputs are twofold. One output of aesthetic processing is an Aesthetic Judgment concerning an object. The other output of the sequence of processing stages is an Aesthetic Emotion, which is a by-product of the cognitive processing levels. The main dependent variables in psychological experiments were the evaluation of pleasure, aesthetic, liking, etc. operationalized by questions such as "How much do you like the artwork?" However, in real life, aesthetic processing is an experience that consists of affective and cognitive features. Affective features comprise feelings of pleasure, arousal, and satisfaction by experiencing an object of art. Cognitive features comprise states of understanding, successful classification, and interpretation. In between input and output there exist a number of processing stages. We have distinguished cognitive and emotional outcomes of the model because sometimes the value of both outcomes is different. For example, a cognitive judgment of an expert can be negative ("this is a poor drawing") but does not exclude that the affective or emotional state could be very positive; this, when the processes involved in the formation of the judgment were pleasing, because the expert was pleased by his feelings of expertise.

What are the levels of information processing depicted in the model? The first level consists of Perceptual Analyses. Here the artwork is

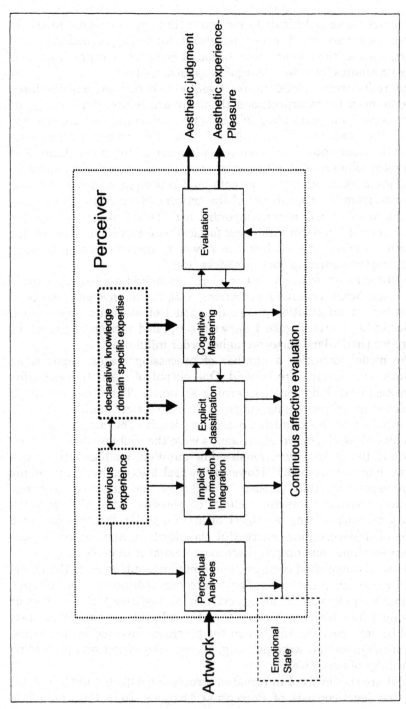

Figure 1. Processing stages in aesthetic experiences (adopted from Leder, Belke, Oeberst, & Augustin, 2004).

visually analyzed using procedures that presumably are not art specific but which are involved in any perceptual analyses. Contrast, color, shape, texture, symmetry, etc. are the products derived from this early processing stage. Tyler (1999) has shown how symmetry is perceived instantly. More important, Locher and Nodine (1987) revealed, using artworks, that symmetry is indeed an important feature in the perception of artworks.

A stage of Implicit Memory Integration was included in our model because several approaches from cognitive psychology assume that rather implicit classifications affect the aesthetic value of an object (Ramachandran & Hirstein, 1999; Zeki, 1999). Prototypicality and familiarity are among these variables. Prototypical faces are particularly attractive, and it seems that some sorts of prototypical artworks also are preferred (Hekkert & van Wieringen, 1990). Familiarity often turned out to be linked with appreciation and preference. Kunst-Wilson and Zajonc (1980) revealed that aesthetic preferences for objects that were familiarized in the laboratory were more sensitive than explicit judgments of familiarity. The mere-exposure hypothesis has had a high appeal to aesthetic research in psychology (Leder, 2002; Martindale, 1984). However, despite the fact that mere repetitions increase liking for many objects, the empirical findings with artworks are rather ambiguous (Bornstein, 1989). This is not surprising when we consider the next levels of processing that are usually involved in aesthetic experiences with art.

In addition to these implicit processing stages, we proposed a stage of Explicit Analyses. Here either the content or the artists' style is represented. Importantly, with increasing art-specific knowledge, style is becoming more dominant. The content can be similar to any other visual identification, such as the identification of a number of strange looking women in "Les demoiselles." Style-related explicit processing would identify the artwork as a cubist-style painting, made by Picasso. While rather naïve perceivers tend to identify the depicted object for experts, the way of depiction becomes more important (Cupchik, 1992). The same would hold for nonrepresentative, abstract paintings. Naïve viewers might classify them as a combination of colors and black lines, while an expert might recognize them as a painting in Mondrian-style for example. Moreover, naïve viewers may show a stronger tendency to interpret abstract paintings in terms of concrete objects, while experts refer to the style per se (Parsons, 1987). Thus, the identification of what we "see" is already depending on the state of expertise and knowledge.

The next processing stage is called Cognitive Mastering, in which the perceiver aims to understand and interpret the results of the previous processing stages. Expertise in art might have an important effect on this processing level as well because with increasing art knowledge and experience, a piece of art should be more easily classified or interpreted. In the following stage of evaluation (which builds an important feedback loop with Cognitive Mastering), the results of the cognitive and the affective processes are measured. Unsatisfying, ambiguous evaluations might trigger further processing of the artwork (which also depends on expertise of the viewer). Importantly, ambiguity in art might not need to be fully resolved as a certain level of ambiguity might be positively experienced as arousing. However, essential is the ability to experience successful understanding and the rewarding experience of cognitive and affective processing stages.

ART AND COGNITION: STYLE-RELATED PROCESSING

Top-down cognitive processes affect most processing levels. As style-related processing seems to be an essential feature of art appreciation, it is proposed that psychological research in aesthetics should particularly focus on this kind of processing. Some related questions already have been addressed. As was shown by Gordon and Holyoak (1983), preferences are affected by familiarity not only through repetition but also by familiarity of the underlying construction principles. Gordon and Holyoak (1983) made people learn letter strings that were constructed according to the artificial grammars. Afterwards, they tested preferences for old and new letter strings, as well as for letter strings that were previously unseen but corresponded to the learned rules. The perceiver liked these latter strings more than new ones. Gordon and Holyoak (1983) argue that this is a hint to a "preference" for abstracting principles and, in terms of art, artist's style.

The underlying mechanism of style learning was explicitly investigated by Hartley and Homa (1981). They showed how exposure to paintings produced implicit and explicit knowledge about artist's styles. In a different approach Hasenfus, Martindale, and Birnbaum (1983) revealed that broader classes of stylistic categories are recognized and used for classification by persons of different levels of expertise. Another way to learn to distinguish aspects of artist's style was proposed by Leder (1994), who claimed that the deviation between the depicted and the depiction results in systematic alienations. Comparing the processing of portraits as photographs with pure line drawings, he showed that alienation of the line-drawing style results in a differential weighting of configural as opposed to local features (Leder, 1996).

Moreover, Leder (2002) has directly investigated whether preferences for a less fluent style (Reber et al., 1998) can be improved by familiarity in the sense of mere exposure. Using pastel-style depictions of portraits, he found evidence for changes in preferences after familiarization with the initially less preferred nonfluent style. These examples somehow show the underlying basis of style-related processing, which is based on implicit abstraction processes. However, in the process of art appreciation, it is particularly style-related processing that can often be explicated and often is the basis for discourses on art for experts.

ART AND COGNITION: EFFECTS OF EXPERTISE IN ART APPRECIATION

Winston and Cupchik (1992) explained how expertise in art comes along with an increase in style-related processing. Expertise in art consists of implicitly and explicitly acquired knowledge about art. Explicitly, we can improve experience through school education, art journals and books, media, and discourse. The variety of appearances of visual art assure that no overall or absolute expertise in art can be gained by a single viewer. As a result, there is a permanent (cognitive) challenge to experience and further explore art in the future, even for art experts. In our model, we have also discussed that the possibility to improve and broaden art-specific knowledge might also be a reason for ongoing aesthetic experiences with the same artwork, as new and unexpected aspects might become important at a different occasion. The more someone knows about art, the more possibilities should turn out to be successful in Cognitive Mastering of an artwork to classify or interpret it successfully.

The most general theory explaining why additional knowledge positively changes aesthetic experiences comes from Martindale (1984). He claimed that the number of associations formed determines the hedonic experience. However, in respect to the model depicted in Figure 1, the possible ways in which art knowledge affects aesthetic experience can also be seen. Expertise increases the likelihood of stylistic processing, which allows experiences of style generalization (Gordon & Holyoak, 1983; Leder, 2002). Moreover, expertise increases the likelihood of a pleasing recognition of acquired knowledge (Martindale, 1984).

Expertise also plays an important role concerning the quality of Cognitive Mastering. The more someone knows about art, the wider the range of hypotheses that can be tested in order to gain a sufficient understanding. This is particularly apparent in respect to contemporary and often conceptual modern art. Thus, knowledge about possible concepts in art directly increases the chance of understanding. In the original version of the model (Leder et al., 2004), we discussed that expertise might affect the level on which "understanding" of an artwork is sought. Experts relate understanding to an art-specific semantic knowledge, while naïve viewers might seek understanding more in respect to personal interpretations.

An approach to classify different approaches (in five levels) and attitudes towards art was provided by Parsons (1987). His approach is based on qualitative interviews, and he describes different ways of dealing with artworks. These different ways bear some similarity to what we call Cognitive Mastering and provide an elaborated version of different qualities of Cognitive Mastering. Parsons (1987) distinguishes responses to art, called Favoritism, which are mainly based on content, but link content with personal beliefs. We call this self-related processing. Reference to beauty and explicit realism in depiction is found at Parsons (1987) level two. Expressiveness (level three) is empathic; the perceiver considers what the artist might have felt and thought while producing the artwork. Level four is similar to our level of Explicit, style-related classification where perceivers focus on style and form. Only at level five, called Autonomy, underlying concepts and thus the "autonomy" of the artwork are analyzed. Locher (2003) recently successfully demonstrated the classification of responses to art according to the schema of Parson in order to test a theory of pictorial rightness. Concerning the cognitive processes involved in aesthetic experience, an understanding of expertise in art in the future will be essential.

CONCLUSIONS AND OUTLOOK

We have described a model of cognitive processing stages involved in art appreciation that particularly focused on aspects of style processing and expertise. Understanding aesthetics in the future presumably needs more research concerning the details of how expertise is acquired. The classification schema provided by Parsons (1987) seems to be promising and might be used to investigate different levels of expertise or at least different attitudes toward art.

Once experimental research has shown what processes are involved, a next step has to identify the relation between rewarding-centers of the brain and elements of aesthetic processing. This is particularly important for the understanding of the affective and emotional components of aesthetic experiences. Neuropsychological methods provide a promising approach to understanding these mechanisms. Recently, Vartanian and Goel (2004) used brain scans to show that during the perception of artworks, emotional and cognitive pathways as well as reward centers are activated. Their findings are in accordance with the components and mechanism proposed in our model.

Understanding art from a psychological perspective has recently started a renaissance of new interest from neuroscience. Cognitive psychologists and neuroscientists mainly focus on visual properties of artworks and aspects of cognitive *and* affective processing. In the present study, to complete our understanding of why people are attracted by art, we add to the existing theories an information-processing model that is explicitly derived from an analysis of twentieth century art.

ACKNOWLEDGMENTS

The writing of this chapter was supported by a Grant SFB 626 C5 of the Deutsche Forschungsgemeinschaft (DFG) to Helmut Leder. We thank Steve Pawlett for helping us preparing the manuscript.

REFERENCES

Aiken, N. E., & Coe, K. (2004). Promoting cooperation among humans: The arts as the ties that bind. *Bulletin of Psychology and the Arts, 5*(1), 5-20.
Arnheim, R. (1954). *Art and visual perception.* Berkeley: University of California Press.
Arnheim, R. (1971). *Entropy and art: An essay on disorder and order.* Berkeley: University of California Press.
Baumgarten, A. G. (1988). *Theoretische Ästhetik. Die grundlegenden Abschnitte der "Aesthetica"* [Theoretical aesthetics. Essential parts of the "aesthetica"]. Hamburg: H. R. Schweizer (1988).
Berlyne, D. E. (1970). Novelty, complexity and hedonic value. *Perception and Psychophysics, 8,* 279-286.
Berlyne, D. E. (1974). *Studies in the new experimental aesthetics.* John New York: Wiley and Sons.
Bornstein, R. F. (1989). Exposure and affect: Overview and meta-analysis of research, 1968-1987. *Psychological Bulletin, 106*(2), 265-289.
Broadbent, D. (1958). *Perception and communication.* New York: Pergamon Press.
Cupchik, G. C. (1992). From perception to production: A multilevel analysis of the aesthetic process. In G. C. Cupchik & J. Laszlo (Eds.), *Emerging visions of the aesthetic process.* New York: Cambridge University Press.
Fechner, G. T. (1871). *Vorschule der Ästhetik.* Hildesheim: Olms.
Gordon, P. C., & Holyoak, K. J. (1983). Implicit learning and generalisation of the "mere exposure" effect. *Journal of Personality and Social Psychology, 45,* 492-500.
Grasskamp, W. (1989). *Die unbewältigte Moderne. Kunst und Öffentlichkeit* (The unmastered moderne: Art and public). München: Beck.
Hartley, J., & Homa, D. (1981). Abstraction of stylistic concepts. *Journal of Experimental Psychology: Learning, Memory, and Cognition, 7,* 33-46.

Hasenfus, N., Martindale, C., & Birnbaum, D. (1983). Psychological reality of cross-media artistic styles. *Journal of Experimental Psychology, 9*(6), 841-863.

Hekkert, P., & van Wieringen, P. C. W. (1990). Complexity and prototypicality as determinants of the appraisal of cubist paintings. *British Journal of Psychology, 81,* 483-495.

Höge, H. (1995). Fechners Experimental Aesthetics and the Golden Section hypothesis today. *Empirical Studies of the Arts, 13,* 131-148.

Kant, I. (1968). *Kritik der Urtheilskraft* (Critique of pure reason). N. K. Smith (trans.). Available online at: http://www.arts.cuhk.edu.hk/Philosophy/Kant/cpr).

Kreitler, H., & Kreitler, S. (1972). *Psychology of the arts.* Durham: Duke University Press.

Kreitler, H., & Kreitler, S. (1984). Meaning assignment in perception. In W. D. Fröhlich, J. G. Smith, & U. Hentschel (Eds.), *Psychological processes in cognition and personality* (pp. 173-191). Washington: Hemisphere Publishing.

Kunst-Wilson, W. R., & Zajonc, R. B. (1980). Affective discrimination of stimuli that cannot be recognized. *Science, 207,* 557-558.

Leder, H. (1994). *Information processing of portraits.* Presentation, XII. IAEA-Congress, Montreal.

Leder, H. (1996). Line drawings of faces reduce configural processing. *Perception, 25,* 355-366.

Leder, H. (2002). *Explorationen in der Bildästhetik* (Explorations in visual aesthetics). Lengerich: Pabst.

Leder, H., Belke, B., Oeberst, A., & Augustin, D. (2004). A model of aesthetic appreciation and aesthetic judgements. *British Journal of Psychology, 95,* 489-508.

Locher, P., & Nodine, C. (1987). Symmetry catches the eye. In J. K. O'Regan & A. Levy-Schoen (Eds.), *Eye movements: From physiology to cognition.* Dordrecht: North Holland Press.

Locher, P. J. (2003). An empirical investigation of the Visual Rightness Theory of picture perception. *Acta Psychologica, 114,* 147-164.

Martindale, C. (1984). The pleasures of thought: A theory of cognitive hedonics. *The Journal of Mind and Behavior, 5,* 49-80.

Martindale, C., & Moore, K. (1988). Priming, prototypicality, and preference. *Journal of Experimental Psychology: Human Perception and Performance, 14,* 661-670.

Parsons, M. J. (1987). *How we understand art: A cognitive developmental account of aesthetic experience.* Cambridge: Cambridge University Press.

Ramachandran, V. S., & Hirstein, W. (1999). The science of art. *Journal of Consciousness Studies, 6*(6-7), 15-51.

Reber, R., Winkielman, P., & Schwarz, N. (1998). Effects of perceptual fluency on affective judgments. *Psychological Science, 9,* 45-48.

Shiff, R. (1986). *Cézanne and the end of impressionism: A study of the theory, technique, and critical evaluation.* Chicago: University of Chicago Press.

Solso, R. L. (1994). *Cognition and the visual arts.* Cambridge: MIT Press.

Tyler, C. W. (1999). Is art lawful? *Journal of Consciousness Studies, 6,* 673-674.
Vartanian, O., & Goel, V. (2004). Emotion pathways in the brain mediate aesthetic preference. *Bulletin of Psychology and the Arts, 5*(1), 37-42.
Winston, A. S., & Cupchik, G. C. (1992). The evaluation of high art and popular art by naive and experienced viewers. *Visual Arts Research, 18,* 1-14.
Wundt, W. M. (1874). *Grundzüge der physiologischen Psychologie* [Principles of physiological psychology]. Leipzig: Engelmann.
Zajonc, R. B. (1968). Attitudinal effects of mere exposure. *Journal of Personality and Social Psychology Monograph Supplements, 9*(2, Pt.2), 1-27.
Zeki, S. (1999). *Inner vision.* Oxford: Oxford University Press.

CHAPTER 11

Literary Creativity: A Neuropsychoanalytic View

Norman N. Holland

> This is a gift that I have, simple; simple, a foolish extravagant spirit, full of forms, figures, shapes, objects, ideas, apprehensions, motions, revolutions. These are begot in the ventricle of memory, nourished in the womb of pia mater, and delivered upon the mellowing of occasion. But the gift is good in those in whom it is acute, and I am thankful for it.
> —William Shakespeare, *Love's Labor's Lost*, 4.2

"Neuropsychoanalysis" is a term that has tumbled newly into the world, and I should explain. We have two perplexingly different things going on inside our skulls: brain processes and mind processes. Although our neurons are just cells spritzing neurotransmitters at one another, they enable our minds to do things as complex as laughing at Holofernes' pedantic preening in the passage above.

Descartes concluded that mind and brain were two entirely different kinds of stuff and gave us "dualism." By contrast, "neuropsychoanalysis" proceeds from what Mark Solms (a leader in the field) has called "dual-aspect monism." That is, we are made of one kind of stuff (cells), but we can study this stuff in two different ways, neurologically and psychoanalytically (Solms & Turnbull, 2002, pp. 45-78).

The neurologist observes "mind" from outside; that is, by means of the neurological examination: questionnaires, the Boston Naming test or Wisconsin Sorting, bisecting lines, acting out how you use a screwdriver, and other "objective" observations and measures. The neurologist compares what such a neurological examination shows with associated changes in the brain, either postmortem or by means of modern imaging technology.

Then there is the layman's (or Descartes' or the psychoanalyst's) way. We can observe "subjectively," from inside a mind, how we feel and what we think. Freud refined this kind of observation into free association, the most powerful technique that we have for perceiving complex mental functions that simple introspection cannot reveal. Cole Porter (1933) contrasted the two ways in a lyric about a lady whose love for her doctor is unrequited:

> He said my cerebellum was brilliant,
> My cerebrum was far from N. G.
>   I know he thought a lotta
>   My medulla oblongata
> But he never said he loved *me*!

"[A] living creature," Oliver Sacks (1984) has wisely written, "and especially a human being is first and last . . . a subject, not an object. It is precisely the subject, the living 'I,' which is excluded from neurology" (Sacks, 1984, p. 164).

Neuropsychoanalysis uses both the neurologist's toolkit and the analyst's. That is, neuropsychoanalysts will investigate cerebellum, cerebrum, and medulla oblongata. They will also consider, though, by means of transference and free association, the words neurological patients choose to express their states of mind. In effect, Descartes' dualistic terms "mind" and "brain" become two ways of looking at the one thing, the mysterious interacting of brain cells that makes consciousness and mind.

With this combined approach, neuropsychoanalysis can look experimentally at brain systems and structures for how they might correspond to traditional psychoanalytic ideas like id, ego, and superego, repression, impulsivity, compulsivity, or, what is important for creativity, regression. Applying neuropsychoanalysis to literature, then, and to my topic, literary creativity, means looking both subjectively and objectively, from inside and from outside.

Alas, most people who write from inside about creativity get very mushy. And indeed that magic moment when you are writing and you hit upon just the right word or the ingeniously perfect turn of plot—such a moment does indeed seem a gift from the gods, mysterious, and a little crazy. The mushiness lies in ignoring the hard work that has to go before the magic, the writer's preparation, the years of training and practice and rejection and the hard work that has to go after, like getting an agent and a publisher, coaxing blurbs from rival authors, or wangling a spot in Oprah's Book Club.

The writer's hard work, though, doesn't differ from other forms of hard work. It is the magic moment, not what comes before or after, that interests psychologists and neuropsychoanalysts. William James (1880) described it as "divergent thinking," the opposite of "convergent thinking," our ordinary problem solving that homes in on one definite answer. "Instead of thoughts of concrete things patiently following one another . . . we have . . . the most unheard of combination of elements, the subtlest associations of analogy . . . a seething cauldron of ideas, where everything is fizzling and bobbling about in a state of bewildering activity" (James, 1880, p. 453). More soberly, Colin Martindale (1999), in an excellent review of the subject, wrote of "the discovery of new combinations of mental elements" (Martindale, 1999, p. 138). Neuropsychologist Kenneth Heilman (2002, 2005) has published a fine book on the neuropsychology of creativity. He suggests that all creativity (both the scientist's and the artist's) is alike in that *all creativity involves making connections between disparate ideas that seemed to have no connection with one another.* He speaks of connecting the previously unconnected and of "unity in diversity," a term traditional among writers on the arts (Beardsley, 1958).

From the psychoanalytic side of neuropsychoanalysis, although scattered through his writings, Freud did give a coherent account of artists' and writers' creativity (see Holland, 1966, ch. 2). He offered as explanation of the mystery of creative inspiration, "flexibility of repression" or "lack of inhibition." Artists and writers have an "extraordinary capacity for sublimating the primitive instincts," "a certain degree of laxity in the repressions which are decisive for a conflict."

Ernst Kris (1952) wrote the formulation that most psychoanalytic critics accept and repeat like a mantra. Creativity is "regression in the service of the ego" (p. 177 and *passim*), akin to dreaming or daydreaming. That is, to be creative, one lets ideas and feelings percolate up from the deeper parts of one's mind. As essayist, Louis Menand (2004), writes of writing: "You have to wait, and what you are waiting for is something inside you to come up with the words" (Menand, 2004, p. 104).

In Kris' phrasing, one regresses, that is, one goes back to early or even childish thoughts and earlier ways of dealing with thoughts. One puts aside ordinary problem solving or reality testing, the kind of thing that comes before or after the magic moment. Instead, one lets unconscious, wishful fantasizing take over. In his summary, Martindale (1999) shows that a good deal of evidence from conventional psychological studies of creative people supports Kris' view.

From the neurological side, Martindale's 1999 summary points to three elements in the relation between brain function and the magic moment of creativity: low levels of cortical activation, comparatively more right- than left-hemisphere activation, and low levels of frontal lobe activation. Highly creative individuals do not show all these characteristics in general, but only when solving creative problems. Martindale (1999) also speaks of defocused attention: "If one can attend to only two things at the same time, only one possible analogy can be discovered at that time; if one could attend to four things at once, six possible analogies could be discovered, and so on" (Martindale, 1999, p. 139).

Kenneth Heilman (2005) comes by way of neurology to a similar, if less arithmetical, conclusion. He notes that, today, most neurologists acknowledge that our brains consist of anatomically distinct systems that perform specific operations (like, say, picking the phonemes out of a stream of sound). The various forms of intelligence (musical, mathematical, verbal, athletic, and so on) are *modular*. Apparently, these modules are loosely connected in our brains. Then, "Creativity may be achieved by applying networks representing internal models in one domain of knowledge to other networks that contain domains of knowledge which share some attributes" (Heilman, 2005, ch. 8). When creative people bring disparate ideas together, Heilman suggests, they are using one module to activate another normally unrelated module.

Similarly, Norbert Jaušovec concluded:

> It seems that creative thinking requires a broader cooperation between different brain areas. . . . The idea that during creative problem solving respondents displayed less mental activity is rather appealing, as it can be brought in relation to subconscious processes and defocused attention. The second finding, namely, that creative thinking required a broader cooperation between brain areas—especially cooperation between frontal, parietal, and occipital areas of the left hemisphere—seems also congruent with creative theories which have stressed the importance of conceiving two or more opposites and combining it in a whole—a gestalt (Jaušovec, 2002, pp. 205-206).

In short, the idea is that the magic moment of creativity, the making of unity from diversity, activates a wider spread of regions and modules in the brain than ordinary thinking can support. Can we say more about the brain activity involved?

Recent lines of experiment suggest something special about the neurotransmitters that enable this wider, horizontal spread across a creative person's brain. Kischka and his associates found that administering L-dopa to subjects made them less likely to connect distantly related words (Kischka et al., 1996). L-dopa reduced the spread of activation processes in semantic networks. It reduced what we might call the sudden connection of modules associated with an "Aha!" In effect, L-dopa reduced creativity.

In the body, however, L-dopa becomes transformed to dopamine, and dopamine activation means the subject will focus on foraging among outside stimuli instead of heeding imaginings and inspirations from within. Dopamine is associated with novelty seeking. It increases signal-to-noise ratio in the brain or, less technically, it increases our attention to outer stimuli and decreases our attention to ideation coming from inside our brains.

Heilman (2005) suggests, however, that the effect does not come from dopamine itself. He points to a different neurotransmitter in the neurochemical cascade that transforms L-dopa to dopamine; namely, norepinephrine. To promote an inspirational moment in creativity, we would want a *de*crease in dopamine but, more generally, all our catecholamines, especially, Heilman (2005, ch. 8) suggests, norepinephrine.

The norepinephrinic system (or, in the U.K., the noradrenergic) affects arousal, alertness, and attention. It generates the "fight or flight" response to stress. Psychologists have long established that stress (beyond that required for intense alertness) impairs performance on cognitive tests and tests of creativity or, to use the term neuropsychologists use, "cognitive flexibility." Students, nervous at being tested, can improve their grades by limiting norepinephrine. (Thus, teenagers, anxious about taking the SAT, were given propanolol, a beta-blocker commonly used to treat high blood pressure by reducing stress hormones and neurotransmitters [Faigel 1991]. Their scores improved by a mean of 130 points! *Verbum sapienti*.)

Heilman (2005) infers that this beta blockade, by reducing the influence of norepinephrine, allowed spreading and larger networks. Cholinergic neurons in the basal forebrain generate norepinephrine and so modulate cortical arousal. (Heilman [2005, ch. 8] singles out the nucleus basalis of Meynert, the diagonal band of Broca, and the medial septum.) The more norepinephrine, the more arousal. He cites research showing that injecting norepinephrine into the basal forebrain induced high frequency brain waves. (This happens during play when animals become especially alert to novelty in their environment.)

The norepinephrine decreased the slow alpha waves that, Colin Martindale and Nancy Hasenfus (1978) have shown, facilitate creativity. They compared more creative with less creative people. In the resting state, they showed no differences in their brains' electrical activity as indicated by EEGs. But during an "innovation stage," the creatives had more alpha brain waves (8-12 cycles per second) than noncreative people. The higher alpha outputs showed they were operating at a *lower level of arousal* at moments of inner creativity (see also Cape & Jones, 1998). "When asked to be original . . . creative people exhibit defocused attention accompanied by low levels of cortical activation" (Martindale, 1999, pp. 141-142).

Heilman (2005, ch. 8) goes on to cite several studies that have shown that increasing norepinephrine decreases the spontaneous activity from within the brain's networks relative to their activity stimulated from without. Neuropsychologists speak of signal-to-noise ratio. But activity from within (noise) one would associate with "Aha!" thinking and "illumination." Activity from without (signal) one would associate with alertness to opportunities in one's environment (Hasselmo, Linster, Patil, Daveena, & Cekic, 1997; Servan-Schreiber, Printz, & Cohen, 1990; Waterhouse & Woodward, 1980). One would not associate activity toward the outer world with inspiration from within. Hence, a *de*crease in norepinephrine, which is associated with states of dreaming, resting, or relaxing (McCarley, 1982), would yield precisely the states of mind needed for that special moment of "illumination" (Martindale, 1999, p. 149).

What controls the amount of circulating norepinephrine? The locus coeruleus, the "blue place" in the brain stem. This tiny bilateral nucleus in the pons spreads norepinephrine widely throughout the brain. The locus coeruleus projects to the limbic system, the thalamus, and the cerebral cortex, and especially to the inferior parietal lobes that are so important in attentional processing. It probably, according to Heilman and others, innervates a greater variety of brain areas than any other single nucleus. High levels of activity in the locus coeruleus make us more alert and favor "bottom-up," stimulus-driven attention to novelty. In particular, this norepinephrine system activates the regions involved in spatial analysis and visuomotor processing (Foote, Berridge, Adams, & Pineda, 1991; Heilman, 2005, ch. 8; Morrison & Foote, 1986).

If high levels of locus coeruleus activity focus us outward, Heilman speculates, the opposite, low levels, would therefore favor inward attention. A less energized locus coeruleus would lead to less norepinephrine which would lead to "top-down" processing, processing driven from within, that would in turn favor the "Aha!" stage of creativity (Aston-Jones, Chiang, & Alexinsky, 1991; Heilman, 2005, ch. 8).

The locus coeruleus is both "phasically" and "tonically" active. That is, it shows spasmodic activity as well as steady. Heilman (2005) suggests that the phasic, transient mode would favor alertness and attention to new outside stimuli, while the tonic, steady mode would lead to wide scanning rather than focused attention. The tonic mode would thus favor the "illumination" or "inspiration" aspect of creativity. The phasic mode would favor the more prosaic and practical aspects of creativity (Heilman, 2005, ch. 8).

But, then, what controls the locus coeruleus? The dorsolateral frontal lobes. The dorsolateral frontal lobes can start or inhibit the chemical cascade that creates dopamine which in turn ends by creating norepinephrine, essential for the stress reaction. It is the dorsolateral frontal lobes, with their ability to delay response to outer stimuli, that allow the brain's activities to focus on internal matters. It is the executive function of the dorsolateral frontal lobes that can switch one module so it connects, not to a stimulus from outside, but to another module inside.

Experiments by Arnsten and Goldman-Rakic (1984) suggest "that the dorsal prefrontal cortex may be the only cortical area to have direct influence on the LC and raphe nuclei and secondary influence on the monoaminergic innervation of large areas of cerebral cortex" (Arnsten & Goldman-Rakic, 1984, p. 9). More specifically, it is the dorsolateral frontal lobes and the dorsal anterior cingulate gyrus, particularly in the right hemisphere (Liotti & Mayberg, 2001), that control the locus coeruleus. These are regions in the brain devoted to planning, decision making, and choosing among possible motor activities. They therefore activate and deactivate the locus coeruleus, and they thereby change the amounts of norepinephrine in the brain and hence the propensity to act. Heilman (2005) speculates:

> Reduced activity in these frontal and cingulate regions, by virtue of reduced input to locus coeruleus, could provide the basis for reductions of cortical norepinephrine, associated reductions in signal-to-noise ratio and the recruitment of widely distributed networks that contain a rich variety of representations. Whereas depression might lead to creative innovation, verification and production [the later, final, outer-directed stages in creation—nnh] are associated with high arousal, and thus these stages of creativity often must await the resolution of depression (Heilman, 2005, ch. 8, citing Damasio 1996).

In short, when we are motivated to act or plan we may be effective vis-à-vis the outer world, but we are not in the relaxed, perhaps even slightly depressed, state that allows for inner illumination, inspiration, and innovation. Conversely, when we are relaxed and open to inspiration, we are not marketing the novel. And which state we are in depends on how much norepinephrine is coursing through our brains. That in turn depends (via the locus coeruleus) on whether or not the frontal lobes are focused on some action or plan for action and are therefore inhibiting the possibly creative or possibly confusing minglings of disparate ideas. In other words, the norepinephrine hypothesis accords with the finding by other researchers of creativity coming from reduced frontal lobe inhibition (Jaušovec, 2000, 2002; Jaušovec & Jaušovec, 2000; Martindale, 1999).

Exploring Heilman's hypotheses about creativity, he and some of his co-workers tested people's ability to solve puzzles under the influence of three different drugs. One was a placebo. The second was ephedrine, which increases the levels of norepinephrine. The third was propranolol. This is the beta-blocker that was administered to the nervous students taking the SAT, that decreases norepinephrine. The experimenters asked their subjects to solve anagrams (for example, KPNNIA or LNHPDIO) as a way to test cognitive flexibility. The drugs that modulated the noradrenergic system affected both the speed and the ability to do the task successfully. With drugs that produced less activity in the norepinephrinic (noradrenergic) system, the subjects did better. They showed more cognitive flexibility and presumably, therefore, more creativity. The experiment tends to confirm that norepinephrine biases frontal lobe processing away from cognitive flexibility and hence away from the inspiration phase of creativity.

> Our results may also explain the 'moment of insight' experiences where a difficult problem is repeatedly approached with effort, only to have the solution come later at a moment of rest, such as just before falling asleep. These moments of insight would therefore occur when arousal and noradrenergic activation are . . . at their nadir (Beversdorf, Hughes, Steinberg, Lewis, & Heilman, 1999, p. 2767; Heilman, Nadeau, & Beversdorf, 2003).

Some indirect confirmation of Heilman's (2004) norepinephrine hypothesis comes from research into depression. Depression is associated with reduced cerebral blood flow to the dorsolateral prefrontal cortex and anterior cingulate (Liotti & Mayberg, 2001). Reduced activity in these regions would lead to reduced input to locus coeruleus and therefore reduction of cortical norepinephrine, reductions in signal-to-noise ratio, and recruitment of widely distributed rather than focused networks. This would lead to the flaccid state of mind receptive to inner inspiration.

Heilman's norepinephrine hypothesis would then explain the apparent links between creativity and depression or bipolar disorder, reported widely in the literature (Jamison, 1989, 1993). Depression or bipolar does not cause creativity. Rather, both stem from a common source: low concentrations of norepinephrine. The brain configuration that favors creativity, unfortunately, favors depression, too.

The traditional lore about creativity also tends to confirm the norepinephrine hypothesis. Again and again, writers on creativity point to Kekulé's discovering the benzene ring through dreaming of a snake with its tail in its mouth. Archimedes shouted his "Eureka!" from the bathtub. Newton conceived of gravity while sitting under an apple tree, and Buddha had his moment of enlightenment under the bo tree. These inspirational moments came at times of relaxation after intense work when less norepinephrine was secreted because of that relaxation.

With a general term like relaxation, we can turn from neuropsychology back to the psychoanalytic side of a neuropsychoanalytic inquiry. I left off the psychoanalytic theories with Ernst Kris' (1952) "regression in the service of the ego." Now we can see what that regression (perhaps all regression) is in a brain sense. We have less of the neurotransmitters driving the systems searching for real-world satisfactions of need. We have more activity in the medial and subcortical regions of our brains that come into being earlier in the development of the individual and the species. These are regions associated with dreaming, daydreaming, and fantasying (Kaplan-Solms & Solms, 2000).

To explore this state of mind psychoanalytically, the question is, what do we hear when we listen (with the proverbial third ear) to people describing their creative moments? I think we hear two (at least two) things.

First, one needs to be passive (as in Heilman's relaxation). I have already cited Louis Menand's (2004) waiting for something to come up from inside, but Keats' statement is classic: "At once it struck me, what quality went to form a Man of Achievement especially in Literature & which Shakespeare possessed so enormously—I mean *Negative Capability*, that is, when a man is capable of being in uncertainties, Mysteries, doubts, without any irritable reaching after fact & reason" (Keats, 1958, 2.213).

Second (and parallel to that motif of passivity), although common sense tells us that an artist's ideas come from the artist, tradition sometimes attributes them to some outside force: a Muse or one of Henry James' "germs" or inspiration (a breathing into) from the gods. Writers and artists themselves say it is not clear whether the creative idea has come from inside or outside. Matisse, for example, said, "I had become possessed by painting and could not abstain . . . something drove me, I do not know what, a force, something alien to my normal life as a man" (Flam, 1995, p. 83). And this is Shelley in "The Defense of Poetry": "Poetry is not like reasoning, a power to be exerted according to the determination of the will. A man cannot say, 'I will compose poetry.' The greatest poet even cannot say it; for the mind in creation is as a fading coal, which some invisible influence, like an inconstant wind, awakens to transitory brightness." So, too, Charlotte Brontë wrote in the 1850 preface to *Wuthering Heights:* "But this I know; the writer who possesses the creative gift owns something of which he is not always master—something that at times strangely wills and works for itself. . . . If the result be attractive, the World will praise you, who little deserve praise; if it be repulsive, the same World will blame you, who almost as little deserve blame" (Sale & Dunn, 1990, p. 322).

From a psychoanalytic point of view, this state, passively waiting for something which may be outside oneself or inside—it's not clear which—duplicates an earlier phase of the human lifespan. These words apply not just to the creative person but also to a baby waiting for its mother to bring nurturance. As described by such baby-watchers as Lynne Murray (1998), Colwyn Trevarthen (1993), or Louis Sander (Condon & Sander, 1974), a baby has a kind of fusion with the mother, moving its limbs in time to her speech, making its facial expressions correspond to hers, responding to her timing with its own, and generally forming an interactive biological system with its caregiver. In the process, the infant develops the systems of affect regulation that will govern its life from then on (Schore, 1994).

The pediatrician and psychoanalyst D. W. Winnicott (1980) described this state of mind as a "potential space."

> From the beginning the baby has maximally intense experiences *in the potential space between the subjective object and the object objectively perceived,* between me-extensions and the not-me.
>
> . . . an intermediate area of *experiencing,* to which inner reality and external life both contribute. It is an area that is not challenged, because no claim is made on its behalf except that it shall exist as a resting-place for the individual engaged in the perpetual human task of keeping inner and outer reality separate yet interrelated.
>
> This intermediate area of experience, unchallenged in respect of its belonging to inner or external (shared) reality, constitutes the greater part of the infant's experience, and throughout life is retained in the intense experiencing that belongs to the arts and to religion and to imaginative living, and to creative scientific work (Winnicott, 1980, pp. 2, 14, 100).

In other words, the artist in a state of relaxation awaiting inspiration from a muse recapitulates the situation of a baby waiting for nurturance from a mother, not clearly defined as within self or not-self. But, of course, this magic moment phase is only part of the artist's state of mind.

I've written one novel, and I won't for a moment claim that it is great literature (Holland, 1995). Writing it, though, did give me a sense of how creativity toggles between deliberate planning—this will work, that won't—and a more mysterious, more satisfying, and (unfortunately) more occasional phase in which ideas just come.

Our brains seesaw. That is, our brains have limited capacity, and if one function is up, another is likely to be down. Greater attention to stimuli coming from without means less attention to stimuli coming from within. I am suggesting that perhaps that particular seesaw moves more easily and quickly in the creative brain of a writer than in, say, an ordinary reader's brain.

Freud thought writers and artists had "a strong capacity for sublimation and a certain degree of laxity in the repressions which are decisive for a conflict." I think that translates into neuropsychological terms. *Artists and writers can with ease swing back and forth from a strongly reality-oriented thinking-and-planning mode to a relaxation into fantasy.* Possibly, then, the gift of creativity includes an ability to switch the reality orientation of the dopaminergic, reward-seeking system more easily than the rest of us. Possibly the switching among modules that Heilman and others describe corresponds to Freud's "flexibility of repression." Possibly the gift of creativity consists simply in the ability to turn norepinephrine on and off more easily.

Even so, in creating, writers toggle between that early infantile state of passivity and fusion (and perhaps reduced norepinephrine) and the very adult state of deploying a sophisticated repertoire of cognitive skills developed in childhood and far beyond. Then, too, however rational and adult those cognitive skills may be, they will nevertheless express the whole development of the individual from infancy to the moment of writing. *Le style c'est l'homme même*, in Buffon's endlessly cited formula. Writers write with a characteristic style that expresses their personality—as a century of psychoanalytic literary criticism has shown and as William James (1880, p. 454) pointed out long ago:

> According to the idiosyncrasy of the individual, the scintillations [of divergent thinking] will have one character or another. They will be sallies for wit and humor; they will be flashes of poetry and eloquence; they will be constructions of dramatic fiction or of mechanical device, logical or philosophic abstractions, business projects, or scientific hypotheses, with trains of experimental consequences based thereon; they will be musical sounds, or images of

plastic beauty or picturesqueness or visions of moral harmony. But, whatever their differences may be, they will all agree in this,—that their genesis is sudden and, as it were, spontaneous. That is to say, the same premises would not, in the mind of another individual, have engendered just that conclusion.

Artists and scientists and other creatives do not then simply have a talent or access to a certain odd state of mind. *Creative people have a talent for a particular style of creation.* And this style is linked to their core identity, itself embodied in corticolimbic pathways in the brain (Schore, 1994).

Allan N. Schore (1994) has marshalled an impressive array of evidence from neurobiology and developmental neurochemistry about the early fit between nurturing mother (or "primary caregiver") and nursing infant. Feeding, handling, bathing, babytalk, the gaze—all these constitute an intricate dance between caregiver and care receiver that affect the growing neurological system. Schore's evidence leads him to conclude that the day-by-day and hour-by-hour fit between baby and mother writes patterns into the infant's brain. Specifically, the right hemisphere, which in most people governs visuospatial organization, notably the recognizing of faces and emotional expressions, develops faster after birth than the left hemisphere. Until the left hemisphere with its handling of sequence and language (in most people) takes over in the third year, the right hemisphere dominates. Therefore the mother/infant transactions write especially to the right brain, which is developing the child's self-regulation of its emotions and relationships, the core of its identity. In effect, that early relationship becomes imprinted on the right orbitofrontal cortex, which is interconnected with a number of subcortical systems. It is, in effect, the hierarchical apex of the limbic system and the major cerebral system involved in social, emotional, and self-regulatory processes. While Schore's (1994) work must be taken as hypothesis rather than established fact, he nevertheless offers an evidenced and reasonable picture of the development of a neuronally configured identity theme in psychoanalyst Heinz Lichtenstein's (1961) sense.

That is, Lichtenstein (1961) observed a core pattern of being around which later developments took place (Holland, 2000; Lichtenstein, 1961). Lichtenstein saw this "identity theme" as coming from the infant's adaptation to be the baby for this particular mother. And, as is well established, after infancy the brain goes through astonishing growth during the prepubescent years, and then that extra growth dies off during adolescence (Purves & Lichtman, 1985). Experience governs what grows and what doesn't, and experience at that early age is mostly of parents. In this way, parenting and other experiences write a character or identity or personal style in our brains. But to thoroughly develop that idea and its relation to a creative style would take another—and quite long—article.

More briefly, creations emerging from the magic moment (or infantile fusion or reduced norepinephrine) will express a style born in infancy. But they will also draw on adult skills grown around and within that core style. They will also use the creative person's personal take on the tastes and intellectual demands of the time. The psychoanalytic side of a neuropsychoanalytic investigation of creativity tells us that in the magic moment, the creative person accesses a very early infantile state of mind, but also a style of creation developed from childhood on and attuned to the adult's environment. A creative person will be continually running up and down that temporal or longitudinal scale.

Finally then, a neuropsychoanalytic view of that special moment of literary creativity (or creativity in general) suggests that the mind expands (or the brain opens connections) in two directions. From the neurological side, we get the picture of a lot of new, but temporary connections among diverse modules in an adult brain. I think of these as a horizontal expansion. By contrast, from the psychoanalytic side, we get the picture of a vertical expansion up and down from the earliest and innermost parts of our brains or minds to the latest. And none of this, of course, changes our feeling that that magic moment is a gift from the gods, mysterious, and perhaps a little crazy.

REFERENCES

Arnsten, A. F., & Goldman-Rakic, P. S. (1984). Selective prefrontal cortical projections to the region of the locus coeruleus and raphe nuclei in the rhesus monkey. *Brain Research, 306,* 9-18.

Aston-Jones, G., Chiang, C., & Alexinsky, T. (1991). Discharge of noradrenergic locus coeruleus neurons in behaving rats and monkeys suggests a role in vigilance. *Progress in Brain Research, 88,* 501-520.

Beardsley, M. (1958). *Aesthetics.* New York: Harcourt Brace.

Beversdorf, D. Q., Hughes, J. D., Steinberg, B. A., Lewis, L., & Heilman, K. M. (1999). Noradrenergic modulation of cognitive flexibility in problem solving. *NeuroReport, 10,* 2763-2767.

Cape, E. G., & Jones, E. B. (1998). Differential modulation of high-frequency gamma-electroencephalogram activity and sleep-wake state by noradrenaline and serotonin microinjections into the region of cholinergic basalis neurons. *Journal of Neuroscience, 18,* 2653-2656.

Condon, W. S., & Sander, L. W. (1974). Neonate movement is synchronised with adult speech: Interactional participation and language acquisition. *Science, 183,* 99-101.

Damasio, A. R. (1996). The somatic marker hypothesis and the possible functions of the prefrontal cortex. *Philosophical Transactions of the Royal Society of London: B Biological Sciences, 351,* 1413-1420.

Faigel, H. C. (1991). The effect of beta blockade on stress-induced cognitive dysfunction in adolescents. *Clinical Pediatrics, 30,* 446-448.

Flam, J. D. (1995). *Matisse on art.* Berkeley: University of California Press.

Foote, S. L., Berridge, C. W., Adams, L. M., & Pineda, J. A. (1991). Electrophysiological evidence for the involvement of the locus coeruleus in alerting, orienting, and attending. *Progress in Brain Research, 88,* 521-532.

Hasselmo, M. E., Linster, C., Patil, M., Daveena, M., & Cekic, M. (1997). Noradrenergic suppression of synaptic transmission may influence cortical signal-to-noise ratio. *Journal of Neurophysiology, 77,* 3326-3339.

Heilman, K. M. (2002). Defining creativity [Lecture, McKnight Brain Institute at the University of Florida].

Heilman, K. M. (2005). *Creativity and the brain.* New York: Psychology Press.

Heilman, K. M., Nadeau, S. E., & Beversdorf, D. O. (2003). Creative innovation: Possible brain mechanisms. *Neurocase, 9,* 369-379.

Holland, N. N. (1966). *Psychoanalysis and Shakespeare.* New York: McGraw-Hill.

Holland, N. N. (1995). *Death in a Delphi seminar.* Albany, NY: SUNY Press.

Holland, N. N. (2000). *Poems in persons: A psychology of the literary process* (Rev. ed.). Christchurch, NZ: Cybereditions. (Accessed May 31, 2001) (http://www.cybereditions.com).

James, W. (1880). Great men, great thoughts, and the environment. *Atlantic Monthly, 46,* 441-459.

Jamison, K. R. (1989). Mood disorders and patterns of creativity in British writers and artists. *Psychiatry, 52,* 125-134.

Jamison, K. R. (1993). *Touched with fire: Manic-depressive illness and the artistic temperament.* New York: Free Press.

Jaušovec, N. (2000). Differences in cognitive processes between gifted, intelligent, creative, and average individuals while solving complex problems: An EEG study. *Intelligence, 28,* 213-237.

Jaušovec, N. (2002). Neuropsychological bases of creativity. In S. P. Shohov (Ed.), *Advances in psychology research* (Vol. 15, pp. 193–219). New York: Nova Science.

Jaušovec, N., & Jaušovec, K. (2000). EEG activity during the performance of complex mental problems. *International Journal of Psychophysiology, 36,* 73-88.

Kaplan-Solms, K., & Solms, M. (2000). *Clinical studies in neuro-psychoanalysis: Introduction to a depth neuropsychology.* London: Karnac Books.

Keats, J. (1958). *The letters of John Keats* (2 vols.). H. E. Rollins (Ed.). Cambridge, MA: Harvard University Press.

Kischka, U., Kammer, T., Maier, S., Weisbrod, M., Thimm, M., & Spitzer, M. (1996). Dopaminergic modulation of semantic network activation. *Neuropsychologia, 34,* 1107-1113.

Kris, E. (1952). *Psychoanalytic explorations in art*. New York: International Universities Press.
Lichtenstein, H. (1961). Identity and sexuality: A study of their interrelationship in man. *Journal of the American Psychoanalytic Association, 9*, 179-260.
Liotti, M., & Mayberg, H. S. (2001). The role of functional neuroimaging in the neuropsychology of depression. *Journal of Clinical and Experimental Neuropsychology, 23*, 121-136.
Martindale, C. (1999). Biological bases of creativity. In R. J. Sternberg (Ed.), *Handbook of creativity* (pp. 137-152). New York: Cambridge University Press.
Martindale, C., & Hasenfus, N. (1978). EEG differences as a function of creativity, stage of the creative process, and effort to be original. *Biological Psychology, 6*, 157-167.
McCarley, R. W. (1982). REM sleep and depression: Common neurobiological control mechanisms. *American Journal of Psychiatry, 139*, 565-570.
Menand, L. (2004). Bad comma [Review of Lynne Truss, *Eats, Shoots and Leaves*]. *The New Yorker*, pp. 102-104.
Morrison, J. H., & Foote, S. L. (1986). Noradrenergic and serotoninergic innervation of cortical, thalamic, and tectal visual structures in Old and New World monkeys. *Journal of Comparative Neurology, 243*, 117-138.
Murray, L. (1998). Contributions of experimental and clinical perturbations of mother-infant communication to the understanding of infant intersubjectivity. In S. Bråten (Ed.), *Intersubjective communication and emotion in early ontogeny* (pp. 127-143). Studies in emotion and social interaction, 2nd series. Paris and Cambridge UK: Cambridge University Press/Editions de la Maison des Sciences de l'Homme.
Porter, C. (1933/1978). The physician. In *The Cole Porter years*. New York: Warner Bros. n.p.
Purves, D., & Lichtman, J. W. (1985). *Principles of neural development*. Sunderland MA: Sinauer Associates.
Sacks, O. (1984). *A leg to stand on*. New York: Summit Books/Simon and Schuster.
Sale, W. M. Jr., & Dunn, R. J. (Eds.). (1990). *Wuthering Heights: Authoritative text, backgrounds, criticism* (3rd ed., A Norton Critical Edition). New York: Norton.
Schore, A. N. (1994). *Affect regulation and the origin of the self: The neurobiology of emotional development*. Hillsdale, NJ: Lawrence Erlbaum.
Servan-Schreiber, D., Printz, H., & Cohen, J. D. (1990). A network model of catecholamine effects: Gain, signal-to-noise ratio, and behavior. *Science, 249*, 892-895.
Shakespeare, W. (1595/1974). *Love's Labor's Lost*, In G. B. Evans (Ed.), *The Riverside Shakespeare* (pp. 174-216). Boston: Houghton Mifflin.
Solms, M., & Turnbull, O. (2002). *The brain and the inner world: An introduction to the neuroscience of subjective experience*. New York: Other Press.

Trevarthen, C. (1993). The self born in intersubjectivity: The psychology of an infant communicating. In U. Neisser (Ed.), *The perceived self: Ecological and interpersonal sources of self-knowledge* (pp. 121-173). New York: Cambridge University Press.

Waterhouse, B. D., & Woodward, D. J. (1980). Interaction of norepinephrine with cerebrocortical activity evoked by stimulation of somatosensory afferent pathways in the rat. *Experimental Neurology, 67*, 11-34.

Winnicott, D. W. (1980). *Playing and reality*. London and New York: Tavistock Publications.

CHAPTER 12

A Neural-Network Theory of Beauty

Colin Martindale

Baumgarten (1750) coined the term "aesthetics." He defined aesthetics as the science of "sensory cognition." By "natural aesthetics" he meant sensory cognition due to innate or unsystematic working of the sensory and perceptual apparatus. Good sensory cognition leads to a sense of beauty, whereas imperfect sensory cognition leads to a feeling of ugliness or deformity. Later usage of the term aesthetics deviated from how Baumgarten used it. This is unfortunate, as Baumgarten was closer to the truth than many later aesthetic theorists. Baumgarten's main error was to differentiate cognition from aesthetics. The laws of aesthetics and of cognition are largely isomorphic. Fechner (1876) guessed this to be the case. In founding psychological aesthetics, he set forth a number of principles. He was explicit that the most are principles of general psychology rather than principles of aesthetics per se. In this chapter, I explain 25 fundamental aesthetic effects on the basis of a simple cognitive theory.

NEURAL NETWORKS

Connectionist or neural-network theories postulate nodes and connections amongst these nodes. Nodes work like neurons but are simpler, and connections work like axons and dendrites but are again simpler. The reason for this simplification is that we do not know enough about the brain to attempt a neuron-by-neuron explanation of cognition. To build a neural network, we need several components (Rumelhart, Hinton, & McClelland, 1986):

1. A set of nodes. These are similar to neurons but not as complicated. In localist models, nodes represent something, such as a cat or a grandmother. I have used localist terminology for purposes of simplicity.
2. A state of activation. If some nodes are activated enough, we are conscious of whatever they code. (Many nodes, such as those controlling motor behavior, operate outside the realm of consciousness.) The one or two most activated nodes correspond to what is in the focus of attention. Less activated nodes are in the fringe of awareness. Nodes differ in strength—that is, how strongly activated they can become (Martindale, 1981, 1991).
3. A pattern of connections amongst the nodes. These connections are excitatory or inhibitory. They compose our long-term memory and the innate connections involved in sensation and perception.
4. Input and output rules about how a node computes its inputs and how outputs relate to inputs and current activation. Activation of a node is a sigmoidal function of its inputs. As excitatory input increases, activation of a node increases in a sigmoidal fashion until it reaches its asymptotic level of activation. This is how neurons work.
5. Learning rules. A variety of learning rules have been proposed. Many are variants of Hebb's (1949) idea that if two nodes are simultaneously activated, the strength of the positive connection between them is increased. At the very least, we need to add to it a rule that the strength of the inhibitory connection between two nodes is increased if one is activated and the other is inhibited.
6. An environment for the network. I have elsewhere argued that the network should be partitioned into modules devoted to specific tasks (Martindale, 1981, 1991). The brain involves extreme division of labor. For example, perception of a moving, colored form involves activation of neurons in discrete modules devoted to location, form, color, and motion. We need to postulate a number of sensory and perceptual modules. We also need modules for semantic memory, episodic memory, and an action module that initiates response to a stimulus. I have also argued that each module is organized into several layers, with vertical connections being excitatory and with lateral inhibition operating on each layer. Connections are usually bidirectional, with the amount of influence being proportional to distance between nodes. This is the way the brain is organized. On any layer of a module, I argue that nodes are arranged in terms of similarity. The more similar two things are, the closer the nodes coding them are. Such

an arrangement allows us to explain a wide variety of cognitive phenomena.

Neural network theories really have only one explanation for everything: how activated the nodes involved in a phenomenon are. We perceive something because a stimulus activated the relevant nodes. We attend to this rather than that because the nodes coding this are a lot more activated than the nodes coding that. We remember something because the nodes coding it are sufficiently activated. We forget something because the nodes coding the to-be-remembered item are not activated enough. Desirable cognitive outcomes are explained in terms of maximizing activation and minimizing inhibition. Undesirable outcomes, such as forgetting or being confused, are attributed to too much inhibition and not enough activation.

We can explain beauty and aesthetic pleasure in the same way (Martindale, 1984a, 1988): These phenomena result when activation is maximized and inhibition of activated nodes is minimized. On any layer of a module, lateral inhibition normalizes or keeps activation relatively constant. Given this, the crucial factor is often how the activated nodes are distributed on each layer. The laws of cognition and of aesthetic pleasure are isomorphic. We could repeat almost any experiment in cognitive psychology for which it were at all reasonable to ask for preference judgments and get a pattern of results similar to that obtained by looking, for example, at reaction times. A corollary is that perception and cognition are, if successful, pleasurable or self-reinforcing. This is not really surprising. Were they not self-reinforcing, we would not bother to think or perceive. It is impossible to list the objective features shared by beautiful objects. Beauty is not in the eye of the beholder, but in the brain of the beholder. According to the theory, stimuli are judged as beautiful to the degree that they elicit similar states in the brain. Below, I give a sample of aesthetic effects for which the theory can account. Because of space constraints, this is only a small sample of the effects for which the theory can account.

AESTHETIC EFFECTS

Simple Strength Effects

We find a number of cases in which preference for simple stimuli can be related to activation of nodes or neurons in a monotonic fashion.

1. Saturation of colors holding hue and lightness constant: preference is related to color saturation in a positive monotonic fashion. This is easily explained if we make the plausible assumption that node

strength is a monotonic function of saturation. Given that the output of a node is a sigmoidal function of its input, we should expect preference to be a sigmoidal function of saturation. Unpublished research from my laboratory shows this to be the case. Though they did not specifically remark upon it, such sigmoidal relations between preference and saturation were also found by Guilford (1939) and Martindale and Moore (1988).

2. Hue preference: There is a fairly universal order of hue preference (Eysenck, 1941). Most people like blue or red best, then green, then orange. Yellow is most peoples' least favorite color. If we consider spectral colors, this makes preference a U-shaped function of hue. However, hues differ considerably in their maximal saturation. Maximal saturation is also a U-shaped function of hue. If we plot hue preference as a function of saturation, we obtain a positive monotonic function.

3. Word frequency: Zajonc (1968) showed that there is a positive monotonic relationship between the frequency with which a word occurs and preference for the thing denoted by the word. There is a variety of experimental evidence that can best be explained by postulating that more frequent words are coded by stronger nodes than are less frequent words.

Strength Effects Involving Distribution of Activation in the Same Module or Layer

A number of aesthetic effects involve maximizing activation and minimizing inhibition of activated nodes by maximizing the distance among activated nodes.

4. Musical notes: A pure tone consists of sinusoidal vibrations at a single frequency. Pure tones induce a neutral reaction or slight displeasure because they do not produce enough activation. At the other end of the spectrum, white noise is displeasurable. White noise is composed of all possible frequencies. Because of this, it produces a lot of activation but also a lot of lateral inhibition. It thus results in a lot of displeasure. Musical notes consist of combinations of sine waves such that the upper partials (harmonics) are integer multiples of the fundamental frequency (Helmholtz, 1877). The first several upper partials of middle C are C', G', C'', E'', G'', etc. Note that the upper partials are all members of the C-major scale. The upper partials of C include the entire C-major scale, but the higher ones produce little activation. Some people can hear the first few upper partials. Consider a one dimensional array of nodes with each representing a musical pitch and arrangement being the same as that found on a piano. Playing

the note C activates not only the node for C but also the nodes for all the upper partials. Thus, activation is greater than for a pure tone, but the activated nodes are distant enough from one another to produce minimal lateral inhibition. The connections among nodes that are simultaneously activated are strengthened. Because there are hypothetically no positive connections among nodes on the same layer, we postulate a node on another level that is activated by the fundamental and its upper partials. We could call such a chunking node the superordinate node for middle C.

5. Musical consonance: Consider the chord C-E-G. The nodes coding E and G are partially activated by C. Specifically, C activates the nodes coding G' and E". Via their respective superordinate nodes, these nodes activate the nodes coding G and E. When actually played along with C, these nodes are thus are more activated than if played alone. There is also enhanced activation of nodes coding other upper partials shared by C, E, and G.

6. Musical dissonance: Dissonance is produced by notes that are close to each other in frequency. Because of the way we arranged the network, C and C# or C and B will be maximally displeasing because in this case we are maximizing rather than minimizing lateral inhibition.

7. Category typicality: Whereas preference is a monotonic function of perceptual typicality, it is a J- or U-shaped function of category typicality (Martindale, Moore, & West, 1988). For example, we like very typical animals such as dogs and cats, but we also like very atypical animals such as kangaroos and are rather indifferent to animals such as cows and sheep of moderate typicality. We can explain this in terms of how strong nodes are, how nodes are arranged in terms of similarity, and the assumption that similarity must be represented on a two-dimensional slab of cortex. Typical exemplars are most similar to each other; moderately typical exemplars are judged to be moderately similar to typical exemplars; atypical exemplars are dissimilar to prototypes and also to each other. The only way to represent this is to put nodes for prototypes in the center, nodes coding moderately typical exemplars in a band around them, and nodes for atypical exemplars in a more remote band or ring. Note that nodes coding exemplars of medium typicality are subject to lateral inhibition from both sides by a few strong nodes coding prototypes and a lot of nodes coding atypical exemplars. Thus, if we are thinking of animals, the nodes coding typical and atypical exemplars will be subject to rather weak lateral inhibition from only one side.

8. Novelty: A novel stimulus is by definition one that differs from preceding or surrounding stimuli. In the latter case, novelty is the analogue of the von Restorff (1933) effect: in a to-be-remembered list, an item that is markedly different from other items is almost certain to

be remembered. In the former case, novelty is analogous to release from proactive inhibition (Wickens, 1973). In a Peterson and Peterson (1959) short-term memory task, three items are given and rehearsal is prevented in some way. If the items all belong to the same category, proactive inhibition caused by lateral inhibition will build up across trials (Martindale, 1991). The more similar things are, the closer the nodes coding them are and the more they laterally inhibit each other. By the third or fourth trial, there is so much proactive inhibition (lateral inhibition) that the items cannot be remembered even after 20 seconds. If items from another category are given on the next trial, recall increases as a function of how different the category is from the category used on the first three or four trials. Novelty, the von Restorff (1933) effect, and release from proactive inhibition can all be explained in the same way. One moves from a field of nodes all laterally inhibiting each other to uninhibited nodes. Hence, the remote node or nodes can become more activated than those inhibiting one another.

9. Aesthetic effects of edge detection and edge enhancement: Ramachandran and Hirstein (1999) argue that the detection of edges in a visual scene is intrinsically reinforcing or pleasurable. They note that there are strong connections from regions of the brain where edge extraction occurs and the limbic system. Furthermore, edge extraction is adaptive. If edges were not extracted from a visual scene, we should not be able to see objects in the first place. If we monitor eye fixations, almost all fixations are on edges as opposed to areas of uniform lightness. When we focus on an edge, a set of nodes coding it is activated and minimally inhibited by surrounding nodes. They are minimally activated because they are stimulated by only the uniform field.

10. Good form Gestalts: Consider the three lines making up a triangle. Let us lay down the lines that could make up a triangle at random. Three line-detecting nodes will be activated. Now consider the situation in which we have articulated the lines so as to compose a triangle. In this case, we shall have activated the three line detectors as well as nodes coding angles and a node coding the triangle we have created. We shall have clearly activated more nodes. Activation is thus greater than in the case of lines placed at random. Preference for any form must be greater than preference for the component lines placed at random.

11. Irregular forms: The same line of reasoning applies to irregular forms. Placing the lines at random so as not to create a form should in general produce less activation than combining them so that they create an articulated form. Berlyne (1971) presented some evidence that preference for random polygons is an inverted-U function of complexity as defined by number of angles and sides. Martindale, Moore, and

Borkum (1990) were at first unable to replicate this finding. We found that preference was a monotonic function of complexity. Our initial experiments were carried out in a large room in which participants were distant from the stimuli. Thus, slightly disparate angles appeared to be identical. We eventually replicated Berlynes's (1971) results when we presented the polygons in a room about the size that Berlyne had used in his laboratory. The room was much smaller, so that the polygons were closer, and participants could discriminate slightly different angles. In this case, lateral inhibition came into play. Increasingly complex polygons activated increasingly similar angles, which presumably activated closer and closer nodes. Rather than reactivating the same angle detectors, as in the case of distant stimuli, we were activating very similar angle detectors that should have exerted more lateral inhibition upon one another. Note that if preference were plotted as a function of net activation, a monotonic relationship between preference and net activation would emerge.

12. Peak shift: Consider an organism that is rewarded for responding to a 1000 Hz tone (the S+). Unsurprisingly, it will respond maximally to the S+. Because of generalization, it will respond somewhat to tones with similar pitches. Now let us introduce a 980 Hz tone (the S-). Responses to the S- are never rewarded. After a few trials, if we test rate of response, we find maximal responding not to the S+ but to a pitch of, say, 1020 Hz (the S++) shifted away from the S-. This is the phenomenon of peak shift (Hanson, 1959). There is a tendency to respond to the S+, which, as noted, generalizes to nearby pitches. There is also a tendency not to respond to the S- which also generalizes. Thus if the S+ and S- are near enough, there will be a strong tendency to respond to the S+ but also a small tendency *not* to respond to it. Maximal responsiveness is shifted to S++ to which the tendency not to respond is absent. It is straightforward to apply this principle to preference (Staddon, 1975): we prefer what he calls supernormal stimuli. If you are complimented for wearing a skirt of a certain length and ignored or criticized for wearing an out-of-fashion skirt that is too long, you will prefer a skirt somewhat shorter than the one you were complimented for wearing.

13. Behavioral contrast: This phenomenon invariably accompanies peak shift. The organism responds more strongly to the S++ than it had to the S+ before discrimination training began. Grossberg (1975) argues that this is a consequence of the normalization caused by lateral inhibition: the amount of activation on a layer of nodes with recurrent lateral inhibition is kept relatively constant. If we subtract tendency not to respond from tendency to respond, we shall have a smaller amount of net activation than before discrimination training began. This is not a

possible state for a layer of nodes, so we end up with net activity being returned to what is was before discrimination training. However, fewer nodes are activated, so the activation of S++ is greater than the initial activity of S+. To continue with the example of selecting a skirt, behavioral contrast means that you will not merely prefer the shorter skirt, you will like it considerably more than the skirt you were complimented for wearing.

14. Simile and metaphor: To paraphrase Poincaré (1913), similes and metaphors join together mental elements previously thought to be strangers to one another. Consider the statement, "I climbed the stairs sadly." It induces no pleasure. Compare this with Victor Hugo's "I climbed the bitter stairs." Hugo's metaphor says the same thing but by activating more remote nodes. Thus, there is more activation and less lateral inhibition.

Effects Due to Activating Nodes in Different Modules

If aesthetic preference or beauty is a function of maximizing activation and minimizing inhibition of activated nodes, then the more modules that are activated, the greater pleasure should be. In general, different modules exert no inhibition upon one another. Thus, the more modules activated, the greater activation should be and the less inhibition should be.

15. Aesthetic effects of binding: When we see a visual scene, form, location, color, motion, and so on are computed in different modules. Binding refers to the process whereby the correct form is connected to the correct location and so on. Ramachandran and Hirstein (1999) argue that binding must be reinforcing or pleasurable for the same reasons that they argue edge detection and Gestalt structuring are reinforcing. Were binding not reinforcing, the brain would not do it, and we would end up not seeing correctly. In our terms, binding consists of connecting nodes in sensory modules with a node or a perceptual module. Net activation is greater than if no binding had occurred.

16. The dominance of meaningfulness: A large number of studies show that meaningfulness is by far the most important determinant of aesthetic pleasure (Martindale et al., 1990). The mind tries to understand the meaning of its inputs. Pleasure can be induced by simple perception, but greater pleasure will be induced if nodes in the semantic module are also activated, if only because more nodes will be activated.

17. Association effects involving episodic memory: If nodes in episodic memory as well as in semantic memory are activated, then net activation will be greater. Such effects are probably rather negligible in determining aesthetic preference. However, the aesthetic theory of

the man in the street is mainly an associationistic one. Consider an experiment on color preference. Saturation is the main determinant of color preference. However, if one asks people why they like a given color, they tend to give episodic associations as the reason; for example, this green reminds me of my father's favorite necktie. Such naive explanations overlook the question of why the father bought that particular necktie: saturation.

Repetition Effects

There are several well-replicated aesthetic repetition effects. Repetition of a stimulus has several effects upon the nodes coding it. Repetitions affect the threshold and activation of nodes. A decrease in threshold or an increase in resting activation level make a node easier to activate. It is reasonable to assume that the resting level of activation and activation produced by directly stimulating the node add together. Thus, a higher resting level of activation will result in greater activation when the node is actually stimulated. A decrease in resting activation or an increase in threshold has an opposite effect.

18. Habituation (massed repetition of the same stimulus): There is a large body of nonhedonic work on habituation. For simple or weak stimuli, responsiveness declines with each repetition, whereas for strong or complex stimuli, responsiveness increases for several trials and then decreases. Groves and Thompson's (1970) dual process model involves the assertion that repetition elicits two effects: habituation (fatigue or decline in firing rate of neurons) and sensitization of associated neurons. Once sensitized, these neurons also begin to fatigue. Complex stimuli have many associations, so sensitization dominates at first, and responsiveness to the stimulus at first increases. Simple stimuli have few associations, so habituation dominates, and there is a monotonic decrease in response to the stimulus. Berlyne (1971) reviews several studies showing analogous results for preference. For example, preference for popular music, which is quite simple, declines monotonically with repeated exposures. On the other hand, preference for classical music at first increases and then decreases with repeated exposures.

19. Mere-exposure effects: Distributed repetition of the same stimulus leads to increases rather than decreases in preference (Zajonc, 1980). This is not due to the fact that repetition of a stimulus increases recognition of it, and this is pleasurable in the sense of seeing an old friend. Kunst-Wilson and Zajonc (1980) presented polygons at subliminal levels. The polygons were presented for one millisecond, so that all people consciously saw were flashes of light. Preference was again a

function of number of exposures, even though recognition memory for them was at chance levels. The mere-exposure effect is in fact stronger with subliminal than with supraliminal stimuli (Bornstein & Pittman, 1992).

If we assume that every time a node is activated, it is subjected to both fatigue and sensitization processes, then we can explain the mere-exposure effect. Because presentation of stimuli is distributed, fatigue can dissipate while sensitization and resting level of activation cumulate. We know that activation and decline in threshold does not go to zero as soon as the stimulus that turned it on is no longer present. In word-recognition studies, the second time a word is presented, it is easier to recognize. This effect can last for up to two weeks. Martindale (1991) explained this in terms of resting activation and threshold very slowly returning to prestimulation levels. It makes sense that the mere-exposure effect is stronger for subliminal stimuli. For such stimuli, there should be little or no fatigue, but resting activation can cumulate.

20. Poetic rhyme: The same phoneme or set of phonemes is repeated with an interval long enough to allow fatigue to dissipate. We can explain their pleasure-inducing properties in the same way that we explained the mere-exposure effect.

21. Poetic alliteration: Alliteration involves repetition of the same phoneme or syllable usually at the beginnings of words. If the repetition is not overdone, the effect is pleasing. Extended alliteration is displeasing. Because the sounds are repeated too quickly, fatigue cumulates rather than dissipates.

Attentional Effects

22. Aesthetic overshadowing: At least for naive observers, the most striking aspect of a stimulus tends to be by far the most important determinant of preference for it. For example, Martindale and Moore (1990) obtained preference ratings for tones varying in intensity (20dB-100dB) and consonance. Intensity accounted for 96% of explained variance, whereas consonance accounted for only about 1%. Martindale et al. (1990) obtained preference ratings for random polygons varying in size and complexity (number of turns). Of explained variance, 52% was due to complexity and 11% to size. In another experiment, they studied preference for random polygons varying in color typicality, color, size, and complexity. In this case, typicality accounted for 79% of explained variance, color for 6%, size for 2%, and complexity for 1%. Martindale et al. (1988) compared meaningfulness and the mere-exposure effect. Of explained variance in preference, meaning accounted for 86% and the mere-exposure effect for 4%. The general rule is that the most salient

determinant included in a study of preference almost completely overshadows other determinants included in the experiment.

In aesthetic overshadowing, people focus their attention so much on the most salient determinant that there is no activation left over for nodes coding other determinants. Aesthetics overshadowing means that most of an artist's efforts are wasted because people do not attend to them. A poet wants readers to attend to the musical qualities of his or her verse, but overshadowing suggests that ordinary readers probably ignore it almost as much as they ignore typeface and attend only to meaning.

23. Distraction effects: The presence of distracting stimuli seems to destroy aesthetic appreciation. Martindale, Moore, and Anderson (2005) used the polygons varying in size, complexity, color, and color typicality that were reported upon in Martindale et al. (1990). In the 1990 experiment, the polygons were shown in silence; and a number of effects were significant at $p < .001$ or better. Martindale, Moore, and Anderson (2005) presented the polygons to one group of subjects in the presence of 65 dB white noise and to another group of subjects in the presence of 90 dB white noise. The presence of either moderately intense or intense white noise had similar effects: it more or less randomized preference ratings. Highly significant effects in the 1990 experiment were vastly reduced in significance or rendered insignificant. There is only so much attention available. If attention is involuntarily seized by white noise, the module processing the distracting stimuli has drawn enough activation from the central pool of attentional capacity that the modules processing the supposed target stimuli are not allocated enough activation to function effectively.

Iteration Effects

24. Iterated peak shift: A number of animals, such as birds of paradise or peacocks, have traits that are clearly maladaptive. The brilliant colors of male birds of paradise or peacocks serve as signals to predators. Darwin (1871) pointed out that animals with such traits do not form pair bonds and that only one sex, usually the males, shows the maladaptive trait, whereas the other sex is suitably camouflaged. If, for whatever reason, females of a species have a preference for, say, red, they will prefer to mate with males that are more vividly red because of peak shift. Thus, these males will leave more offspring. The same thing will happen the next generation, and so on. This will lead to a runaway trend toward more and more vividly red red-colored males across time. Because males in such species do not help in raising offspring, they are dispensable once they have mated. Staddon (1975) pointed out that

this is an example of peak shift iterated across generations. Martindale (1990) invoked iterated peak shifts to explain trends in fashion and the arts.

25. Iterated habituation: Martindale (1975, 1990) invoked habituation cumulated across generations as a basis for his theory of literary and artistic change. Because artists are more or less continually exposed to art, they tire of the old and are under a continual pressure to seek novelty. The theory, the details of which need not concern us, attributes the cause of artistic change mainly to artists. If the audience had much say in matters, we might expect iterated mere-exposure and thus little systematic change in the arts. The audience does not have much say, as I have demonstrated that literature and the arts show continual change of the type predicted by the theory (Martindale, 1990).

BEAUTY AND CREATIVITY

Martindale (1995), explains having a creative idea as reaching an energy minimum in what is called a Hopfield (1982) neural network. My theory of creativity and my theory of aesthetics may seem to be contradictory; in fact, they are almost identical. The apparent contradiction arises from the way energy and energy minima are defined in Hopfield nets. An energy minimum does not correspond to a minimum of activation. It corresponds to maximizing activation and minimizing inhibition of activated nodes. Thus, the act of creation and the perception of beauty are isomorphic.

REFERENCES

Baumgarten, A. G. (1750). *Aesthetica.* Hildesheim: Georg Olms Verlag, 1970.
Berlyne, D. E. (1971). *Aesthetics and psychobiology.* New York: Appleton-Century-Crofts.
Bornstein, R. F., & Pittman, T. S. (Eds.). (1992). *Perception without awareness: Cognitive, clinical, and social perspectives.* New York: Guilford.
Darwin, C. (1871). *The descent of man, and selection in relation to sex.* London: J. Murray.
Eysenck, H. J. (1941). A critical and experimental study of colour preferences. *American Journal of Psychology, 54,* 385-394.
Fechner, G. T. (1876). *Vorschule der Aesthetik* [Introduction to aesthetics]. Leipzig: Breitkopf und Härtel.
Grossberg, S. (1975). A neural model of attention, reinforcement, and discrimination learning. *International Review of Neurobiology, 18,* 262-327.
Groves, P. M., & Thompson, R. E. (1970). Habituation: A dual-process theory. *Psychological Review, 77,* 419-450.
Guilford, J. P. (1939). A study in psychodynamics. *Psychometrika, 4,* 1-23.

Hanson, H. M. (1959). Effects of discrimination training on stimulus generalization. *Journal of Experimental Psychology, 58,* 321-334.
Hebb, D. O. (1949). *The organization of behavior.* New York: Wiley.
Helmholtz, H. (1877). *On the sensations of tone as a physiological basis for the theory of music.* New York: Dover, 1954.
Hopfield, J. J. (1982). Neural networks and physical systems with emergent collective computational abilities. *Proceedings of the National Academy of Sciences, USA, 79,* 2554-2558.
Kunst-Wilson, W. R., & Zajonc, R. B. (1980). Affective discrimination of stimuli that cannot be recognized. *Science, 207,* 557-558.
Martindale, C. (1975). *Romantic progression: The psychology of literary history.* Washington, DC: Hemisphere.
Martindale, C. (1981). *Cognition and consciousness.* Homewood IL: Dorsey.
Martindale, C. (1984). The pleasures of thought: A theory of cognitive hedonics. *Journal of Mind and Behavior, 5,* 49-80.
Martindale, C. (1988). Aesthetics, psychobiology, and cognition. In F. Farley & R. Neperud (Eds.), *The foundations of aesthetics, art, and art education.* New York: Praeger.
Martindale, C. (1990). *The clockwork muse: The predictability of artistic change.* New York: Basic Books.
Martindale, C. (1991). *Cognitive psychology: A neural-network approach.* Pacific Grove CA: Brooks/Cole.
Martindale, C. (1995). Creativity and connectionism. In S. M. Smith, T. B. Ward, & R. A. Finke (Eds.), *The creative cognition approach.* Cambridge, MA: MIT Press.
Martindale, C., & Moore, K. (1988). Priming, prototypicality, and preference. *Journal of Experimental Psychology: Human Perception and Performance, 14,* 661-670.
Martindale, C., & Moore, K. (1990). Intensity, dissonance, and preference for pure tones. *Empirical Studies of the Arts, 8,* 125-134.
Martindale, C., Moore, K., & Anderson, K. (2005). The effect of extraneous stimuli on aesthetic preference. *Empirical Studies of the Arts, 23,* 83-91.
Martindale, C., Moore, K., & Borkum, J. (1990). Aesthetic preference: Anomalous findings for Berlyne's psychobiological theory. *American Journal of Psychology, 103,* 53-80.
Martindale, C., Moore, K., & West, A. (1988). Relationship of preference judgments to typicality, novelty, and mere exposure. *Empirical Studies of the Arts, 6,* 79-96.
Peterson, L. R., & Peterson, M. J. (1959). Short-term retention of individual verbal items. *Journal of Experimental Psychology, 58,* 193-198.
Poincaré, H. (1913). *The foundations of science.* Lancaster, PA: Science Press.
Ramachandran, V. S., & Hirstein, W. (1999). The science of art: A neurological theory of aesthetic experience. *Journal of Consciousness Studies, 6,* 15-51.
Rumelhart, D. E., Hinton, G. E., & McClelland, J. L. (1986). A general framework for parallel distributed processing. In. D. E. Rumelhart &

J. L. McClelland (Eds.), *Parallel distributed processing: Explorations in the microstructure of cognition* (Vol. 1). Cambridge, MA: MIT Press.

Staddon, J. E. R. (1975). A note on the evolutionary significance of 'supernatural' stimuli. *American Naturalist, 109,* 541-545.

von Restorff, H. (1933). Über die Wirkung von Bereichsbildungen im Spurenfeld [The effects of field formation in the trace field]. *Psychologie Forschung, 18,* 242-299.

Wickens, D. D. (1973). Some characteristics of word encoding. *Memory and Cognition, 1,* 485-490.

Zajonc, R. B. (1968). Attitudinal effects of mere exposure. *Journal of Personality and Social Psychology Monographs, Supplement 9*(2, pt. 1): 1-27.

Zajonc, R. B. (1980). Feeling and thinking: Preferences need no inferences. *American Psychologist, 35,* 151-175.

CHAPTER 13

Neural Correlates of Creative Cognition

Oshin Vartanian and Vinod Goel

INTRODUCTION

Currently, there is general consensus that creativity is not mediated by a single process or mechanism, but that it is brought about by the interaction of several cognitive, emotional, and social processes (see Sternberg, 1999). Of particular interest to us are some of the component processes that mediate creative cognition, such as divergent thinking, hypothesis generation, and set shifting or lateral transformations. Specifically, we are interested in discovering the brain areas that each of these processes can be mapped onto. This goes hand in hand with a resurgence of interest in the role of the brain in creative cognition (e.g., Feist, 2004). Equally important is determining whether the cortical structures that underlie creative cognition also mediate other related phenomena that have been linked to creativity, such as insight solution. The basic reasoning behind this line of research is that discovering the mappings of component processes of creativity onto cortical networks will provide a first step in constructing a model for understanding how these networks or structures interact in bringing about creative cognition.

CREATIVITY AND HEMISPHERIC ASYMMETRY

Much of the earlier work that was conducted in investigating the neural bases of creativity was motivated by some version of a hemispheric asymmetry hypothesis (see Martindale, 1999). These hypotheses were based on physiological evidence that linked the right hemisphere to engagement in creative tasks (e.g., Martindale, Hines, Mitchell, & Covello, 1984). However, the mechanisms that may underlie this hemispheric difference remain to be explicated. After conducting an extensive review of the historical and contemporary work in neuroscience and neuropsychology on hemispheric asymmetry, Springer and Deutsch (1998) suggest that on the whole, the differences in the modes of information processing by the left and right hemispheres can be characterized as "analytic" and "holistic" respectively. They argue that the traditional association of the left hemisphere with linguistic processing and the right hemisphere with spatial processing can be subsumed under the more global analytic and holistic banners. In addition, they emphasize that the two hemispheres do not always process information in the expected manner, and that it is the task rather than the stimuli that determines the mode of processing. The observation that task demands rather than the nature of the stimuli trigger the involvement of a particular hemisphere has found recent support in the literature (Stephan et al., 2003).

Along similar lines but using a different terminology, Goldberg and colleagues have argued that what engages the left and right hemispheres respectively is the extent to which a situation involves the engagement of routine versus novel cognitive strategies (Goldberg, Podell, & Lovell, 1994). They introduce the distinction between *veridical* and *adaptive* decision making to highlight this key functional difference between the right and left prefrontal cortex (PFC) (Goldberg & Podell, 1994). Veridical decision making is engaged in the process of identifying a correct response, and it is determined primarily by the parameters of the situation and independently of the decision maker. Thus, when a person is engaged in a problem with a recognizable structure and a predetermined correct response, then veridical decision making occurs. Typical tasks of this sort are the Wisconsin Card Sorting Task and the Tower of London Task. In contrast, adaptive decision making occurs when there are no readily available patterns to be extracted from the task environment. In such cases, the priorities of the agent become important in choosing the correct course of action. These constitute the majority of situations in open-ended settings in the real world where the agent interacts with the environment in choosing one course of action among many.

Based on the performance of patients with focal brain lesions on a test designed to measure differences in processing between the left and right frontal cortex, Goldberg and colleagues have shown that the decisions of the left frontal cortex are more likely to be in tune with the parameters or features of the environment, whereas those of the right frontal cortex are more likely to deviate from environmental cues and are more likely to be influenced by the preferences of the agent (Goldberg & Podell, 1999; Goldberg, Podell, Harner, Riggio, & Lovell, 1994). The implication of right prefrontal cortex in mediating internally motivated preferences can be contrasted with an alternative view that the emotional brain mediates the interaction between preferences and cognitive demands via orbitofrontal cortex (e.g., Bechara, Damasio, & Damasio, 2000; Bechara, Damasio, Damasio, & Lee, 1999). Nevertheless, Goldberg has argued that the differential performance of patients with frontal lesions supports the notion that the left PFC is more likely than the right PFC to be influenced by the patterns and features of the environment and explains why the right hemisphere is more likely to be engaged in cognitively novel situations where such patterns or features are absent or fail to be detected. In essence, Goldberg's work offers a "hemispheric specialization" account of laterality.

In contrast, Gazzaniga (1985, 1995, 1998) has proposed a rather different model for hemispheric asymmetry. Based on data from split-brain patients, he has demonstrated that following surgical division of the hemispheres, the ability of the left hemisphere to engage in problem solving and reasoning remains intact, whereas the ability of the right hemisphere is seriously impoverished. In a recent demonstration of this, Wolford, Miller, and Gazzaniga (2000) tested the performance of split-brain and focal-lesion patients in a task where they were required to predict the occurrence of events based on exposure to previously presented sequences. However, unbeknownst to the subjects, the sequences that were presented to them were random. The results of this task demonstrated that the left frontal cortex performed worse because of its tendency to extract patterns despite the random nature of the sequences. Based on such data, Gazzaniga postulates the existence of a structure called the "interpreter" in the left hemisphere whose function is to make sense of the environment by extracting patterns—be they causal, logical, or statistical—from events. The right hemisphere, in contrast, is not ascribed such pattern extraction tendency. In fact, Gazzaniga (2000) argues that the right hemisphere performs better than the left hemisphere because it "approaches the task in the simplest possible manner with no attempt to form complicated hypotheses about the task" (Gazzaniga, 2000, p. 1316). In fact, in general, animals perform better than humans on this task as well, presumably because they pursue a strategy similar to the one used by the right hemisphere. Thus, Gazzaniga's account can be best understood as a "hemispheric dominance" account whereby the left hemisphere is viewed to mediate most types of intelligent behavior, with the right hemisphere performing a supporting role, such as processing spatial information (Corballis, 2003; Gazzaniga, 2000).

NEURAL BASES OF HYPOTHESIS GENERATION

We have conducted a series of fMRI studies to elucidate the neural bases of creative cognition. As mentioned above, creativity can be broken down into component processes, and research has shown that one of the features of creative cognition that sets it apart from routine problem solving is the ability to generate hypotheses (Vartanian, Martindale, & Kwiatkowski, 2003). We were interested in determining whether the right and left PFC would be engaged differently as a function of hypothesis generation, especially those requiring set shifts (lateral transformations). For our first study, we used a modification of Guilford's (1967) classic Match Problems. Briefly, this task involves presenting the subject with a particular configuration of matches that make a number of complete squares. On each trial, the subject is instructed to remove a particular number of matches to generate another number of complete squares. The dependent variable is the number of solutions that a subject can generate in response to each problem instruction, with higher solutions being indicative of higher divergent thinking ability.

Guilford (1967) argued that the key feature of performing well on this task is the ability to engage in *set shifts*. Set shifts are analogous to what Goel (1995) has referred to as "lateral transformation." A lateral transformation is a movement from one state in a problem space to a horizontally displaced state rather than a more detailed version of the same state (i.e., vertically displaced state). Mental representations that are imprecise, ambiguous, fluid, indeterminate, vague, etc., facilitate lateral transformations. Mental representations that are overly precise and concrete can hinder lateral transformations. Lateral transformations allow the problem solver to remain noncommittal about the state he or she is in and to move easily between them. As such, lateral transformations are necessary for overcoming set effects and facilitate *widening* of the problem space.

Goel (2002) has argued that indeterminate mental representations, such as those that are described by set shifts or lateral transformations, are mediated by right PFC. We tested this hypothesis by presenting subjects with two versions of Match Problems in the scanner (Goel & Vartanian, 2005). In each trial of the divergent version, they were presented with a match problem and asked to determine the number of ways in which it could be solved. We argued that this required the generation and verification of hypotheses. In contrast, in baseline trials, subjects were presented with hypothetical solutions to match problems and instructed to determine whether the solution was correct. We argued that the baseline condition required the verification of hypotheses only. Therefore, a comparison of Match Problems versus baseline trials would highlight those brain areas that are involved in hypothesis generation. The results indicated that hypothesis generation activated left dorsal lateral PFC (BA 46) and right ventral lateral PFC (BA 47) (Figure 1).

The above comparison of Match Problems vs. baseline trials isolated brain regions involved in hypotheses generation in set-shift problems. This generation process will include both lateral and nonlateral transformations. To identify specifically the neural correlates of lateral transformations, we isolated match problems that had correct solutions and compared those for which at least one correct solution was generated versus those for which no correct solution was generated (Successful vs. Unsuccessful). This resulted in activation in right ventral lateral PFC (BA 47), left middle frontal gyrus (BA 9), and left frontal pole (BA 10). This result demonstrated that although left dorsal lateral PFC (BA 46) and right ventral lateral PFC (BA 47) mediate hypothesis generation in Match Problems, it is only the latter area that also mediates generating hypotheses that require set shifts.

In our final analysis, we examined the proportion of responses that were generated on each trial of Match Problems. This was done because there is a conceptual difference between generating *any* hypothesis versus generating *multiple* hypotheses. In essence, this second analysis was conducted to highlight those brain regions where activation increased in response to generating more hypotheses. The results revealed that activation in right dorsal lateral PFC (BA 46) and cerebellum covaried as a function of the number of solutions that were generated in response to match problems (Figure 2). This activation can be attributed to at least three different processes, namely, working memory (WM), cognitive monitoring, and conflict resolution. Activation in right dorsal lateral PFC (BA 46) could be due to increased WM involvement because as one generates more hypotheses, one has to maintain a larger amount of information in mind. Alternately, this activation could be due to cognitive monitoring because generating more hypotheses places a larger supervisory demand on the system. Finally, as one generates more hypotheses, there is likely to be conflict in terms of what the correct response should be. Of course these three processes are not mutually exclusive, and data from imaging studies have linked activation in right dorsal lateral PFC (BA 46) to all three processes (Barch et al., 1997; Braver & Bongiolatti, 2002; Braver et al., 2001; Cohen et al., 1997; Goel, Buchel, Frith, & Dolan, 2000; Leung, Gore, & Goldman-Rakic, 2002; Zurowski et al., 2002).

The results from our second fMRI study demonstrated that the findings from Match Problems can be extended to the verbal domain as

200 / EVOLUTIONARY AND NEUROCOGNITIVE APPROACHES

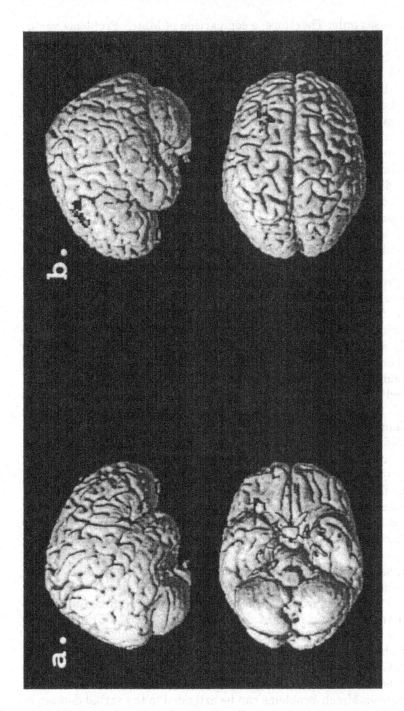

Figure 1. A comparison of Match Problems vs. baseline trials revealed significant activation in (a) right ventral lateral PFC (BA 47) and (b) left dorsal lateral PFC (BA 46).

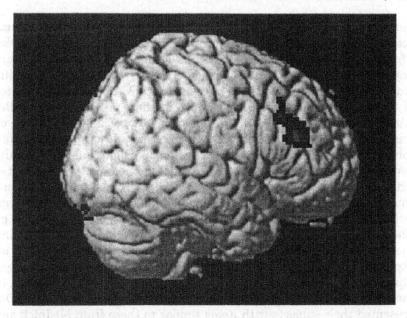

Figure 2. Activation in right dorsal lateral PFC (BA 46) and cerebellum covaried as a function of the number of solutions in Match Problems.

well (Vartanian & Goel, 2005). For this study, we presented subjects with different types of anagram problems in the scanner. Anagram problems require rearranging strings of letters (e.g., KEROJ) to form words (JOKER), and they are known to embody a hypothesis generation component (Greeno, 1978). Our results demonstrated that solving anagrams in a relatively unconstrained way (e.g., "Can you make a word with CENFAR?") compared to a condition where solutions were restricted to particular semantic categories (e.g., "Can you make a country with CENFAR?") activated a network of areas including the right ventral lateral PFC (BA 47). The combined results from Match Problems and the anagram task demonstrated that hypothesis generation in relatively more open-ended settings activates a network that includes right ventral lateral PFC (BA 47), regardless of the spatial or linguistic nature of the stimuli.

NEURAL BASES OF INSIGHT SOLUTIONS

Historically, there has been a close relation between insight problems and problems that require creative solutions, although the mechanisms that are thought to mediate these two types of problem solving are considered to be different (see Sternberg & Davidson, 1996). For our purposes, it is interesting to determine whether insight problems activate the same neural structures as do divergent thinking tasks. This may inform us about whether creative and insight problems share any underlying cognitive mechanisms. Recently, a number of imaging studies using different methods have investigated the neural correlates of insight, with surprising convergence in their results. In an earlier study, Schneider et al. (1996) presented their subjects with solvable or unsolvable anagrams in the PET scanner. The authors reasoned that solving the former would result in a feeling of insight, and their results demonstrated that engagement in solvable anagrams was associated with increased regional cerebral blood flow (rCBF) to the hippocampus. In a more recent fMRI study, Luo and Niki (2003) presented their subjects with Japanese riddles that they knew they could not solve (e.g., The thing that can move heavy logs, but can not move a small nail) and then presented them with the answer (i.e., river) in order to generate an experience of insight. The results showed that activation in the right hippocampus was associated with the experience of insight. Finally, in the most recent fMRI study on this topic, Jung-Beeman et al. (2004) presented their subjects with items similar to those from Mednick and Mednick's (1967) Remote Associates Test (e.g., pine, crab, sauce), in response to which subjects had to generate a single word that would be common to all three (i.e., apple). Because this problem can be solved with or without insight, the authors relied on subjective reports to determine whether the problems were in fact solved with insight or not. The results revealed that solving problems with a subjective feeling of insight activated the right superior temporal gyrus. The results of these three imaging studies on insight converge on the role of the right temporal lobe and in particular the hippocampus in insight solutions. Equally important, they demonstrate that insight problems activate different neural structures than do hypothesis generation tasks.

A NEURAL MODEL FOR CREATIVE COGNITION

Based on the evidence presented above, a few useful trends have emerged for understanding the neural bases of creative cognition. First, the neural bases of creative cognition, in particular those related to hypothesis generation including set shifts (lateral transformations), differ from the neural correlates of insight solutions. Specifically, insight problems seem to engage consistently the right temporal lobe and the hippocampus. Insight and creative problems differ in at least two important ways. First, whereas it is still unclear whether insight solutions are all-or-nothing phenomena or occur as a result of the gradual accumulation of information (e.g., Novick & Sherman, 2003), creative problems tend to involve movement through successive hypothesis generation-and-evaluation cycles until satisfactory solutions are reached (e.g., Eysenck, 1993). Second, strictly speaking, insight problems are not open-ended because they entail the discovery of a predetermined correct response, whereas some types of creative problems are open-ended in that they allow for the discovery of multiple correct solutions. Third, the role of emotion may differ in insight and creative problems, especially in the final phase of solution recognition, and this may give rise to different neural profiles for the two processes. For example, arrival at an insight solution tends to be accompanied by an emotional component (Gick & Lockhart, 1996), whereas this effect may be less general regarding creative solutions.

In the second trend, left and right hemispheres appear to function differently based on the nature of the problem at hand. The left PFC is more likely to be engaged when a problem allows for the extrapolation of patterns to reach correct solutions (e.g., Wolford et al., 2000). In line with this thesis, our lab has accumulated considerable evidence to support the critical role of the left PFC in extracting logical patterns in reasoning tasks (Goel & Grafman, 2000; Goel & Dolan, 2003, 2004; Goel, Gold, Kapur, & Houle, 1998; Goel, Shuren, Sheesley, & Grafman, 2004. In contrast, the right PFC is more likely to be engaged by problems that do not have a single predetermined correct response, but allow the agent to generate multiple strategies (i.e., plans, hypotheses) that will guide movement in the problem space toward a solution (Goel & Grafman, 2000; Goel & Vartanian, 2005). Therefore, it is perhaps not surprising that situations that appear novel to the agent, or real-life situations that provide the agent with multiple paths of action, engage the right PFC (Burgess, 2000; Goldberg et al., 1994).

Third, rather than having a unified role, different regions of right PFC may have different functions in the creative process. Specifically, the *ventral* aspect of right PFC appears to mediate the generation of set-shift hypotheses (Figure 1), whereas the *dorsal* region of right PFC appears to mediate the executive aspects (e.g., conflict resolution, cognitive monitoring, WM, etc.) of the creative process. This dissociation between the ventral and dorsal aspects of right PFC is consistent with evidence from patient studies. For example, the critical role of the right ventral PFC in set-shift hypothesis generation was reinforced in a study of patients with focal brain lesions and normal controls on Match Problems (Miller & Tippett, 1996). The authors administered two types of match problems to their subjects. One type required set shifting to arrive at correct solutions, whereas the other type consisted of problems that required straightforward match removal for solution. They reported that patients with focal right-PFC lesions were impaired specifically on those match problems that required set shifts. This selective impairment in performance was especially apparent in patients with lesions to right *ventral* (as opposed to dorsal) PFC, suggesting that this region is not only critical but necessary for set-shift transformations.

Additional support for the functional distinction between the ventral and dorsal aspects of right PFC is available from imaging studies. For example, Newman, Carpenter, Varma, and Just (2003) investigated the neural correlates of engagement in the Tower of London Task. Their results demonstrated that engagement in plan generation (which would involve a generation component) activated the right PFC, including right inferior frontal gyrus and dorsal lateral PFC. However, varying task difficulty (i.e., number of moves to solution), and thereby cognitive load, modulated activity in dorsal lateral PFC, but not in the right inferior frontal gyrus. This again suggests that right inferior frontal gyrus is involved in the generation of solutions per se, whereas the involvement of right dorsal lateral PFC is a function of cognitive load or executive control.

These trends can be used in the construction of a model for creative cognition, particularly because there is an indication that cognitive flexibility can be understood in two different ways (Eslinger & Grattan, 1993; Feist, 2004). First, within the context of veridical problems where one is in search of a predetermined correct solution, cognitive flexibility involves an ability to react to environmental feedback as one moves toward the correct solution. In contrast, in the context of adaptive problems, cognitive flexibility involves the ability to generate cognitive strategies (i.e., plans, hypotheses) that can be pursued until solutions are reached. This distinction has been referred to as reactive vs. spontaneous cognitive flexibility (Eslinger & Grattan, 1993), and it may involve the left and right (ventral) PFC respectively. Imaging and patient studies can be designed to study the nature of this possible double dissociation. Second, apart from a divergent production (hypothesis generation) component, creative tasks also involve an executive component that can monitor and guide the results of the generative process, and there is reason to believe that this involves the dorsal aspect of right PFC (Goel & Vartanian, 2005). Therefore, creative cognition appears to involve at least two aspects of right PFC that are integral components of a larger cortical framework.

ACKNOWLEDGMENTS

This research was supported by grants from NSERC and CIHR, and a Premier's Research Excellence Award to Vinod Goel.

REFERENCES

Barch, D. M., Braver, T. S., Nystrom, L. E., Forman, S. D., Noll, D. C., & Cohen, J. D. (1997). Dissociating working memory from task difficulty in human prefrontal cortex. *Neuropsychologia, 35*, 1373-1380.

Bechara, A., Damasio, H., & Damasio, A. R. (2000). Emotion, decision making and the orbitofrontal cortex. *Cerebral Cortex, 10*, 295-307.

Bechara, A., Damasio, H., Damasio, A. R., & Lee. G. P. (1999). Different contributions of the human amygdala and ventromedial prefrontal cortex to decision-making. *Journal of Neuroscience, 19*, 5473-5481.

Braver, T. S., Barch, D. M., Kelley, W. M., Buckner, R. L., Cohen, N. J., Miezin, F. M., Snyder, A. Z., Ollinger, J. M., Akbudak, E., Conturo, T. E., & Petersen, S. E. (2001). Direct comparison of prefrontal cortex regions engaged by working and long-term memory tasks. *Neuroimage, 14*(1 Pt 1), 48-59.

Braver, T. S., & Bongiolatti, S. R. (2002). The role of frontopolar cortex in subgoal processing during working memory. *Neuroimage, 15*, 523-536.

Burgess, P. W. (2000). Strategy application disorder: The role of the frontal lobes in human multitasking. *Psychological Research, 63*, 279-288.

Cohen, J. D., Perlstein, W. M., Braver, T. S., Nystrom, L. E., Noll, D. C., Jonides, J., & Smith, E. E. (1997). Temporal dynamics of brain activation during a working memory task. *Nature, 386*, 604-608.

Corballis, P. M. (2003). Visuospatial processing and the right-hemisphere interpreter. *Brain & Cognition, 53*, 171-176.

Eslinger, P. J., & Grattan, L. M. (1993). Frontal lobe and frontal-striatal substrates for different forms of human cognitive flexibility. *Neuropsychologia, 31*, 17-28.

Eysenck, H. J. (1993). Creativity and personality: Suggestion for a theory. *Psychological Inquiry, 4*, 147-178.

Feist, G. (2004). Creativity and the frontal lobes. *Bulletin of Psychology & the Arts, 5*, 21-28.

Gazzaniga, M. S. (1985). Organization of the human brain. *Science, 24*, 947-952.

Gazzaniga, M. S. (1995). Principles of human brain organization derived from split-brain studies. *Neuron, 14*, 217-228.

Gazzaniga, M. S. (1998). *The mind's past*. Berkeley: University of California Press.

Gazzaniga, M. S. (2000). Cerebral specialization and interhemispheric communication: Does the corpus callosum enable the human condition? *Brain, 123*(Pt 7), 1293-1326.

Gick, M. L., & Lockhart, R. S. (1996). Cognitive and affective components of insight. In R. J. Sternberg & J. E. Davidson (Eds.), *The nature of insight* (pp. 197-228). Cambridge, MA: MIT Press.

Goel, V. (1995). *Sketches of thought*. Cambridge, MA: MIT Press.

Goel, V. (2002). Planning: Neural & psychological. In L. Nadel (Ed.), *Encyclopedia of cognitive science* (pp. 697-703). New York: Macmillan.

Goel, V., Buchel, C., Frith, C., & Dolan, R. J. (2000). Dissociation of mechanisms underlying syllogistic reasoning. *NeuroImage, 12*, 504-514.

Goel, V., & Dolan, R. J. (2003). Explaining modulation of reasoning by belief. *Cognition, 87,* B11-B22.

Goel, V., & Dolan, R. J. (2004). Differential involvement of left prefrontal cortex in inductive and deductive reasoning. *Cognition, 93,* B109-B121.

Goel, V., Gold, B., Kapur, S., & Houle, S. (1998). Neuroanatomical correlates of human reasoning. *Journal of Cognitive Neuroscience, 10,* 293-302.

Goel, V., & Grafman, J. (2000). The role of the right prefrontal cortex in ill-structured problem solving. *Cognitive Neuropsychology, 17,* 415-436.

Goel, V., Shuren, J., Sheesley, L., & Grafman, J. (2004). Asymmetrical Involvement of Frontal Lobes in Social Reasoning. *Brain, 127,* 1-8.

Goel, V., & Vartanian, O. (2005). Dissociating the roles of right ventral lateral and dorsal lateral prefrontal cortex in the generation and maintenance of hypotheses in set shift problems. *Cerebral Cortex, 15,* 1170-1177.

Goldberg, E., & Podell K. (1999). Adaptive versus veridical decision making and the frontal lobes. *Consciousness and Cognition, 8,* 364-377.

Goldberg, E., Podell, K., Harner, R., Riggio, S., & Lovell, M. R. (1994). Cognitive bias, functional cortical geometry and the frontal lobes: Laterality, sex and handedness. *Journal of Cognitive Neuroscience, 6,* 276-296.

Goldberg, E., Podell, K., & Lovell, M. (1994). Lateralization of frontal lobe functions and cognitive novelty. *Journal of Clinical and Experimental Neuropsychiatry, 22,* 56-68.

Greeno, J. G. (1978). Natures of problem solving abilities. In W. K. Estes (Ed.), *Handbook of learning and cognitive processes* (Vol. 5, pp. 239-270). New York: John Wiley and Sons.

Guilford, J. P. (1967). *The nature of human intelligence.* New York: McGraw-Hill.

Jung-Beeman, M., Bowden, E. M., Haberman, J., Frymiare, J. L., Arambel-Liu, S., Greenblatt, R., Reber, P. J., & Kounios, J. (2004). Neural activity when people solve verbal problems with insight. *PLoS Biol, 2,* E97.

Leung, H. C., Gore, J. C., & Goldman-Rakic, P. S. (2002). Sustained mnemonic response in the human middle frontal gyrus during on-line storage of spatial memoranda. *Journal of Cognitive Neuroscience, 14,* 659-671.

Luo, J., & Niki, K. (2003). Function of hippocampus in "insight" of problem solving. *Hippocampus, 13,* 316-323.

Martindale, C. (1999). Biological bases of creativity. In R. J. Sternberg (Ed.), *Handbook of creativity* (pp. 137-152). New York: Cambridge University Press.

Martindale, C., Hines, D., Mitchell, L., & Covello, E. (1984). EEG alpha asymmetry and creativity. *Personality and Individual Differences, 5,* 77-86.

Mednick, S. A., & Mednick, M. T. (1967). *Examiner's manual: Remote Associates Test.* Boston, MA: Houghton Mifflin.

Miller, L. A., & Tippett, L. J. (1996). Effects of focal brain lesions on visual problem-solving. *Neuropsychologia, 34,* 387-398.

Newman, S. D., Carpenter, P. A., Varma, S., & Just, M. A. (2003). Frontal and parietal participation in problem solving in the Tower of London: fMRI and computational modeling of planning and high-level perception. *Neuropsychologia, 41,* 1668-1682.

Novick, L. R., & Sherman S. J. (2003). On the nature of insight solutions: Evidence from skill differences in anagram solution. *Quarterly Journal of Experimental Psychology, 56A*, 351-382.

Schneider, F., Gur, R. E., Alavi, A., Seligman, M. E., Mozley, L. H., Smith, R. J., Mozley, P. D., & Gur, R. C. (1996). Cerebral blood flow changes in limbic regions induced by unsolvable anagram tasks. *American Journal of Psychiatry, 153*, 206-212.

Springer, S. P., & Deutsch, G. (1998). *Left brain, right brain* (5th ed.). San Francisco, CA: W. H. Freeman.

Stephan, K. E., Marshall, J. C., Friston, K. J., Rowe, J. B., Ritzl, A., Zilles, K., & Fink, G. R. (2003). Lateralized cognitive processes and lateralized task control in the human brain. *Science, 301*, 384-386.

Sternberg, R. J. (1999). *Handbook of creativity*. New York: Cambridge University Press.

Sternberg, R. J., & Davidson, J. E. (1996). *The nature of insight*. Cambridge, MA: MIT Press.

Vartanian, O., & Goel, V. (2005). Task constraints modulate activation in right ventral lateral prefrontal cortex. *Neuroimage, 27*, 927-933.

Vartanian, O, Martindale, C., & Kwiatkowski, J. (2003). Creativity and inductive reasoning: The relationship between divergent thinking and performance on Wason's 2-4-6 task. *Quarterly Journal of Experimental Psychology, 56A*, 641-655.

Wolford, G., Miller, M. B., & Gazzaniga, M. (2000). The left hemisphere's role in hypothesis formation. *Journal of Neuroscience, 20*, RC64.

Zurowski, B., Gostomzyk, J., Gron, G., Weller, R., Schirrmeister, H., Neumeier, B., Spitzer, M., Reske, S. N., & Walter, H. (2002). Dissociating a common working memory network from different neural substrates of phonological and spatial stimulus processing. *NeuroImage, 15*, 45-57.

CHAPTER 14

Creativity, DNA, and Cerebral Blood Flow

Rosa Aurora Chávez-Eakle

INTRODUCTION

If we had to select one trait crucial for the human species, or if we were asked to choose a desirable attribute, in both cases, perhaps many of us would choose creativity. Creativity not only enables us to adapt to the environment (which has been relevant for the survival and evolution of our species), it also enables us to transform it, to generate multiple possible alternatives for a single challenge, and allows us to give birth to aesthetic products. Creativity gives foundations to science, art, philosophy, and technology. In addition, creativity is important for social survival and individual well-being (Tiedt, 1976; Torrance & Safter, 1999). Understanding how creativity occurs and what brain processes are involved with it is challenging, and such an understanding might transform our view of ourselves and our societies (Zeki, 2001).

Creativity is a process that leads to the generation of something, transforming and transcending the existent (Chávez, 1999). This process is integrated by three overlapping and highly dynamic phases: (a) Association/Integration phase where the individual connects previously unrelated elements of inner and outer experiences. That is, the individual makes associations between elements of the external world and their subjectivity, becoming aware of these associations, continuing to incorporate new elements from external reality and from the interior world; connecting ideas, images, sensations, emotions, all kinds of sensory perceptions, sometimes with periods of apparent latency. During this phase there occurs a perceptual, sensory, cognitive, and affective integration. Different levels of consciousness are involved in this phase. (b) The Elaboration phase involves the individual deliberately working with these associations and developing them in detail and building a product by using her or his particular talents and abilities. This phase is conscious and involves volition. (c) The Communication phase involves sharing the creative product; the associations are transmitted to and reproduced in others, as well the sensory and emotional experiences. This leads those who encounter the creative product to produce new associations in themselves. Communication ends the process, but at the same time there begins new creative processes in other people, thus making creativity contagious. Consequently, reality is understood from a new perspective, and conceptual and aesthetic fields might be expanded (Chávez, 1999). Indeed, multiple neuromental functions take place during the creative process.

THE INQUIRY INTO CREATIVITY FROM A NEUROBIOLOGICAL PERSPECTIVE

Galton's (1892) work was seminal for its inquiry into creativity from the perspective of natural science, which considers creative ability and genius as natural and heritable. However, Galton worked more to elucidate the heritability of genius than to understand the creative process. He studied families with a high incidence of geniuses (such as his own family) and applied statistical procedures to evaluate his observations. Galton (1880) also found that synaesthesia, to experience a particular sense through the modality of other senses (e.g., to see numbers in specific colors, to taste shapes, or to have a tactile experience with sound) is seven times more frequent among highly creative individuals than in the general population.

Galton's work was also seminal for the development of genetics (from the Greek root *gen* which means "becoming"), which began as a science in 1865 under two paradigms (both great examples of creative thinking): Galton's (1892) application of statistical methods to biological phenomena and Mendel's observations concerning the distribution of traits among generations and his contribution to the concept of the gene, even before DNA was discovered (Lisker & Armendares, 2001).

Further, Galton (1892) developed the principles that are now used in the field of genetics to study the heritability of different kinds of traits, including personality and intelligence. After Galton, the interest in genius and creativity among geneticists almost disappeared. Nonetheless, the field of genetics is a good source of interesting examples of the creative process; that is the case of the controversial discovery of the DNA structure: "In 1953 James Watson and Francis Crick *deduced* the three dimensional structure of DNA and immediately *inferred* its mechanism of replication . . . (they) analyzed x-ray diffraction photographs of DNA fibers taken by Rosalind Franklin and Maurice Wilkins and derived a structural model that has proved to be essentially correct" (Stryer, 1995, p.80, emphasis added). The inquiry of molecular genetic variations became possible in 1984 after Mullis had a powerful insight while driving. He had a vivid visualization of DNA replicating that led him to devise an ingenious method for amplifying specific sequences of DNA, the polymerase chain reaction or PCR (Luque-Cabrea & Herráez-Sánchez, 2001; Stryer, 1995). Through this method, millions of copies of a single targeted gene can be obtained and analyzed. From this, molecular genetics has advanced tremendously. Nonetheless, it was not until the 1990s that the interest in complex traits, in particular in cognitive ability, reappeared among geneticists (e.g., Bouchard, 1990; Plomin, 2002); and a great amount of molecular genetic research about personality has been performed (see Benjamin, Ebstein, & Belmaker, 2002 for a review). However, no molecular genetics research that focused on creativity has been conducted until the recent study detailed later in this chapter (Chávez-Eakle, 2004).

However, researchers have been interested in investigating the neurophysiological processes involved in the act of creation. For example, Arieti (1976) proposed that creativity is associated with an increase in the temporo-occipito-parietal cortex's functioning, and also with an increase in the interactions between these areas and the prefrontal cortex, independently from the stimuli intensity, keeping the mentioned areas a disposition to activation. In addition, Martindale pioneered work in this field, finding that highly creative individuals have a tendency to be physiologically overreactive to stimulation when compared to less creative subjects. For instance, the highly creative exhibit prolonged alpha blocking in response to tones; they habituate slower to stimuli; and rate electric shocks as being more painful (Martindale, 1978; Martindale, Anderson, Moore, & West, 1996; Martindale, Hines, Mitchell, & Covello, 1984). Moreover, Martindale and his colleagues found large and consistent electroencephalographic (EEG) differences between high and low creative individuals, observed only during creative task performance. The right-hemisphere EEG activity in parieto-temporal areas tends to be significantly higher than left-hemisphere activity in highly creative individuals during the performance of creative tasks (Martindale, 1990; Martindale et al., 1984). Further, less creative individuals tend to show alpha blocking on all types of cognitive tasks, including creative ones, while highly creative participants tend to be differentially reactive, exhibiting alpha blocking during the performance of noncreative tasks but showing alpha enhancement during creative tasks (Martindale & Hasenfus, 1978). Furthermore, highly creative individuals exhibited higher alpha indices during an analog of creative inspiration than during an analog of creative elaboration, which was not found in less creative participants (Martindale, 1978).

Brain-function imaging is becoming a promising alternative for the study of creativity. Carlsson, Wendt, and Risberg (2000) compared the regional cerebral blood flow (rCBF) between low and highly creative individuals during the performance of a divergent thinking task. Highly creative participants showed more prefrontal rCBF in both right and left hemispheres, whereas low creative individuals had activation predominantly in the left cerebral hemisphere. In addition, Bekhtereva, Dan'ko, Starchenko, Pakhomov, and Medvedev (2001) compared the results of electroencephalography and CBF measurements from two different samples of students. Participants were not selected by their creativity indexes, but the same verbal creative tasks were administered to all the subjects. It was found that greater creative performance was related to higher values of spatial synchronization in anterior cortical areas and a general increase of the coherence in both frontal areas. Highly creative performance was also associated with higher CBF in both frontal lobes, particularly the Brodmann's areas (BA) 8–11 and 44–47 (Bekhtereva et al., 2001).

Indeed, there is still much to inquire about the neurobiology of the creative process. In the following sections of this chapter, the results of a research project that studied creativity from a multiple perspective, including the study of some specific molecular genetic variation and its association with creativity, and the evaluation of the cerebral blood flow during creative performance will be presented. To my knowledge this is the first molecular genetic study to focus on creativity and the first brain images study using the Torrance Tests of Creative Thinking.

CREATIVITY AND MOLECULAR VARIATIONS IN CANDIDATE GENES

Genes have variations, and some of these variations are responsible for variability in and between species; other gene variations can be a consequence of mutations that might lead to better environmental adaptations or to pathological conditions. When variations are present in more than 1% of the population, and are not associated with a pathological condition, these are known as polymorphisms. When studying the associations between polymorphic variations and a specific trait, it is important to choose carefully the most appropriate genes from all the genes that are available. One criterion in selecting appropriate genes is to choose those that are related to a system that could be physiologically involved with the trait being investigated. In this research, some specific molecular genetic variations were analyzed in order to find whether these could be associated with the creative potential and with some of the temperamental and behavioral traits present in highly creative individuals (Chávez-Eakle, 2004). Two candidate genes were chosen: the gene that codes for the serotonin transporter and the gene that codes for the Dopamine receptor DRD4.

Serotonin is a major modulator of emotional behavior (Westenberg, Murphy, & Den Boer, 1996); it integrates cognition and has been found to be involved in the modulation of sensory input, the experience of time, sleep and dreaming, anxiety traits, fear, and pain (Rhawn, 1996). Further, serotonin orchestrates the activity and interaction of several other neurotransmitter systems, and its action is primarily terminated by reuptake via the serotonin transporter (Lesch, Greenberg, Higley, Bennett, & Murphy, 2002). In addition, it has been reported that there is an association between harm avoidance (a temperament trait related to anxiety behaviors) and a variation of the serotonin transporter gene (Lesch, Bengel, & Heils, 1996; Lesch et al., 2002), and harm avoidance is a temperament dimension that scores low among highly creative individuals (Chávez-Eakle, Lara, & Cruz-Fuentes, 2006).

Dopamine was another interesting candidate to explore, for it is known to play an important role in cognition and motor functioning, is a modulator of exploratory behavior in animals and humans, is involved with euphoria stimulation, and with emotion, mood, and reward. Further, the dopamine receptor DRD4 gene has been described as having an association with novelty seeking (Ebstein, 1997; Prolo & Licinio, 2002), a personality trait that involves seeking new situations and sensations (Cloninger, Svrakic, & Przybeck, 1993). However, other research teams have reported negative associations between the DRD4 and the novelty seeking trait (e.g., Sullivan, Fifiels, & Kennedy, 1998). Interestingly, a positive, significant correlation has been found between the creativity index and the exploratory excitability, a component of the Novelty Seeking dimension (Chávez-Eakle, Lara, & Cruz-Fuentes, 2006).

For this research, 100 individuals were recruited. Forty percent were famous scientists or artists with national and international awards and with a sustained productive activity in their fields. They were members of the Mexican National System of Researchers, the National System of Creators, or were awarded as Young Creators. These three systems provide economic support to the most productive scientists and artists, and in order to remain in these systems, members have to prove a relevant and constant production in their fields. The remaining participants were healthy control individuals or psychiatric outpatients without pharmacological treatment at the moment of the evaluations. All the participants were tested with the Torrance Tests of Creative Thinking, Verbal and Figural forms (Torrance, 1990). The Torrance Tests are the most acknowledged and employed creativity instruments; they have shown high reliability and high predictive validity in longitudinal studies (Torrance, 1993; Torrance & Safter, 1999). The figural and verbal TTCT provide a creativity index, which is an indicator of creative potential. The figural TTCT provides scores on the following creative dimensions: fluency, originality, elaboration, abstraction, and premature closure resistance. The verbal TTCT provides scores of fluency, flexibility, and originality (Torrance, 1990). The Temperament and Character Inventory (Cloninger, Svrakic, & Przybeck, 1993) and the Overexcitability Questionnaire OEQII (Falk, Lind, Miller, Piechowski, & Silverman, 1999) were also administered. The temperament and character inventory is based on the psychobiological model of personality (Cloninger et al., 1993), which considers four temperament and three character dimensions. In this model, temperament was defined in terms of individual differences in learning everyday behaviors. Temperament involves heritable neurobiological dispositions to early emotions and their related automatic behavior and responses to specific environmental stimuli. Character refers to self-concept and individual differences in goals and values and involves higher-order cognitive processes such as logic, formal construction, symbolic interpretation, and creation. The Overexcitability Questionnaire is based on Dabrowsky's theories. After working with gifted children and highly creative adults, Dabrowsky found that they tend to react with more intensity and more frequency to diverse kinds of stimuli, naming this as "overexcitability." There are five kinds of overexcitabilities: sensual, intellectual, imaginational, emotional, and psychomotor (Dabrowski, Kawczak, & Piechowski, 1970). Overexcitabilities have been described as indicators of giftedness (Falk, Manzanero, & Miller, 1997).

Blood samples were taken from 90 individuals, and DNA was extracted. The serotonin-transporter-gene regulatory region (5'SLC6A4) and the dopamine receptor DRD4 gene were amplified using the PCR method mentioned in the previous section, and typified through electrophoresis. The serotonin-transporter gene (5'SLC6A4) modulates the transcriptional activity of the serotonin-transporter gene and is unique in humans and other primates (Lesch et al., 2002). In humans, most of its alleles are composed of either 14- or 16-repeat elements (short s and long l alleles). The following allele frequency was found in our sample: ss = 45.56%, ls = 41.11%, ll = 13.33%. These frequencies were under Hardy-Weinberg equilibrium, which means that in the absence of disturbing forces such as selection, mutations, or migrations the allele frequencies show equilibrium in populations (Lisker & Armendares, 2001). An association was not found between the polymorphic variation of the serotonin-transporter gene and the creativity index. However, we found a significant association between the short allele and the harm-avoidance temperament trait, $F(1, 89) = 3.8$, $p = 0.06$, which is similar to what has been found by previous research groups investigating molecular genetics of human personality (Lesch, 2003; Lesch, Bengel, et al., 1996; Lesch, Greenberg et al., 2002). Another interesting discovery in this research was the significant association observed between the polymorphic variation of the 5'SLC6A4 gene and the emotional overexcitability, $F(1, 89) = 4.09, p = 0.05$. Higher scores on emotional overexcitability were found among individuals carrying two copies of the long allele (Chávez-Eakle, 2004). Emotional overexcitability corresponds to the intensity and frequency of responses when exposed to emotional stimuli.

The gene that codes for the dopamine receptor DRD4 has more polymorphic variations than the 5'SLC6A4 gene, which increases the complexity of the analysis. Allelic variations correspond to the number of repetitive units of 48 pairs of bases (Ebstein & Auerbach, 2002). It has been described that longer alleles correspond to more excitable receptors. The 7-repeated unit allele was the last appearing during evolution. The following allele frequency was found in our sample: 24 = 8%, 27 = 2.7%, 34 = 1.3%, 44 = 36.0%, 46 = 5.3%, 47 = 44%, 66 = 2.7%. These frequencies were not under Hardy-Weinberg equilibrium, which could suggest that the genetic variation is related to the trait investigated or that there are other traits involved in such variation. A significant association between the polymorphic variation of the DRD4 gene and the sensual overexcitability, $F(6, 74) = 3.74$, $p = 0.003$ was found (Chávez-Eakle, 2004). Sensual overexcitability corresponds to the intensity and frequency of responses to different kinds of sensorial stimuli: visual, auditory, tactile, olfactory, and gustative (Dabrowski et al., 1970). This is an important finding considering the role dopamine has in the modulation of exploratory behavior.

A principal finding of this research was the significant association observed between the creativity index obtained with the Torrance Test of Creative Thinking Verbal form and the polymorphic variation of the DRD4 gene, $(F(1, 74) = 3.50, p = 0.07)$; the level of significance increased when associating the genotype with verbal creativity fluency scores, $(F(1, 74) = 4.6, p < 0.05)$. In both cases, individuals carrying the 7-allele had the higher creativity scores (Chávez-Eakle, 2004).

This is the first study reporting an association between molecular genetic variations and creativity. The observed significant associations between overexcitabilities and molecular genetic variations are relevant findings suggesting that overexcitabilities have a biological correlate. However, it is very important to say that to find an association does not indicate that the associated gene is responsible or causal for the trait investigated; other genes and several environmental factors probably intervene. Creativity is such a crucial trait in the evolution of our species that the likelihood of it depending upon a single gene is small, and it is important to mention that different genes interact differently during fetal neural development than in later life (Lesch et al., 2002). In the case of complex traits (like creativity) the contribution of a single gene to the variance of the trait is a small 1.5-3%. Having found an association between the creativity index and the molecular variation in the dopamine transporter gene DRD4 means that there is a positive sign in this direction, and further studies involving more genes of the dopaminergic system are needed. Other research alternatives might be to evaluate the activation of specific brain areas during the creative performance.

CEREBRAL BLOOD FLOW ASSOCIATED WITH HIGHLY CREATIVE PERFORMANCE

In other research, we evaluated the cerebral blood flow (CBF) associated with the figural and verbal creativity indexes (Chávez-Eakle, 2004; Chávez, Graff-Guerrero, García-Reyna, Vaugier, & Cruz-Fuentes, 2004) using the Torrance Tests of Creative Thinking (TTCT) Figural and Verbal (Torrance, 1990), Single Photon Emission Computerized Tomography (SPECT), and statistical parametric mapping. Participants were recruited from the cohort mentioned in the previous section of this chapter. Twelve individuals were invited to participate in the functional brain images project and were selected using their creativity indexes (Verbal and Figural TTCT). Six of these individuals had creativity scores above the 99th percentile, whereas the remainder corresponded to the 50th percentile. The twelve subjects did not present medical, neurological, or psychiatric disorders, were not under medication, and did not consume any psychoactive drug. Two TTCT verbal tasks were used when performing the brain images acquisition. The first task ("Just Suppose") was a warm-up activity, whereas the second ("Unusual Uses") was administered after intravenous injection of the radiotracer Tc99m-ECD. CBF was determined using SPECT. The image processing and analysis were performed using statistical parametric mapping SPM2. The SPECT images were visually inspected for image quality. All the images were transformed to the ANALIZE format for their further automatic realignment (Friston et al., 1995). The images were spatially normalized using the SPECT image template from the Montreal Neurological Institute (MNI). The significant threshold for *a priori* regions (fronto-temporal) was $t > 3$, *p-corrected* < 0.01, and clusters formed by more than 10 voxels were analyzed. Linear correlations between the figural and verbal creativity indexes and the CBF were also completed. Results were graphically presented using the Talairach-Tournoux coordinates system (Talairach & Tournoux, 1988).

We found a positive, significant correlation between the figural and verbal creativity indexes and the CBF in the right precentral gyrus, Brodmann area (BA) 6. The figural creativity index also showed a positive, significant correlation with the CBF in the right anterior cerebellum. The creativity index obtained with the TTCT verbal showed a positive, significant correlation with the CBF in the right postcentral gyrus, BA 3; the left middle frontal gyrus, BA 11; the right rectal gyrus, BA 11; the right inferior parietal lobule, BA 40; and the right parahippocampal gyrus, AB 35. Results are summarized in Table 1 and Figure 1.

To my knowledge, this was the first study correlating the CBF with the figural and verbal creativity indexes obtained by the Torrance Tests of Creative Thinking. Our results showed that a bilaterally distributed brain system is involved in creative performance. Most of the brain areas that showed a correlation correspond to the right cerebral hemisphere; however, correlations were observed in both cerebral hemispheres, suggesting that creative thinking involves bilateral activation. Both figural and verbal creativity indexes showed a significant positive correlation with the CBF in the right precentral gyrus; this area has been involved in association processes, the assimilation of sensorial information, the modulation of impulses transmitted to motor areas, motor learning, in the perception of phantom limb movements, and in sexual arousal (Malouin, Richards, Jackson, Dumas, & Doyon, 2003, Mouras et al., 2003; Rhawn, 1996). The right frontal rectal gyrus has been related with emotion processing and to complex cognitive tasks such as meditation (Newberg et al., 2001). The inferior parietal lobule is a multimodal assimilation area and the right postcentral gyrus, a primary sensory area (Rhawn, 1996). The right cerebellum (culmen) is involved in emotional reactions and is directly linked to the amygdala, hippocampus, temporal lobe, hypothalamus, thalamus, anterior cingulate, and orbital frontal lobes (Rhawn, 1996). The right cerebellum is interconnected with the left hemisphere and becomes activated in some verbal tasks such as the production of verbs in response to nouns. Furthermore, it has been reported that individuals with lesions in the

EVOLUTIONARY AND NEUROCOGNITIVE APPROACHES

Table 1. Coordinates and anatomical localization of clusters for the regions of correlation between the CBF and the creativity indexes obtained with the Torrance Tests of Creative Thinking (Figural and Verbal forms). Z, r, p corrected, and p uncorrected correspond to the values obtained through linear correlation for the voxel with maximum significance of each cluster. BA, Brodmann area. Coordinates correspond to the Montreal Neurological Institute (MNI). Size of cluster corresponds to the number of voxels for each clusters.

Creativity Index	Coordinate (MNI) X	Y	Z	Hemisphere	Region	BA	Cluster size	r	Z	p-corr	p-no corr
Figural											
	58	−6	48	Right	Precentral gyrus	6	20	0.78	3.07	0.01	0.001
	22	−34	−28	Right	Anterior cerebellum		16	0.74	2.61	0.03	0.005
Verbal											
	54	−8	52	Right	Postcentral gyrus	3	148	0.83	3.58	0.003	0.000
	62	6	28	Right	Precentral gyrus	6	15	0.78	3.0	0.01	0.001
	−42	48	−18	Left	Middle frontal gyrus	11	13	0.78	2.89	0.02	0.002
	10	10	−22	Right	Rectal gyrus	11	21	0.78	2.82	0.02	0.002
	64	−28	38	Right	Inferior parietal lobe	40	16	0.75	2.75	0.02	0.003
	24	−34	−26	Right	Parahippocampal gyrus	35	14	0.74	2.52	0.04	0.006

Source: Published in *Salud Mental*, 27(3), 2004. p. 47, reproduced with authorization from the editor.

CREATIVITY, DNA, AND CEREBRAL BLOOD FLOW / 219

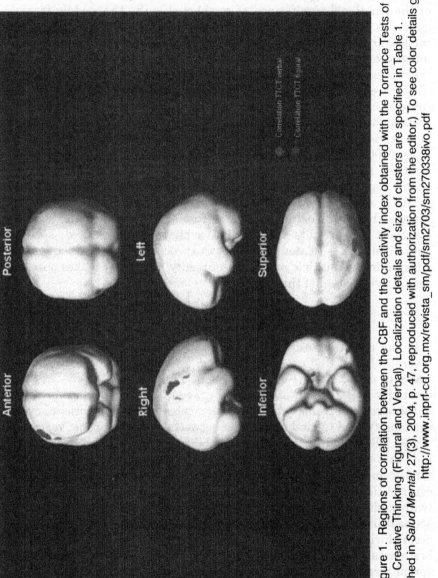

Figure 1. Regions of correlation between the CBF and the creativity index obtained with the Torrance Tests of Creative Thinking (Figural and Verbal). Localization details and size of clusters are specified in Table 1. (Published in *Salud Mental*, 27(3), 2004, p. 47, reproduced with authorization from the editor.) To see color details go to http://www.inprf-cd.org.mx/revista_sm/pdf/sm2703/sm270338ivo.pdf

right cerebellum have disturbances in verbal association and spatial tests (Rhawn, 1996) and show frontal hypoactivity (Arai et al., 2003). The middle frontal gyrus is a structure related to higher level processing of the emotional significance of complex stimuli. The middle frontal gyrus, in association with the mediofrontal and anterior cingulate cortices are sites of convergence for limbic inputs and are involved in the integration of cognition and emotion, affect and meaning, and also in the representation of the mental states of others (Berthoz et al., 2002). These areas maintain rich interconnections and are related to the conscious experience of emotion (Lane et al., 1998). Higher activation in these areas could be related to the vivid conscious experience of feelings and perceptions described in highly creative individuals (Chávez & Lara, 2000; Dabrowski et al., 1970). The latter, combined with higher symbolic abilities that are processed mainly in frontal lobes, might enable highly creative individuals to translate their experiences into creative works. Creativity is a complex, dynamic, multi-integrative process that involves perceptual, volitional, cognitive and emotional functions. Our results suggest that a bilateral, distributed, specific neural network is related to the creative process. These brain areas are engaged in the multiple processing of reality. Creativity makes possible the transformation of this reality.

CONCLUSIONS

In the research described in the previous sections of this chapter, several relevant findings were reported: (a) an association between the presence of the allele 7 of the dopamine receptor DRD4 gene and the creativity index; (b) an association between the polymorphic variation of the serotonin-transporter/promoter region gene and emotional overexcitability; and (c) and association between the polymorphic variation of the DRD4 and sensual overexcitability. These associations do not implicate causality; however, they suggest a promising starting point for further molecular genetic exploration of the creative potential. The contribution of a single gene for a complex trait is small, other genes (with additive and no-additive effects) and other environmental and sociocultural factors might be involved. Multiple neuromental processes occur during creative acts. When evaluating the activation of specific brain areas during creative performance, it was found that figural and verbal creativity indexes correlated with CBF in specific areas in both cerebral hemispheres; these areas are involved in multimodal processing, in complex cognitive functions (such as imagery, memory, and novelty processing among others) and in all levels of emotion processing. This suggests that creativity is performed by a highly distributed bilateral brain system. The brain-culture interactions, and the gene-environment interactions as well, are fascinating and challenging issues; creativity involves both sociocultural and psychobiological complex processes; therefore research on creativity could be a promising field that would lead us to increase our understanding of these topics. Neuroscience and molecular genetics offer rich possibilities to explore further the creative process. This knowledge is not separate from the experience of creating and could provide significant data for other researchers interested in creativity in various disciplines.

ACKNOWLEDGMENTS

I am grateful to Dr. Ramón de la Fuente who made this research possible, to Dr. Carlos Cruz , to Dr. Ariel Graff, and to Dr. A. Jonathan Eakle.

REFERENCES

Arai, M., Tanaka, H., Pascual-Marqui, R. D., & Hirata, K. (2003). Reduced brain electric activities of frontal lobe in cortical cerebellar atrophy. *Clinical Neurophysiology, 114*, 740-747.
Arieti, S. (1976). *Creativity: The magic synthesis.* New York: Basic Books.
Bekhtereva, N. P., Dan'ko, S. G., Starchenko, M. G., Pakhomov, S. V., & Medvedev, S. V. (2001). Study of the brain organization of creativity: III. Brain activation assessed by the local cerebral blood flow and EEG. *Human Physiology, 27*, 390-397.
Benjamin, J., Ebstein, R. P., & Belmaker, R. H. (2002). *Molecular genetics and the human personality.* Washington, DC: American Psychiatric Publishing.
Berthoz, S., Artigues, E., Van de Moortele, P.-F., Poline, J.-B., Rouquette, S., Consolli, S. M., et al. (2002). Effect of impaired recognition and expression of emotions on frontocingulate cortices: An fMRI study of men with alexithymia. *American Journal of Psychiatry, 159*, 961-967.
Bouchard, T. J. J. (1990). Sources of human psychological differences: The Minnesota study of twins reared apart. *Science, 250*, 223-328.
Carlsson, I., Wendt, P. E., & Risberg, J. (2000). On the neurobiology of creativity. Differences in frontal activity between high and low creative subjects. *Neuropsychologia, 38*, 873-885.
Chávez-Eakle, R. A. (1999). *What is creativity?* Unpublished Psychiatry Thesis. Universidad Nacional Autónoma de México UNAM, Mexico City.
Chávez-Eakle, R. A. (2004). *Integral evaluation of the creative personality: Clinical, genetic and phenomenological features.* Unpublished Doctoral Dissertation, Universidad Nacional Autonoma de Mexico UNAM, Mexico City.
Chávez, R. A., Graff-Guerrero, A., García-Reyna, J. C., Vaugier, V., & Cruz-Fuentes, C. (2004). Neurobiology of creativity: Preliminary results of a brain activation study. *Salud Mental, 27*(3).

Chávez, R. A., & Lara, M. C. (2000). Creativity and psychopathology. *Salud Mental, 5*, 1-9.

Chávez-Eakle, R. A., Lara, M. C., Cruz-Fuentes, C. (2006). Personality: A possible bridge between Creativity and Psychopathology. *Creativity Research Journal, 18*(1), 27-38.

Cloninger, C. R., Svrakic, D. M., & Przybeck, T. R. (1993). A psychobiological model of temperament and character. *Archives of General Psychiatry, 50*, 975-990.

Dabrowski, K., Kawczak, A., & Piechowski, M. (1970). *Mental growth through positive disintegration*. London: Gryf Publications.

Ebstein, R. P., & Auerbach, J. G. (2002). Dopamine D4 receptor and serotonin transporter promoter polymorphisms and temperament. In J. Benjamin, R. P. Ebstein, & R. H. Belmaker (Eds.), *Molecular genetics and the human personality* (pp. 137-150). Washington, DC: American Psychiatry Publishing, Inc.

Ebstein, R. P., & Belmaker, R. H. (1997). Saga of an adventure gene: novelty seeking, substance abuse and the dopamine D4 receptor (DRD4) exon III repeat polymorphism. *Molecular Psychiatry, 2*, 381-384.

Falk, R. F., Lind, S., Miller, N., Piechowski, M., & Silverman, L. (1999). *The Overexcitability Questionnaire-Two (OEQ II): Manual, Scoring System, and Questionnaire*. Denver, CO: Institute of Advanced development.

Falk, R. F., Manzanero, J., & Miller, N. (1997). Developmental potential in Venezuelan and American artists: A cross cultural validity study. *Creativity Research Journal, 10*, 201-206.

Friston, K., Ashburner, J., Poline, J., Frith, C., Heather, J., & Frackowiak, R. (1995). Spatial registration and normalisation of images. *Human Brain Mapping, 2*, 165-189.

Galton, F. (1880). Visualised numerals. *Nature, 22*, 494-495.

Galton, F. (1892). *Hereditary genius, an inquiry into its laws and consequences*. New York: Macmillan and Co.

Lane, R. D., Reiman, E. M., Axelrod, B., Yun, L.-S., Holmes, A., & Schwartz, G. E. (1998). Neural correlates of levels of emotional awareness: Evidence of an interaction between emotion and attention in the anterior cingulate cortex. *Journal of Cognitive Neuroscience, 10*, 525-535.

Lesch, K. P. (2003). Neuroticism and serotonin: A developmental genetic perspective. In R. Plomin, J. C. Defries, I. W. Craig, & P. McGuffin (Eds.), *Behavioral genetics in the postgenomic era* (pp. 389-424). Washington, DC: American Psychological Association Press.

Lesch, K. P., Bengel, D., & Heils, A. (1996). Association of anxiety-related traits with a polymorphism in the serotonin transporter gene regulatory region. *Science, 274*, 1527-1531.

Lesch, K. P., Greenberg, B. D., Higley, J. D., Bennett, A., & Murphy, D. L. (2002). Serotonin transporter, personality and behavior: Toward dissection of gene-gene and gene-environment interaction. In J. Benjamin, R. P. Ebstein, & R. H. Belmaker (Eds.), *Molecular genetics and the human personality* (pp. 109-136). Washington, DC: American Psychiatry Publishing, Inc.

Lisker, R., & Armendares, S. (2001). *Introducción a la genética humana* [Introduction to human genetics]. Mexico City: Manual Moderno-Facultad de Medicina UNAM.

Luque-Cabrea, J., & Herráez-Sánchez, Á. (2001). *Texto ilustrado de biología molecular e ingeniería genética. Conceptos, técnicas y aplicaciones en ciencias de la salud* [Illustrated text of molecular biology and genetic engineer concepts, techniques and applications in health sciences]. Madrid, España: Harcourt.

Malouin, F., Richards, C. L., Jackson, P. L., Dumas, F., & Doyon, J. (2003). Brain activations during motor imagery of locomotor-related tasks: A PET study. *Human Brain Mapping, 19*, 47-62.

Martindale, C. (1978). Creativity, consciousness and cortical arousal. *Journal of Altered States of Consciousness, 3*, 68-87.

Martindale, C. (1990). Creative imagination and neural activity. In R. Kunzendorf & A. Sheikh (Eds.), *The psychophysiology of mental imagery*. Amityville, NY: Baywood.

Martindale, C., Anderson, K., Moore, K., & West, A. N. (1996). Creativity, oversensitivity, and rate of habituation. *Personality and Individual Differences, 20*, 423-427.

Martindale, C., & Hasenfus, N. (1978). EEG differences as a function of creativity, stage of the creative process, and effort to be original. *Biological Psychology, 6*, 157-167.

Martindale, C., Hines, D., Mitchell, L., & Covello, E. (1984). EEG alpha asymmetry and creativity. *Personality and Individual Differences, 5*, 77-86.

Mouras, H., Stoleru, S., Bittoun, J., Glutron, D., Pelegrini-Issac, M., Paradis, A. L., & Burnod, Y. (2003). Brain processing of visual sexual stimuli in healthy men: A functional magnetic resonance imaging study. *NeuroImage, 20*, 855-869.

Newberg, A., Alavi, A., Baime, M., Pourdehnad, M., Santanna, J., & d'Aquili, E. (2001). The measurement of regional cerebral blood flow during the complex cognitive task of meditation: A preliminary SPECT study. *Psychiatry Research, 106*, 113-122.

Plomin, R. (2002). Quantitative trait loci and general cognitive ability. In J. Benjamin, R. P. Ebstein, & R. H. Belmaker (Eds.), *Molecular genetics and the human personality* (pp. 211-230). Washington, DC: American Psychiatry Publishing, Inc.

Prolo, P., & Licinio, J. (2002). DRD4 and novelty seeking. In J. Benjamin, R. P. Ebstein, & R. H. Belmaker (Eds.), *Molecular genetics and the human personality* (pp. 91-108). Washington, DC: American Psychiatry Publishing, Inc.

Rhawn, J. (1996). *Neuropsychiatry, neuropsychology, and clinical neuroscience*. Baltimore, MD: Williams & Wilkins.

Stryer, L. (1995). *Biochemistry* (4th ed.). New York: W. H. Freeman and Company.

Sullivan, P. F., Fifiels, W. J., & Kennedy, M. A. (1998). No association between novelty seeking and the type 4 dopamine receptor gene (DRD4) in two New Zealand samples. *American Journal of Psychiatry, 155*, 98-101.

Talairach, J., & Tournoux, P. (1988). *Co-Planar Stereotaxic Atlas of the Human Brain: 3-Dimensional Proportional System: An approach to cerebral imaging.* New York: Thieme Medical Pub.

Torrance, E. P. (1990). *Torrance Tests of Creative Thinking.* Bensenville, IL: Scholastic Testing Service.

Torrance, E. P. (1993). The beyonders in a thirty year longitudinal study of creative achievement. *Roeper Review, 15,* 131-135.

Torrance, E. P., & Safter, H. T. (1999). *Making the creative leap beyond.* Buffalo, NY: Creative Education Foundation Press.

Westenberg, H. G., Murphy, D. L., & Den Boer, J. A. (1996). *Advances in the neurobiology of anxiety disorders.* New York: Wiley.

Zeki, S. (2001). Artistic creativity and the brain. *Science, 293,* 51-52.

CHAPTER 15

Artistic Creativity and Affective Disorders: Are They Connected?

Dennis K. Kinney and Ruth L. Richards

INTRODUCTION

Associations between great creativity and serious disturbances of mood have been observed for millennia, as a number of creative geniuses in ancient Greece appear to have had severe mood disorders. A century ago, the eminent psychiatrist, Emil Kraepelin, noted that some features of mania might facilitate creativity in certain artistic endeavors. However, while there has long been extensive speculation about relations between creativity and psychopathology, most empirical research on the topic has been conducted in recent decades.

In this chapter, we first review lines of empirical research that bear on the question and that suggest that there are indeed significant relationships between creativity and mood disorders or liability for these disorders. Next, we review complementary evidence for a relationship between creativity and mood elevation. We then discuss factors that may mediate these associations, with a particular focus on evidence for personality traits that are associated with both familial liability for mood disorders and enhanced creative potential. Finally, we discuss clinical and social implications of this research and make recommendations for future research.

EVIDENCE FOR ASSOCIATION OF CREATIVITY WITH LIABILITY FOR MOOD DISORDERS

Biographical and Anecdotal Reports of Links between Creativity and Mood Disorders

The likely presence of major mood disorders in a number of artistic geniuses, such as Van Gogh, has prompted much theorizing about associations between creativity and mood disorders (e.g., Jamison, 1990; Kinney, 1992; Runco & Richards, 1997). In the last twenty years, persuasive data to support such associations has accumulated from research that used rigorous methods, including reliable and valid criteria for making psychiatric diagnoses.

Scientific Evidence for a High Prevalence of Mood Disorders in Artistic Geniuses

Several careful studies have found a significantly elevated prevalence of major mood disorders—especially manic-depressive illness, or **bipolar disorder**, and related conditions—in distinguished creators in the fine arts. These investigations were conducted by several different groups of researchers. Groups of extremely eminent artists, writers and composers were studied in three different samples, from Continental Europe, England, and the United States, respectively (Akiskal & Akiskal, 1988; Andreasen, 1987; Jamison, 1989). All studies found extremely high prevalences of mood disorders among these artistic geniuses, supporting earlier research (see also reviews by Jamison, 1990; Kinney, 1992; Richards, 1981). These studies **raise several key questions.**

i) Does the association of creativity with mood disorders also extend to **noneminent**, or "everyday," levels of creativity?

ii) Is the association limited to the **fine arts**, or does it extend to other fields?

iii) Is the link limited only to patients with mood disorders, or does it extend to people with milder mood swings and even to patients' clinically **unaffected relatives**?

iv) Is great suffering associated with severe mood swings a "price" one must pay for unusual creativity, or are other, **non**pathological, characteristics associated with liability for mood disorders actually the important factors that are conducive to creativity? In particular, do key **personality** characteristics, such as greater interest in new ideas or experiences, or greater achievement-striving and self-confidence, *mediate* group differences in creative achievement?

Greater Noneminent Creativity in Bipolar-Spectrum Persons and Their Healthier Relatives

Richards, Kinney, Lunde, Benet, and Merzel (1988a) extended this link between creativity and mood disorders by finding that, even when using broader measures of "everyday," noneminent creativity, creative accomplishment was higher in subjects with bipolar disorder or cyclothymia and their psychiatrically normal relatives than in controls.

Thus, the positive relation between mood disorders and enhanced creativity appears to go beyond a small number of artistic geniuses and may in fact be relevant to 5% or more of the population at large. To be able to study the relation of creativity to mood disorders, Richards et al. (1988a) devised a new psychological measure (**The Lifetime Creativity Scales, or LCS**) for rating a wide variety of creative accomplishments, including avocational as well as work-related achievements. Research using the LCS has produced evidence for the reliability of creativity ratings using these scales (Kinney, Richards, & Southam, in press; Richards, Kinney, Benet, & Merzel 1988b). These creativity scales were used by the investigators, while blind to diagnoses, to rate information obtained from interviews on the job and hobby activities of persons with a history of bipolar disorder or cyclothymia, their unaffected relatives, and groups of control subjects without mood disorders.

In this research, Richards et al. (1988a, 1988b) noted, creativity was viewed as a characteristic that is not limited to artistic geniuses, but rather is present in widely ranging degrees in the general population and can be displayed in almost any field of endeavor—a conception of creativity similar to that expressed not only by distinguished psychologists, such as Maslow (1968), but also by eminent biologists such as Dobzhansky (1962). The scientific support for this approach to the assessment of creativity was provided by empirical evidence for a general capacity for originality and other personality traits associated with creativity that are manifested across many different types of endeavors (see e.g., Barron, 1969). Assessment of creativity by the LCS was based on subjects' real-life vocational and avocational activity. In accord with Barron (1969), in order to be judged creative, activities had to be both original and meaningful to other people. Data from three large samples provided several complementary types of evidence for the validity of these scales, including content, convergent, and discriminant validity, as well as good inter-rater agreement (Richards et al., 1988b).

Richards et al. (1988a) compared assessments of the creative activities of bipolar I subjects, cyclothymes, and their first-degree normal relatives with those of psychiatrically normal and ill comparison subjects who had no personal or family history of mania or depression. The research took into account the psychiatric histories of both subjects and their relatives, and the investigators used information from personal interviews as the basis for independently assessing subjects' creativity and mental health. Statistical analyses of creativity ratings controlled for background variables such as years of education and intelligence.

The sample of 77 subjects was previously ascertained and diagnosed by an international team of investigators (Wender et al., 1986). The combined **index** subjects (bipolar disorder patients, cyclothymes, and normal relatives) were rated significantly higher on Overall Peak Creativity than all control subjects combined. Within the index group, the first-degree normal relatives of bipolar disorder patients and cyclothymes were higher in creativity than the bipolar subjects themselves. In other words, the mean level of peak creativity was an "inverted-U" function of increasing liability for bipolar disorder. Thus it was a subject's relationship to a bipolar patient or cyclothyme, rather than psychiatric illness or health itself, that was most strongly associated with greater creativity. Because of a narrow focus on pathological, rather than beneficial behaviors, most investigations have failed to examine the possibility that the healthy relatives of bipolar patients may actually tend to have superior creative potential.

This study had several important practical implications. First, the scales assessed a wide range of levels of creativity, across a variety of work and leisure activities. The results therefore suggest that the association of mood disorders and creativity is not restricted simply to artistic genius, or even to the fine arts. Rather, the association seems to extend to noneminent forms of creative achievement in a wide variety of activities. Second, among the mood-disordered patients and their relatives, it was the healthier persons—those who either had mild mood disorders or had no mental disorder at all—who had the highest average creativity. This suggests that increased creative potential is not limited to persons with severe mood swings, but may instead extend to include their unaffected relatives.

Several lines of evidence indicate that there is a "bipolar spectrum" of disorders that extends beyond frank bipolar I disorder to a variety of milder disorders. These "spectrum" disorders, including bipolar II disorder (BP-II) and cyclothymia, have an elevated prevalence among the relatives of individuals with bipolar I disorder (McInnis & DePaulo, 1996). A "softer" end of this spectrum may even extend to persons who, while not meeting full diagnostic criteria for mood disorders, still manifest above-average levels of hypomanic symptomatology. Thus the creativity link may be relevant, not only to the millions of persons with bipolar disorder itself, but also to tens of millions who may carry genes for the disorder but either have only mild symptoms or are completely healthy.

CREATIVITY AND MOOD ELEVATION

Thus if there are indeed some advantages for creativity that are associated with risk for mood disorders, the advantages may be due not to the psychiatric illness itself, but rather to other psychological characteristics, such as increased access to unusual ideas, or greater striving in pursuing unconventional ideas despite personal and financial risks. These kinds of personality features have been found to be associated with greater creativity in research on the personality correlates of creativity in a number of different occupations (e.g., Barron & Harrington, 1981). Thus there are several converging lines of scientific evidence that support the view that it is mild, or even subclinical, elevations of mood that are likely to be most conducive to creative activity.

Support for this view also comes from other research, such as studies of artistic geniuses, who described their most creative periods as occurring during episodes of mild mood elevation (Jamison, 1989). The same finding also comes from studies of noneminent persons with mood disorders. Thus Richards and Kinney (1990) confirmed the finding of Jamison, Gesner, Hammen, and Padesky (1980) that bipolar patients report that mild mood elevations most often facilitated their creativity.

Richards and Kinney (1990) asked persons with histories of cyclothymia, unipolar depression, or bipolar disorders how low and high moods affected their creativity; each diagnostic group reported that mildly elevated moods significantly enhanced their creativity, whereas low moods decreased it. The creativity-enhancing effects of high moods were particularly marked for patients with a history of hypomania. By contrast, most of these patients indicated that full-blown mania did not tend to facilitate creativity. To the contrary, these more extreme swings in mood tended to be destructive, rather than helpful, to creative efforts. These data provide further support for the hypothesis that creativity is an "inverted-U" function of increasing levels of hypomanic or manic symptomatology (Richards et al., 1988a). This inverted-U hypothesis proposes that several behavioral characteristics aid creativity when they are moderately elevated, as often occurs with mild mood elevation, but become harmful when the characteristic becomes too great, as often occurs during the extreme mood elevation of mania. For example, greater access to original ideas or unusual associations during mild mood elevation (potentially helpful in generating creative ideas) can escalate into flight of ideas (unhelpful) during the extreme mood elevation of mania, or heightened confidence and ambition (helpful in pursuing creative ideas despite the criticism they often engender) can grow into delusions of grandeur (unhelpful) during manic episodes.

FACTORS THAT MAY MEDIATE ASSOCIATIONS OF CREATIVITY WITH MOOD DISORDERS

What could account for associations between creativity and mood disorders (or liability for these disorders)? Table 1 describes several ways in which creativity and mood disorders could be related (see Richards, 1999). The last relationship listed, however, appears to be the one most strongly supported by research. That is, research suggests that enhanced creativity may actually be related, not so much to mood disorders per se, but rather to personality characteristics that are conducive to creativity and are more prevalent in persons who are temperamentally disposed to bipolar disorders.

If this is true, it is of clinical as well as theoretical interest. For example, it is sometimes suggested that the extreme emotions and unusual experiences associated with mania and major depression may actually deepen artists' sense of empathy and facilitate their creativity. Individuals with bipolar disorder who work in artistic professions sometimes voice concerns that mood-stabilizing medications may impair their creativity (e.g., Schou, 1979). However, extremes of mood may actually be a liability to the creative process.

Three types of psychological characteristics seem of particular relevance in this regard. These three variables are theoretically interesting as potential facilitators of different aspects of the creative process. First, the **ability to generate many and varied ideas**—to engage in **creative thinking**—seems likely to be of fundamental importance, particularly in the initial stages of creative achievements. Increased access to unusual ideas or associations in elevated mood states has long been noted by clinicians. Indeed, racing thoughts or flight of ideas can be viewed as an extreme, and dysfunctional, form of this process that, at this severe level, is likely to impair rather than facilitate creativity. Second, **an interest in, and receptiveness to, new ideas and experiences** may facilitate creativity by increasing the reservoir of psychological material on which the creator can draw for the generation of creative ideas. **Openness to Experience**, for example, assessed using the **NEO Personality Inventory** (Costa & McCrae, 1992), is correlated with measures of divergent thinking and with Gough's Creative Personality Scale (McCrae, 1987). The **NEO** Openness to Experience construct is characterized by active imagination, aesthetic sensitivity, attentiveness to inner feelings, preference for

Table 1. Typology of Relations of Creativity to Mood Disorders

1. Direct relationship of pathology to creativity (P→C)

Aspects of psychopathology (P) can contribute directly to creative outcomes or processes (C). Consider Kay Jamison's *An unquiet mind*, a first-person account of manic-depressive illness by an internationally known expert. Personal experience is relevant both to the content of the book and to aspects of creative process in writing it.

2. Indirect relationship of pathology to creativity (P→T→C)

Here, a third factor (T) intervenes between pathological and creative factors. Consider a person who does journal writing about mood states or conflicts, for personal reasons of catharsis, but comes to discover greater creative potential and rewards. Nobelist John Cheever, who suffered from depression, did youthful writings about family and school situations, which are thought to have helped him personally. Such creative expressions can enhance perspective, empowerment, and general health and, at best, put one in touch with more universal themes and altruistic motives. Individuals like Cheever may end up creating for the benefit of others.

3. Direct relationship of creativity to pathology (C→P)

Humanistic psychologist Rollo May, among others, wrote about the anxiety that may at times attend creative expression. Especially in the arts, one must be open to whatever comes up. The heightened sensitivity reported by people with mood disorders could raise the odds at times of distress. In the best circumstances, such psychological discomfort and anxiety during the creative process can be an important step along the way to a more healthy and open personality. Hence, if creativity leads to pathology in the short term, it can ultimately lead to greater health.

4. Indirect relationship of creativity to pathology (C→T→P)

Here, the third or intervening factor is the emergent conflicts that come to consciousness during the act of creation. Consider problems with substance abuse as a less healthy response to conflict than the working through in # 3 above. Substance abuse occurs more often in individuals with mood disorders than in the general population. Another example is the creative and outspoken schoolchild who is ostracized by peers and misunderstood by teachers. Sometimes a seeming hyperactivity is an early indicator of later bipolar disorder. With a more supportive environment, a better outcome can be possible.

5. Third factor which can affect both creativity and pathology (T→C & P))

An important potential third factor is **familial liability** for mood disorders, particularly bipolar disorder. Having this liability may raise the odds of both (a) problems related to mood swings and (b) positive qualities related to creativity or leadership. These may occur separately or together in individuals, or across different family members as found, for instance, by Richards and Kinney (1990). This third factor could involve cognitive, affective, and motivational factors—thus bringing along with mood elevation, for example, an over-inclusive cognitive style (ranging from adaptive levels of original thinking to a maladaptive level seen in thought disorder), heightened emotional sensitivity (ranging from increased depth of appreciation to a maladaptive level of emotional instability), and inspired motivation (ranging from energetic confidence to maladaptive grandiosity).

Source: Modified from Richards (1999); reprinted with the permission of the publisher.

variety, intellectual curiosity, and nondogmatic thinking (Costa & McCrae, 1992). In previous research, higher scores on the Openness to Experience scale have been associated with higher levels of hypomanic symptomatology (Meyer, 2002) and outright mania (Lozano & Johnson, 2001). Could the Openness trait, likely to have a strong genetic component (Plomin & McClearn, 1990), explain the finding that unaffected relatives of bipolar probands showed heightened levels of creativity?

Finally, **an increased level of self-confidence, perseverance, and striving for achievement** is likely to be important for the creator to elaborate and develop an innovative idea into a creative product or accomplishment that can be shared with other people—and to persuade other people to recognize and appreciate the worth of that creative idea or product. Indeed, Csikszentmihalyi (1998) argues this latter process is an integral part of "creativity," because it is so crucial for a creator to persuade the "gatekeepers" of a discipline (e.g., agents, gallery owners, reviewers, and publishers) that a novel idea has merit. If the creator cannot succeed in persuading such gatekeepers to value his or her innovation, then even the most creative idea will, in effect, die with the creator. Csikszentmihalyi's (1998) argument highlights how important it is to develop the creative kernel of an idea into a form that can be communicated to, and appreciated by, other people.

There is evidence that bipolar disorder is often associated with personality characteristics that include heightened self-esteem, and perseverance in pursuing goals (e.g., Hirschfeld & Klerman, 1979). Do these tendencies extend to unaffected relatives of bipolar disorder probands and provide a crucial link in bringing social recognition to a new idea or creative product?

SOCIAL AND CLINICAL SIGNIFICANCE

Implications of Increased Creativity in Persons with Mood Disorders and Their Relatives

If it can be shown that familial risk for bipolar disorder is associated with creativity-enhancing traits, this will have important implications for how to apply new genetic knowledge. As discovery of genetic markers makes it possible to identify individuals who carry susceptibility genes for mood disorders, it becomes increasingly important to know whether familial risk for mood disorders is also associated with **positive** behavioral phenotypes.

It is thus not only persons with frank bipolar I disorder, but also this larger group of bipolar spectrum patients and the patients' relatives—and their mates—who are deeply concerned about issues of stigma and self-esteem, and how to weigh the potential risks and benefits of familial/genetic risk for bipolar disorder in making crucial life decisions such as whether to marry or have children. These decisions become increasingly pressing with advances in genetic research that are beginning to identify specific genes that increase liability for bipolar disorder. The research reviewed earlier suggests that familial (most likely genetic) liability for bipolar disorder is associated with increased creative potential. That is, the research suggests that persons with bipolar disorders tend to carry a familial liability that increases their potential, not only for developing the mood disorders, but also for being unusually creative. In a favorable setting, this increased creative potential will be realized and manifested as a higher-than-normal average level of creative **accomplishment**.

A corollary of this hypothesis is that persons who carry familial liability for bipolar disorder, but escape frank illness itself, will tend to be more creative than people in the general population. Bipolar patients' unaffected relatives may therefore tend to be more creative, on average, than persons without a personal or family history of major mood disorders. The relatives may also be more creative on average than persons with mood disorders themselves whose severe symptoms may tend to disrupt creative thinking and accomplishment.

There are decidedly **optimistic implications of this hypothesis**. First, bipolar patients are most likely of all to carry liability and have great creative *potential;* Second, *if* they can obtain treatment to control their symptoms and realize their creative potential, they should tend to be unusually creative. If the link between creativity and liability for mood disorders is supported, it could have several significant clinical implications:

a. *Fighting stigma and increasing patients' morale and self-esteem.* Patients have repeatedly told the authors that the research linking mood disorders and creativity has this effect on their morale. (This is important because of the very high suicide rate—an estimated 15%—in bipolar-I and II disorders);

b. *Encouraging medication compliance.* This is important because poor medication compliance is a particularly severe problem in treating bipolar disorder, with research reporting that half or more of bipolar patients fail to adhere to medication regimens in either the year before or after hospitalization (e.g., Scott & Pope, 2002);

c. *Identifying creative potential as a strength.* This is important because empirical research on psychotherapies has found that an approach that emphasizes patients' *strengths* is significantly more effective than other approaches (Barry, Zeber, Blow, & Valenstein, 2002);

d. *Debunking myths about the relation between creativity and mental illness.* One such myth is the view that severe mood swings are a "price" unusually creative people must pay for their creativity. (This is important because if these views are false, as preliminary research suggests they are, then these myths may discourage persons with mood disorders from seeking treatment, because of unfounded fears that mood-stabilizing medications will make them less creative);

e. *Improving educational, occupational, and avocational guidance for people with mood disorders or at high risk for them.* (This is important, because helping persons with great creative potential to find careers or avocations that enable them to develop those creative talents is likely to benefit both the individuals, who are likely to be happier and more productive, and society at large, which is likely to benefit from the innovations produced by unusually creative people).

More broadly still, a better understanding of the psychological processes that contribute to creativity is itself also an extremely important issue, with implications for improving the creativity of clinical research as well as practice. Elucidation of the psychological factors and personality traits that underlie the link between creativity and liability for mood disorders may clarify how liability for these disorders leads to illness in some persons at risk, but not in others.

The research on relations between creativity and mood disorders may *also* have significant implications for patients' **unaffected relatives**, including potential programs aimed at genetic counseling and primary prevention in persons at high risk for developing mood disorders. If patients and their unaffected relatives have unusual creative potential, as research noted earlier suggests, then educational/career counseling and job placement programs could potentially optimize the chances of both recovered patients **and** their as-yet-unaffected relatives staying well—if they are helped to find educational, vocational, and avocational programs that enable them to develop and express their creative potential. Finally, society as a whole could benefit significantly from programs that help unusually creative people express their talents.

Importance of Creativity for Individual and Societal Well-Being

A further benefit of research on creativity and mood disorders is the information that it will provide about correlates of actual real-life creative accomplishments, which are so crucial for cultural, scientific, and technological innovation. IQ scores and other *tests* of cognitive performance account for only a modest portion of individual differences in **real-life** accomplishments (e.g., Barron & Harrington, 1981; Jencks et al., 1979; Wallach, 1985). If it can advance scientific understanding of the psychological factors that contribute to creative thinking and problem solving, research on creativity and mood disorders may potentially have implications, not only for persons with mood disorders and their relatives, but also for broader issues of human health and well-being.

CONCLUSION

Several lines of research suggest that the association between increased creative potential and liability for major mood disorders, particularly bipolar disorder, may extend to *everyday* as well as eminent levels of creativity and thus may be relevant to millions of people who have bipolar disorder or are related to a person with this disorder. These findings are potentially of great clinical significance for patients' self-esteem and medication compliance, for how patients and their families view liability for mood disorders, and for combating the social stigma that is still often attached to these disorders. The results of studies reviewed here highlight the need for further research on the relation of creativity to mood disorders, using more sensitive measures of clinical and subclinical mood states, richer descriptions of subjects' creative activities, and investigation of creative thinking and personality variables that may mediate associations of creativity with liability for mood disorders.

REFERENCES

Akiskal, H. S., & Akiskal, K. (1988). Reassessing the prevalence of bipolar disorders: Clinical significance and artistic creativity. *Psychiatry and Psychobiology, 3,* 29-36.

Andreasen, N. C. (1987). Creativity and mental illness: Prevalence rates in writers and their first-degree relatives. *American Journal of Psychiatry, 144,* 1288-1292.

Barron, F. (1969). *Creative person and creative process.* New York: Holt, Rinehart and Winston.

Barron, F., & Harrington, D. M. (1981). Creativity, intelligence, and personality. *Annual Review of Psychology, 32,* 439-476.

Barry, K. L., Zeber, J. E., Blow, F. C., & Valenstein, M. (2002). Effect of strengths model versus assertive community treatment model on participant outcomes and utilization: Two-year follow-up. *Psychiatric Rehabilitation Journal, 26,* 268-277.

Costa, P. T., & McCrae, R. R. (1992). *Revised NEO Personality Inventory (NEO-PI-R) and NEO Five-Factor Inventory (NEO-FFI) Professional Manual.* Odessa, FL: Psychological Assessment Resources.

Csikszentmihalyi, M. (1998). Creativity and genius: A systems perspective. In A. Steptoe (Ed.), *Genius and mind: Studies of creativity and temperament* (pp. 39-64). New York: Oxford University Press.

Dobzhansky, T. (1962). *Mankind evolving.* New Haven, CT: Yale University Press.

Hirschfeld, R. M., & Klerman, G. L. (1979). Personality attributes and affective disorders. *American Journal of Psychiatry, 136,* 67-70.

Jamison, K. R., Gesner, R. H., Hammen, C., & Padesky, C. (1980). Clouds and silver linings: Positive experiences associated with primary affective disorders. *American Journal of Psychiatry, 137,* 198-202.

Jamison, K. R. (1989). Mood disorders and patterns of creativity in British writers and artists. *Psychiatry, 52,* 125-134.

Jamison, K. R. (1990). Manic-depressive illness and accomplishment: Creativity, leadership, and social class. In F. K. Goodwin & K. R. Jamison (Eds.), *Manic-depressive illness.* Oxford: Oxford University Press.

Jencks, C., Smith, M., Acland, H., Bane, M. J., Cohen, D., Gintis, H., Heyns, B., & Michelson, S. (1979). *Inequality.* New York: Basic Books.

Kinney, D. K. (1992). The therapist as muse: Greater roles for clinicians in fostering innovation. *American Journal of Psychotherapy, 18,* 434-453.

Kinney, D. K., Richards, R. L., & Southam, M. (in press). Everyday creativity and the Lifetime Creativity Scales. In M. A. Runco (Ed.), *Handbook of creativity research.* Cresskill, NJ: Hampton Press.

Lozano, B. E., & Johnson, S. L. (2001). Can personality traits predict increases in manic and depressive symptoms? *Journal of Affective Disorders, 63,* 103-111.

Maslowm, A. H. (1968). *Toward a psychology of being.* New York: Van Nostrand.

McCrae, R. R. (1987). Creativity, divergent thinking, and openness to experience. *Journal of Personality and Social Psychology, 52,* 1258-1265.

McInnis, M. G., & DePaulo, Jr., J. R. (1996). Major mood disorders. In D. L. Rimoin, J. M. Connor, & R. E. Pyeritz (Eds.), *Emery and Rimoin's principles and practice of medical genetics* (3rd ed., Vol. II). New York: Churchill Livingstone.

Meyer, T. D. (2002). The Hypomanic Personality Scale, the Big Five, and their relation to depression and mania. *Personality and Individual Differences, 32,* 649-660.

Plomin, R., & McClearn, G. E. (1990). Human behavioral genetics of aging. In J. E. Birren, & K. W. Schaie (Eds.), *Handbook of the psychology of aging* (3rd ed., pp. 67-78). New York: Academic Press.

Richards, R. L. (1981). Relationships between creativity and psychopathology: An evaluation and interpretation of the evidence. *Genetic Psychological Monographs, 103,* 261-324.

Richards, R. L., Kinney, D. K., Lunde, I., Benet, M., & Merzel, A. P. C. (1988a). Creativity in manic-depressives, cyclothymes, their normal relatives, and control subjects. *Journal of Abnormal Psychology, 97,* 281-288.

Richards, R. L., Kinney, D. K., Benet, M., & Merzel, A. P. C. (1988b). Assessing everyday creativity: Characteristics of the Lifetime Creativity Scales and validation with three large samples. *Journal of Personality and Social Psychology, 54,* 476-485.

Richards, R. L., & Kinney, D. K. (1990). Mood swings and everyday creativity. *Creativity Research Journal, 3,* 202-217.

Richards, R. L. (1999). Affective disorders. In M. A. Runco & S. Pritzker (Eds.), Encyclopedia of creativity (Vol. 1, p. 40). San Diego, CA: Academic Press, Elsevier, 1999. Table reprinted with permission of the publisher.

Runco, M., & Richards, R. L. (1997). *Eminent creativity, everyday creativity, and health.* Stamford CT: Ablex/Greewood Publ. Co.

Schou, M. (1979). Artistic productivity and lithium prophylaxis in manic-depressive illness. *British Journal of Psychiatry, 135,* 97-103.

Scott, J., & Pope, M. (2002). Nonadherence with mood stabilizers: Prevalence and predictors. *Journal of Clinical Psychiatry, 63,* 384-390.

Wallach, M. A. (1985). Creativity testing and giftedness. In F. D. Horowitz & M. O'Brien (Eds.), *The gifted and talented: Developmental perspectives.* Washington, DC: American Psychological Association.

Wender, P. H., Kety, S. S., Rosenthal, D., Schulsinger, F., Ortmann, J., & Lunde, I. (1986). Psychiatric disorders in the biological and adoptive families of adopted individuals with affective disorders. *Archives of General Psychiatry, 43,* 923-929.

Index

Abstract thinking, 89-91
  See also Alphabet and creativity: East Asia
Adaptive and veridical decision making, distinction between, 196
Adaptive function, variety of suggestions about art's, 2-3
Aesthetics/art/creativity, advances in the study of, v-vii
  See also individual subject headings
Affective disorders. *See* Mood disorders and creativity
Affect/pitch and rhythmical performance of poetry, 69-70
Affiliation needs, creative content of scientific journals and, 119, 122, 123
Alphabet and creativity: East Asia
  cognitive model, the alphabet as a, 91-94
  distancing thoughts from the words that bind them, 93-94
  orthography/writing system, Asian, 94-97
  phonemes, learning, 92-93
Analytical information processing, 141-142
Ancestral arts, Western view of, 9-10
Anthropomorphism, 32

Appreciation, cognitive processes in art
  aesthetic experiences are fundamental to human experience, 149-150
  art, features that make, 154
  Cognitive Mastering, 157-160
  expertise in art appreciation, effects of, 159-160
  history of cognition in empirical aesthetics, 150-153
  model of aesthetic experience, 153-158
  modernist era and dominance of style over content, 154-155
  processing stages, 155-158
  style-related processing, 158-159
  summary/conclusions, 160-161
Archaeologists and the function of the arts, 6
Aristotle, 48-50
Arnheim, Rudolf, 151
Art/aesthetics/creativity, complexity/confusion around and studies of, v-vii, 2-3, 7-10, 192, 209-210
  See also individual subject headings
Artification, 9
Asia (East) and creativity, 89-91
  See also Alphabet and creativity: East Asia

239

Association/Integration phase in creativity, 209
Asymmetry of cognitive mechanisms, model of, 141-142
Attentional effects and neural-network theory of beauty, 190-191

Barney, Tom, 67
Barrow, John D., 18
Baum, Richard, 89-90
Baumgarten, Alexander, 150, 151, 181
Beauty. *See* Neural-network theory of beauty
Belle-lettristic criticism, 40
Berlyne, Daniel, 151-152
Bipolar disorder, 172-173
  See also Mood disorders and creativity
Bolinger, Dwight, 70-71
Book of Three, The (Alexander), 112
Boston Naming Test, 165
Brain, the human, 15, 142, 153
  See also Neur listings
Bruner, Jerome, 34
By-product, art as, 6-7, 17-18, 32, 33-35

California Psychological Inventory, 106, 107
Callow, Simon, 84
Candide (Voltaire), 52
Centralization and information approach to human sciences/aesthetics, 136-138
Cerebral blood flow (CBF) and creativity, 212, 216-220
Cézanne, Paul, 154
Channel-capacity and rhythmical performance of poetry, 66
Charlie and the Chocolate Factory (Dahl), 112
Charlotte's Web (White), 108, 112

Children and developmental evidence for artistic/aesthetics domain, 23-25
Children of Green Knowe, The (Boston), 101
China, 89-90
  See also Alphabet and creativity: East Asia
Cingulate gyrus and neuropsychoanalytic view of literary creativity, 171
Cognitive mapping, 32
  See also Appreciation, cognitive processes in art; Neu listings
Cognitive mechanisms, model of asymmetry of, 141-142
Collective understanding and literary criticism, 42-43
Commitment, religious behavior evolving as honest signals of, 5
Communication phase in creativity, 210
Compound stress rule and rhythmical performance of poetry, 81
Conceptual analysis of happiness, 49-52
Confusion and cognitive flexibility, 36
Consilience, 41
"Constructive Conceptualism" (Gribkov & Petrov), 136
Continuity and rhythmical performance of poetry, 67
Control/manipulate people, the arts functioning to, 6
Cooperation/social cohesion, the arts functioning to enhance, 6, 7-8
Core of the system and information approach to human sciences/aesthetics, 137-139
Costs and tradeoffs, the principle of, 35-36
Creativity/aesthetics/arts, complexity/confusion around and studies of, v-vii, 2-3, 7-10, 192, 209-210
  See also individual subject headings

Crick, Francis, 210-211
Criticism and collective understanding, literary, 42-43
Csikszentmihalyi, Mihaly, 52-53, 59-60
Cultural beings, humans are biologically disposed to be, 1-3

Dadaism, 154
Darwin, Charles, 1, 3-4, 18, 31, 39, 41
Death/separation and the origins of art, 11
Deductive method and information approach to human sciences/aesthetics, 132
Defense of Poetry, The (Shelley), 173-174
Depression and norepinephrine, 172
Derrida, Jacques, 40
Descartes, René, 165, 166
Descent of Man, and Selection in Relation to Sex (Darwin), 39
Destiny view and literature/happiness connection, 50
Determinism, psychological, 124, 126
Developmental evidence for artistic/aesthetics domain, 23-25
Discontinuation and rhythmical performance of poetry, 67-68
Disorders, affective. *See* Mood disorders and creativity
Distraction effects and neural-network theory of beauty, 191
DNA and creativity, 210-216
Domains of the mind. *See under* Selection theories of creativity/aesthetics
Dopamine, 169, 213
Dualism, 165, 166

Einstein, Albert, 143
Elaboration phase in creativity, 210
Empirical Studies of the Arts, 119, 120

Encodedness and rhythmical performance of poetry, 68-69
Enjambment and rhythmical performance of poetry, 66, 72-73
Epicurus, 51
Epigenetic rules, 37
Eudaimonia (happiness), 49, 50
Evolutionary hypotheses, overview of art, complexity/confusion of notions of human, 2-3
  cultural beings, humans are biologically predisposed to be, 1-2
  nine hypotheses about what art does/is, 3-7
  psychologists of art relying on restricted samples, 1-2
  what is art?, 7-10
  why do/did people ever begin to artify, 10-12
  See also individual subject headings
Existentialism, 143-144
Experience Sampling Method (EMS), 53
Expressionism, 154

Fantasy stories directed at children, authors of
  characteristics of creative books, 104
  dimensions of fantasy, identifying, 104
  gender context, stylistic motive pattern in, 105-106, 112-113
  historical periods, comparing writings in different, 109-113
  measuring creativity, 103
  overview, 101-102
  personality/creativity/work style, 106-109
  sample, selecting a, 102
  stylistic/motive patterns, identifying, 105-106
  summary/conclusions, 113-114

Fechner, Gustav, 150-151
Flow concept and literature/
    happiness connection, 52-54
    See also Happy, does literature
    make people
Folk knowledge of human nature,
    38-39
Fónagy, Iván, 68
Formalism, 143
Fossil evidence for artistic/aesthetics
    domain, 20-21
Foucault, Michel, 40
Franklin, Rosalind, 211
Freud, Sigmund, 166, 167, 175
"Frogs" (Aristophanes), 120
Frontal cortex, left/right. See Neur
    listings
Frontotemporal dementia (FTD), 21
Frye, Northrop, 40
Functional magnetic resonance
    imaging (fMRI), 198-201

Galton, Francis, 210
Gammage Cup, The (Kendall), 113
Gender and authors of fantasy
    stories, 105-106, 112-113
Gestalt psychology, 85, 151, 188
Gielgud, John, 84
Golitsyn, G., 130
Greece and literature, ancient, 44-49

Happy, does literature make people
    conceptual analysis, 49-52
    flow concept, 52-54
    historical background, 48-49
    study 1, 54-58
    study 2, 58-62
    summary/conclusions, 62
Harvard Business Review, 119
Hasenfus, Nancy, 169
Heilman, Kenneth, 167, 168
Hemispherical (brain) activity and
    information processing, 142
    See also Neur listings
Herbig, Paul, 89

Hierarchical structures and
    information approach to
    human sciences/aesthetics,
    reflexion-based, 134,
    135-136
Hijacking hypothesis, 35
Hobbit, The (Tolkien), 101
Humanitarian studies, 129-131
    See also Information approach to
    human sciences/aesthetics
Human nature and understanding
    literature, 38-39, 41

Iambic pentameter, 65
Ideational systems of culture, 119,
    120
Identity theme, neuronally
    configured, 176-177
Individual competition, rethinking
    the fixation on, 8
Individualism and sensate systems,
    119
Industrial and Labor Relations
    Review, 120
Information approach to human
    sciences/aesthetics
    alteration of styles dominating the
    humanities, 143
    humanitarian studies, 139-145
    information maximum, principle of
    the, 131, 144, 146-147
    mental life, the sphere of, 133,
    136-139
    new paradigm: levels of analysis,
    131-132
    practical human activity,
    132-136
    reflexion/reflexive processes, 134,
    135-136, 140
    reflexivity in the humanities,
    movement toward, 142-143
    See also Appreciation, cognitive
    processes in art
Insight solutions, neural bases of,
    201-202
Instinct, art taking the place of, 37

Interation effects and neural-network theory of beauty, 191-192
Interest in other people, creativity associated with, 119
Intonation contours and rhythmical performance of poetry, 69-71, 76-77, 80, 83
Isolation, humanitarian studies existing in, 129
Iteration effects and neural-network theory of beauty, 190-191

James, Henry, 173
James, William, 167, 175-176
Japan, 89
  See also Alphabet and creativity: East Asia
Jausovec, Norbert, 168
Joule, J., 139
Journal of Applied Psychology, 119, 120
Journal of Criminal Law and Criminology, 119
Journals, scientific. *See* Scientific journals, creative content of
Jung, Carl, 110

Kant, Immanuel, 50, 150
Keats, John, 173
Knowles, Gerry, 67, 76
Korea, 96
Kraepelin, Emil, 225
Kreitler, Hans, 152
Kreitler, Shulamath, 152
Kris, Ernst, 167, 173
"Kugelmass Episode, The" (Allen), 34, 35

Lacan, Jacques, 40
Ladd, Robert D., 70
Language development and human evolution, 31
L'Année Psychologique, 119

L-dopa, 169
L'éducation sentimental (Flaubert), 124, 126
Left-track analysis and right-track solutions, 92
Lexical analysis, 42
Liberty and literature/happiness connection, 51, 52
Lifetime Creativity Scales (LCS), 227
Literature, the adaptive function of
  assimilating language functions, 31-32
  belle-lettristic impressionism, 40
  by-product, art as, 33-35
  cognitive mapping, 32
  common ground, a recognized, 41
  confusion and cognitive flexibility, 36
  costs and tradeoffs, the principle of, 35-36
  criticism and collective understanding, literary, 42-43
  emotionally driven needs, 37
  folk traditions of human nature, 38-39
  human nature, understanding, 38-39, 41
  hypotheses about literary art, 5
  instinct, art taking the place of, 37
  lexical analysis, 42
  point of view as central locus of meaning, 43
  poststructuralism, 40-41
  sexual selection, art as manifestation of, 32-33
  subjectively meaningful cognitive map, 37
  survival value inherent in literature, 47-48
  understanding of the world, affirming a certain, 43-44
  See also Happy, does literature make people; Neuropsychoanalytic view of literary creativity; Rhythmical performance of poetry; Scientific journals, creative content of

Little Prince, The (St. Exupery), 112
Locus coeruleus and neuropsychoanalytic view of literary creativity, 170-171

MacDonald, Kevin, 37
Madame Bovary, 34, 35
Manipulate/control people, the arts functioning to, 6
Margolles, Teresa, 155
Marlowe Society, 84
Martindale, Colin, 167, 169
Marx, Karl, 139
Match Problems, 198-201
Mating opportunity, art/creativity and the, 4-5
  See also Selection theories of creativity/aesthetics
Mayer, J. R., 139
Meaningfulness and neural-network theory of beauty, 188
Menand, Louis, 167, 173
Mental systems and information approach to human sciences/aesthetics, 133, 136-139
Meta-arts and information approach to human sciences/aesthetics, 136
Meter, perception-oriented theory of, 66
Mexican National System of Researchers, 213
Miller, Bruce, 21
Miller, Geoffrey, 32
Miller, George, 66
Monotonic trend and information processing, 142
Mood disorders and creativity
  biographical/anecdotal reports, 225-226
  factors accounting for associations between, 230-232
  genetic knowledge, applying new, 232-234
  mild/subclinical elevations, 229-230

[Mood disorders and creativity]
  noneminent creativity, 226-228
  scientific evidence, 226
  social/clinical significance, 232-235
  summary/conclusions, 235
  well-being, importance of creativity for individual/societal, 234-235
Morals, connecting creativity in science with, 119, 126
Morton, Eugene, 72
Motive Dictionary, 119, 122
Motive dispositions, evolved, 37
Mouse and His Child, The (Hoban), 108
Multiple arts occurring at once, 7-8
Music, 19-23
  See also Rhythmical performance of poetry

National System of Creators, 213
Natural selection theories
  See also Selection theories of creativity/aesthetics
Needham, Joseph, 90
NEO Personality Inventory, 230, 232
Neural correlates of creative cognition
  cerebral blood flow, 212, 216-220
  component processes that mediate cognition, 195
  DNA, 210-216
  function, neurocognitive approach to, 3, 5
  functional magnetic resonance imaging studies, 198-201
  hemispheric asymmetry, 195-197
  insight solutions, 201-202
  model for creative cognition, 202-203
  neuroscience evidence, 21-23
Neural-network theory of beauty
  attentional effects, 190-191
  creativity and beauty, 192
  interation effects, 191-192

[Neural-network theory of beauty]
  module/layer, distribution of activation in the same, 184-188
  modules, effects due to activating nodes in different, 188-189
  networks, components of, 181-183
  repetition effects, 189-190
  strength effects, simple, 183-184
Neuropsychoanalytic view of literary creativity
  cingulate gyrus, 171
  cortical activation, 168
  distant systems, cooperation between, 168-169
  frontal lobe activation, 168, 171
  hemisphere activation, 168, 176
  identity theme, neuronally configured, 176-177
  L-dopa, 169
  locus coeruleus activity, 170-171
  neuropsychoanalysis, defining, 165-166
  norepinephrine, 169-173
  passivity/relaxation while awaiting inspiration, 173-175
  psychoanalytic side of neuropsychoanalytic inquiry, 167, 173-174
  style of creation, talent for a particular, 176
  subjectively/objectively and from inside/outside, looking, 166-167
"New Criticism," 40
New Guinea, 10-11
Nonfunction for the arts, hypothesis of, 6-7
Norepinephrine and neuropsychoanalytic view of literary creativity, 169-173

Optimality principles and information approach to human sciences/aesthetics, 137, 139
Oral literary forms, 47

Overarticulation and rhythmical performance of poetry, 69, 77, 79
Overexcitability Questionnaire, 214

Parody and information approach to human sciences/aesthetics, 136
Passivity and neuropsychoanalytic view of literary creativity, 173-175
Peaking and rhythmical performance of poetry, 67
Phonemes and alphabet/creativity connection, 92-93
Pinker, Steven, 32
Pitch and rhythmical performance of poetry, 69-71, 82
Plato, 48
Play/make-believe as a function of art, 5
Poetry and the power of literature, 48-49
  See also Rhythmical performance of poetry
Point of view as central locus of meaning, 43
Popper, Karl, 47
Porter, Cole, 166
Poststructuralism, 40-41, 143-144
Potential space (state of mind), 174
Primordial/symbolic thought contents and content analysis, 118-119, 142-143
Propanolol, 169
Proximal mechanisms, by-products of, 34
Psychological Review, 119, 120
Psychologists, evolutionary, 1-2
  See also Neur listings

Reader, The (Schlink), 59
Reflexion-based hierarchical structures and information approach to human sciences/aesthetics, 134, 135-136, 140

Reflexivity in the humanities, movement toward, 142-143
Regression, 173
Regressive Imagery Dictionary, 118, 122
Religion/religious behavior, 5, 9, 138
Repetition effects and neural-network theory of beauty, 189-190
Republic, The (Plato), 48
Resources and information approach to human sciences/aesthetics, 134-135
Rhythmical performance of poetry
　cognitive and phonetic assumptions, 65-66
　enjambment, 72-73
　summary/conclusions, 83-86
　syllables, strings of consecutive stressed, 74-83
　vocal style, expressive functions of, 68-72
Right-track solutions and left-track analysis, 92
Ritual ceremony and the arts, 7-9

Schore, Allan N., 176
Scientific investigation, 89-91
　See also individual subject headings
Scientific journals, creative content of
　method, study, 120-122
　morals, connecting creativity with, 119, 126
　novelty, pressures toward, 118, 126
　primordial and symbolic thought contents, 118-119
　results, study, 122-126
　sensate and ideational systems of culture, 118-119
　titles of articles, 117, 119-120
Selection theories of creativity/aesthetics
　co-opted adaptations, 17-18
[Selection theories of creativity/aesthetics]
　domains of the mind
　　developmental evidence, 23-25
　　as domains of the art, 19-20
　　fossil evidence, 20-21
　　neuroscience evidence, 21-23
　　overview, 18-19
　natural selection theories, 16, 17
　sexual selection theories, 16-17
　summary/conclusions, 26
Sensate systems of culture, 118-119
Serotonin, 213
Set shifts and neural correlates of creative cognition, 196
Sexual selection theories, v, 2, 4-5, 32-33
　See also Selection theories of creativity/aesthetics
Simon, Denis, 90
Single photon emission computed tomography (SPECT), 216
Skill and debate over what art does/is, 3
Snow, C. P., 129
Social cohesion/cooperation, the arts functioning to enhance, 6, 7-8
Sociobiological revolution, 39
Sociopsychological sphere and information approach to human sciences/aesthetics, 142, 143
Solms, Mark, 165
Speculative theory, 40
Structuralism, 143, 144
Superstructures, information approach to human sciences/aesthetics and building, 135-136
Surrealism, 154
Survival value inherent in literature, 47-48
Syllabic writing and alphabet/creativity connection, 97
Syllables and rhythmical performance of poetry, stressed, 74-83

Synthetic information processing, 141-142

Temperament and Character Inventory, 214
Temporality and literature/happiness connection, 50-52
Tension/anxiety, art relieving, 10
Therapeutic nature of artification, 11
Tibet, 97
Torrance Tests of Creative Thinking (TTCT), 214, 216-217
Tower of London Task, 196
Trehub, Sandra, 25
Trilling, Lionel, 40
Trobriand people, 7
Trotter, David, 124, 126
True and Only Heaven, The (Lasch), 117
Turner, Mark, 34
Twentieth Century Words (Ayto), 117

Uncertainty, art helping to cope with, 10

Veridical and adaptive decision making, distinction between, 196

Versification patterns. *See* Rhythmical performance of poetry
Vietnam, 96
Visual art and neurocognitive approach to function, 3, 5
Volitionality and literature/happiness connection, 50, 52
Vorschule der Ästhetik (Fechner), 151

Watson, James, 210-211
Weber, Max, 139
Wilkins, Maurice, 211
Wilson, E. O., 36, 40
Winnicott, D. W., 174
Wisconsin Sorting Test, 165, 196
Wizard of Earthsea, The (LeGuin), 113
Writers Q Sort, 106, 107
Writing systems and alphabet/creativity connection, 94-97
See also Lit listings; Scientific journals, creative content of
Wundt, Wihelm, 150-151
Wuthering Heights (Brontë), 174

Young Creators, 213